BRITAIN AND THE BOMB

BRITAIN AND THE BOMB

TECHNOLOGY, CULTURE AND THE COLD WAR

W.J. NUTTALL

Whittles Publishing

Published by
Whittles Publishing Ltd,
Dunbeath,
Caithness, KW6 6EG,
Scotland, UK
www.whittlespublishing.com

© 2019 W. J. Nuttall
ISBN 978-184995-389-4

Efforts have been made to establish and contact copyright holders for all
images presented in this book. We are most grateful to all the various rights
holders who have kindly granted permission for reproduction. Despite our
best endeavours there may be instances where the rights of third parties
have been overlooked. In such cases, we apologise and we ask that rights
holders make contact and we will endeavour to resolve matters.

Quoted textual material is presented for the
purposes of criticism and in a spirit of scholarship.

Cover art: 'Before the Axe Fell' painting by Charles Thompson
(with kind permission)

CONTENTS

for Florence

FOREWORD

by the Rt Hon. Lord Owen, CH, PC

This book contributes to a much-needed understanding of the concepts relating to the UK building and retaining its own nuclear weapons-based deterrence strategy against evolving threats and huge technological advances. It covers the late 1950s and the 1960s from the RAF V-bombers to Polaris, through to the origins of the Chevaline programme.

It is now crystal clear that after the fall of the Berlin Wall in 1989, democratic politicians in NATO took a peace dividend far too rapidly. It was always going to be a fraught and volatile transition. At the time of writing, we face Putin's Russia, which, though very different from the Soviet Union, has become a threat unlike the Gorbachev-Yeltsin- Putin period from 1986 to 2010. Putin, starting his third term as president, following Medvedev's period as president, moved into an aggressive period. The Russian military intervention over Georgia had started to set new limits on the borders of the Russian Federation. Putin's annexation of Crimea in 2014 was, however, of quite a different scale in assertiveness.

Ukraine returned the nuclear weapons on its territory to the Russian Federation in exchange for assurances in the December 1994 Budapest Memorandum that their territorial integrity would be respected by the US, UK and Russia. Yet Russia was still, in effect, occupying a large part of Ukraine in 2019.

Alongside that reality China's global power has progressed at a striking rate: China is destined to become not just the largest economic power but much closer to being equal to the United States in the military projection of power.

The UK response took a number of forms firstly on 23 June 2016, in a highly significant referendum, 17,410,742 million people voted to leave the EU, with 16,141,241 million voting to remain. Just over a year later, on 18 July 2017 in a debate in the House of Commons, a majority of 355 MPs out of a total of 650 voted to build four new Dreadnought submarines capable of launching US-purchased intercontinental missiles with UK-manufactured nuclear warheads into the 2070s. That vote had an internal political dimension, in that 140 Labour MPs voted for that particular sophisticated nuclear deterrent. Only 47 voted against, including the leader of the Labour party, Jeremy Corbyn; but he thereafter accepted that Labour would not campaign against the building of those submarines. It is hard to see a Labour government, if returned to power in a general election even as late as 2022 after a fixed five-year parliament, being able to assemble enough MPs to form a majority to cancel these Dreadnought submarines having five years earlier reaffirmed their building. Labour MPs, under Corbyn or any other leader, have decided – and are likely to continue to decide – not to make unilateral nuclear disarmament a feature of Labour's future policy, but Labour will continue to take seriously the longer-term commitment to phase out nuclear weapons as a Nuclear Weapon State, NWS, and a signatory to the Non-Proliferation Treaty, NPT. The collapse of the INF Treaty at the start of August 2019 may be, to some extent, defused if the US Senate's bipartisan initiative making it clear that they want President Trump to extend New Start covering their and Russian nuclear weapons due to expire in 2021 makes headway. This will certainly be supported by other NATO countries.

The UK has, therefore, as part of the Brexit debate which at the time of writing continues, made a meaningful shift to 'move the emphasis from a European focus on world events, to a global focus through diplomacy, military support and freer trade.'[1] In this book Bill Nuttall takes us back to the period before Britain's overriding focus on European-based prosperity and security. As we turn once again towards a more global focus, it is appropriate that we should start this new phase by developing and retaining our own nuclear deterrent. Such a political consensus builds on the earlier decision to build two large aircraft carriers with a base in Oman – but it will have to be accompanied by a readiness to increase defence spending from the 2 per cent of GDP target for all NATO countries to 2.5 per cent, and eventually later to 3 per cent of GDP. In the Conservative Party leadership election, increasing the defence budget was advocated by the two candidates, though Boris Johnson, who became Prime Minister, was less specific than Jeremy Hunt who gave defence spending a very high priority. Time will tell: but at least defence is being given a higher priority in UK thinking than since the fall of the Berlin Wall and Brexit is matched by a higher commitment to NATO.

These decisions are linked to the fact that President Putin admitted that he had considered putting Russian nuclear forces on full alert at the time of maximum tension over his decision to annexe Crimea; he has threatened to base nuclear weapons there and has deployed missiles capable of carrying nuclear weapons in Kaliningrad, the Russian enclave on the Baltic Sea that neighbours Poland and Lithuania.

The UK National Security Council established in 2010 has a mixed membership; in addition to ministers, the military heads of the Ministry of Defence, and the heads of M16, MI5 and GCHQ all attend as of right. It will be a profound and sensible geopolitical development if the UK, probably in association with Australia, New Zealand and maybe Canada, now decides to build its own global positioning system. It would come as a consequence of the EU prohibiting the UK from continuing its full participation as a third party in their Galileo system. But that decision, even if there were to be an attempt to reverse it, would betoken an underlying EU attitude to defence which we must not just brush off as of little consequence. The US, of course, already has its own system, but it may not be averse to having access to another NATO country's system; in the era of cyber warfare,

---

1   David Owen and David Ludlow, *British Foreign Policy After Brexit*, Biteback Publishing, 2017, p.3

keeping more than one option available at any one time is prudent. Initially the drive to even consider such a development by the UK was a hesitant one, but very quickly it assumed its own dynamic. It soon became obvious that we should question whether or not to continue, as before, as a key partner in developing this highly encrypted service with the EU. The UK blocked the ongoing transfer of critical technology when it found its own companies being squeezed out. Then the UK decided to transfer to the RAF control of military space operations and to focus on our own satellite navigation system. In a sense we were accepting the logic of Brexit that satellites are a crucial feature of modern life and technology, and one from which we dare not risk exclusion. There will be those who will hope that the EU will shift their position in negotiations and let us participate fully, but there was a red flag warning message put up which the UK will have to give very serious regard to and now take this direction of travel even if the EU softens its current hostility.

On the sharing of nuclear technology with the US, the picture now is very different from that in the 1950s and 1960s, as touched on in this book. As far as the AWE (Atomic Weapons Establishment) is concerned, cooperation has vastly improved since the time of the 1958 Mutual Defence Agreement (MDA) with the Lawrence Livermore National Laboratory, California, and Los Alamos in New Mexico. The process of collaboration has moved considerably in the UK's favour over nearly six decades: AWE's work is now at the cutting edge of nuclear warhead design and development, and it is conducted with the benefit of exchanges on specific issues with the American nuclear weapons facilities, along with a small number of civilian contractors. These exchanges at the technical 'working level' were conducted through Anglo-American Joint Working Groups (JOWOGs) created through the 1958 MDA.[2] Following the 1963 Polaris Sales Agreement (PSA) these activities became linked to the strategic nuclear weapons programmes of the US Navy and their Special Projects Office (SPO) – now the Strategic Systems Project Office – through the Department of Defense (DoD), Atomic Energy Commission (AEC) and Lockheed Missile and Space Company (LMSC), the manufacturers of Polaris, Poseidon and Trident.[3] The 1959 follow-on agreement to the MDA made available special nuclear materials such as tritium, which the US supplied to the UK, and which have periodically taken place as 'barter arrangements' whereby the UK supplies the US Atomic Energy Commission with highly enriched uranium or plutonium and the US supplies the UK with the special nuclear materials. Ultimately the MDA has been the enabler for the transfer of nuclear warhead designs and techniques between the US and UK, and this has meant that Britain has been able to test devices at the

---

2   The Joint Working Groups (JOWOGs) had first been set up as part of the 1958 MDA, along with the Joint Atomic Energy Information Group (JAEIG) which provided a mechanism for passing information along with regular 'stocktakes' or reviews which ensured that everyone employed in each specialist area worked to mutual advantage. Although the MDA was published as a government Command Paper the substance of the agreement remained hidden in a series of classified annexes. The same was also true for the 1959 US/UK agreement relating to nuclear materials and the specific terms of the 'barter exchanges' under the MDA. TNA, PREM 13/3129, S. Zuckerman to prime minister, 16 December 1964.

3   Now Lockheed Martin. As with the UK effort, a large number of both government and private contractors each played a part.

Nevada test site. This collaboration has been followed in other areas such as the storage of missiles, and it could go much further in this area.

US and UK exchanges are becoming – and should become ever more so – a two-way street. We see this over the Joint Strike Fighter (JSF) production. It is time to finally put aside the drying-up of information exchanges that took place in the 1950s, and the problems over UK nuclear explosive testing between 1965 and 1973. The UK–US nuclear relationship is sustained by the UK being able to offer the US unique alternative technical pathways to develop and produce future nuclear weapons. This development was one of the beneficial effects of the hugely costly Chevaline programme. The period following the years considered by this book included a two-way series of exchanges from AWE and elsewhere, to the US laboratories and nuclear weapons facilities. These exchanges helped enable the US to transfer technology for MIRV warheads. The MDA was dovetailed with the PSA and the 1980 and 1982 agreements to supply Trident and its associated technology, and hence will prompt crucial considerations for all successor systems.

The transition on nuclear negotiations between Conservative and Labour governments should pose no problems in 2022 were Jeremy Corbyn to become prime minister after accepting that the majority of Parliament are in favour of nuclear deterrence and NATO. It is more than possible, however, that Corbyn will not be the Labour leader. But in fairness on these defence issues, as on EU membership, he has been far more respectful of Labour MPs views than ever Michael Foot was from 1980 to 1983 when Labour suffered a huge defeat in the General Election that year. The years ahead are hard to predict but that this Parliament will last a full five years from 2017–2022 looks unlikely and in an era of multi-party politics with the Brexit Party potentially challenging the Conservatives, almost any electoral outcome is possible.

Harold Wilson was no great supporter of Polaris when he took over from Sir Alec Douglas-Home in 1964, but in 1974 he took over Edward Heath's warhead modernisation programme. James Callaghan, on leaving office, gave Margaret Thatcher a summary of his recent meeting with President Carter, and his Polaris replacement file to assist her with the deliberations regarding a successor system. Thatcher followed up the discussions with the Carter Administration from the point where they had been left off by Callaghan. There was also the prospect of Anglo-French nuclear cooperation – a prospect raised by President Giscard d'Estaing on 5 June 1979. Although there were some political attractions in closer Anglo-French defence collaboration, there was also felt to be a need to 'avoid anything which might damage our nuclear links with the Americans on which our present deterrent depended'.[4] This is a view long held by defence officials and confirmed by ministers.

While Bill Nuttall's book closes with the beginnings of the Chevaline era, later events are also interesting and relevant to today. As regards the Trident replacement to Polaris/Chevaline, a deal was eventually reached on 2 June 1980 with Harold Brown, US Defense

---

4 It was also noted that there might be West German objections to Anglo-French collaboration, as it might undermine US commitments to Europe.

Secretary, and Margaret Thatcher in No. 10: the US had agreed to waive the bulk of the pro rata research and developments costs of the Trident missiles for greater American usage for military purposes of the island, Diego Garcia, in the Indian Ocean. Britain paid a nominal US$100 million towards R&D costs and agreed to cover the cost of manning air defence systems at US bases in the UK. Yet in August 1981 the new US Defense Secretary under President Reagan informed the UK that they had finally decided to upgrade the C-4 missiles to the D-5. The question of the cost of D-5 was raised by Thatcher with Reagan on 1 February 1982, and it was clear the Administration wanted to help. Keeping within the US legal requirement that development costs could only be waived in the national interest, Britain agreed on 11 March 1982 – just before the Falklands War – first to maintain a stronger naval capability than had been envisaged in John Nott's initial defence cuts, and secondly that in exchange for a waiver for the R&D costs of D-5, the Royal Navy would keep its amphibious capability with HMS *Fearless* and HMS *Intrepid*. Margaret Thatcher did agree to reduce the minimum number of missiles and warheads.[5] If Jeremy Corbyn became prime minister he would have to decide on the command and control of these weapons, and discuss all matters relating to nuclear policies fairly soon after taking office with the President of the US.

In this book Bill Nuttall considers our earlier national journey from Empire to Europe, and the transition of British nuclear weapons from the Royal Air Force to the Royal Navy. He reminds us that the relationship of Britain with the Bomb runs deeper than any one system or context. Indeed, while we might look forward to sincere moves towards global nuclear disarmament, realistically it looks as if the UK will continue to be an NWS for over 100 years from now, well into the second half of the 22nd century.

David Owen
August 2019

---

5 Charles Moore, *Margaret Thatcher. The Authorised Biography Volume I: Not For Turning* (Allen Lane, 2013), pp.572–3.

THE AUTHOR

Bill Nuttall is a technology policy specialist expert in nuclear issues. He is the author of *Nuclear Renaissance – technologies and policies for the future of nuclear power* (2005) and many academic works on related matters. He is a Professor in the School of Engineering and Innovation at The Open University and a Fellow of Hughes Hall, a college of the University of Cambridge.

ACKNOWLEDGEMENTS

This book has come together over many years and I am enormously indebted to a very large number of people that assisted the project in various ways.[1] So I would like to take this opportunity to list just some of the people who helped me along the way. Some of the names relate to people who sadly are no longer with us; I thank them and remember them fondly.

I am most grateful to:

John Ash, Bill Bardo, Wayne Cocroft, Jean-Pierre Contzen, Owen Cote, Den Davies, Frank Donagh, Charles W. Gill, Peter Halford, Richard Hamilton, Glen Hartley, Dan Hastings, Denis Healey, Matthias Holweg, Colin Hughes, Ken Johnston, Matthew Jones, Misha Leybovich, Shelley Lockwood, Phil Long, James and Sandy Lovelock, Douglas Lowe, Brian Manley, Brian Mann, Hironori Matsunaga, Richard Moore, Mary Nuttall, Nicholas Oliver, Robin Pittman, Kate Pyne, John Simpson, Simon Smith, Stephen Smith, Elaine Steel, Neil Taylor, Simon Taylor, Jonathan Trevor and Ivor Warne. In addition I am particularly grateful to the British Rocketry Oral History Project/British Nuclear History (Charterhouse) Conferences and the UK Programme on Nuclear Issues of the Royal United Services Institute for the rich intellectual forums they provide.

British society during the early Cold War was much more rigid than it is today. The top echelons of defense engineering were not welcoming to women and minorities. Thankfully, while not perfect, things are somewhat better now.

I would like to express my thank to my commissioning editor, Keith Whittles, for his kind support of this project. I am also most grateful to Caroline Petherick for her careful editing and advice on the text.

Perhaps part of my journey to this book relates to my late uncle, Jeff Nuttall. In 2018 MIT Press reissued what they described as 'legendary exploration of radical 1960s art, music, and protest movements': the book *Bomb Culture*. Arguably, that book and this one look at the same story from two perspectives: Jeff provided the perspective of the anti-nuclear campaigner and protestor in 1960s Britain, whereas this book seeks to gain insight into what was occurring on the other side of the razor wire fences of the Cold War.

Of course, all responsibility for the ideas expressed in this book rests with the author alone.

---

1 Of course, one should not assume that those that helped me necessarily agreed with what I have written.

TIMELINE

3 October 1952	Operation Hurricane: first British nuclear test explosion
April 1954	Blue Danube nuclear weapon enters service with the Royal Air Force
November 1956	Soviet Union crushes Hungarian Revolution
November 1956	Suez Crisis ends. UK cessation of military activity following US pressure
November 1956	Douglas Lowe and John Hayhurst's specification for the TSR2 made official and public as GOR-339
4 October 1957	Soviet Union launches Sputnik-1 – the first artificial satellite
3 July 1958	US–UK Mutual Defence Agreement signed – modified many times subsequently
April 1960	Cancellation of Blue Streak British medium-range ballistic missile
1 May 1960	Francis Gary Powers' U-2 aircraft shot down over Sverdlovsk, USSR
October 1962	Cuban Missile Crisis
December 1962	Skybolt air-launched nuclear missile project cancelled by USA, and Polaris submarine-launched system proposed as an alternative.
March 1963	Profumo scandal starts to appear in the British press
April 1963	US–UK Polaris Sales Agreement
2 August 1964	Gulf of Tonkin incident escalates the Vietnam War
16 October 1964	Labour government formed under PM Harold Wilson
6 April 1965	TSR2 strike aircraft cancelled by Labour government – replaced with option on US F-111 aircraft
January 1968	Labour government announces intention to greatly reduce UK military commitments East of Suez from 1971, and F-111 aircraft acquisition plans cancelled.
15 June 1968	First UK Polaris submarine, HMS *Resolution*, starts her first patrol
24 January 1980	Chevaline Polaris upgrade announced to Parliament
1982	Chevaline enters service

PROMINENT CHARACTERS

Roland Beamont
Wing Commander Roland Prosper 'Bee' Beamont, CBE, DSO & Bar, DFC & Bar
Second World War fighter pilot, Cold War test pilot and aviation author

Jimmy Dell
Wing Commander James Leonard Dell, OBE
Cold War test pilot, later director flight operations for British Aerospace

Alec Douglas-Home
Baron Home, Alexander Frederick Douglas-Home, KT
Sickness prevented service in the Second World War. Conservative party politician, served twice as foreign secretary, and as prime minister for one year (October 1963–October 1964)

George Edwards
Sir George Robert Freeman Edwards, OM, CBE, FREng, FRS, DL
Initially an aircraft designer, later managing director of Vickers-Armstrongs Ltd, and subsequently executive director of the merged British Aircraft Corporation

Denis Healey
Baron Healey, Denis Winston Healey, CH, MBE, FRSL
Second World War Army officer, Labour party politician, Cold War defence secretary, later chancellor of the exchequer

Douglas Lowe
Air Chief Marshal Sir Douglas Charles Lowe, GCB, DFC, AFC
42 years of service to the Royal Air Force, from Second World War RAF Bomber Command pilot to air chief marshal

Harold Macmillan
First Earl of Stockton, Maurice Harold Macmillan, Earl of Stockton, OM, FRS
Wounded serving in the Army in the First World War, Conservative party politician serving as foreign secretary, chancellor of the exchequer and prime minister (January 1957–October 1963)

Louis Mountbatten

First Earl Mountbatten of Burma, Louis Francis Albert Victor Nicholas Mountbatten, KG, GCB, OM, GCSI, GCIE, GCVO, DSO, FRS

Royal Navy midshipman in the First World War, and Royal Navy officer in the Second, last viceroy and first governor-general of India, Cold War naval officer rising to be admiral of the fleet, first sea lord and chief of the defence staff

Duncan Sandys

Baron Duncan-Sandys, Edwin Duncan Sandys, CH

Second World War Army officer, Conservative party politician, Cold War minister of defence and then minister of aviation in the government of Harold Macmillan

George Wigg

Baron Wigg, George Edward Cecil Wigg

Long service with the Army in the inter-war period, Second World War Army officer in the Educational Corps, Labour party politician, and close confidant of Prime Minister Harold Wilson especially on matters relating to security

Harold Wilson

Baron Wilson, James Harold Wilson, KG, OBE, FRS, FSS

Oxford University academic, later civil servant and Labour party politician, prime minister (October 1964 – June 1970 and March 1974 – April 1976)

CHAPTER ONE – RATIONALE

In the early years of the 21st century Britain has been on a journey to an important decision: whether and how to replace an ageing fleet of nuclear-powered submarines capable of firing devastating weapons thousands of miles. During those years the decision centred around what was known in official circles as the 'Successor', but in more common parlance it is known as the Trident Replacement Decision. On 19 July 2016 the House of Commons of the British Parliament voted by 472 votes to 117 to renew the UK's Trident nuclear weapons. It was also decided that the next phase of the deterrent was to be a continuation of the concept of four large Royal Navy submarines, each capable of firing nuclear missiles. In October 2016 it was announced that the first boat would be named *Dreadnought*, and following tradition the new class of submarines would be the Dreadnought class, taking its name from the first boat.[1]

This book is written to help the British people understand the issues involved in this important contemporary political decision; a decision that will not be fully implemented until the 2030s, and one which faces internal technical challenges and external risks of change and innovation along the way. This book is also intended to help the British consider their place in the world. The two issues of strategic nuclear weapons and Britain's place in the world are intimately connected, but remain separate. For the last 400 years, Britain has been a trading nation, and for much of that time, an imperial power. The days of Empire are long gone, but Britain maintains a global outlook matching afresh to an era of economic globalisation. Geographically Britain is a European country facing local and regional opportunities and threats. Britain has long been a cornerstone of the NATO alliance supporting, and more importantly being supported by, a perceived special relationship with the United States of America. As we shall see, during the late 1950s the UK made a slow but clear decision to establish its economic and strategic future on a regional basis involving Europe and the North Atlantic, and in security terms the Arctic Ocean. Britain retreated from colonialism and turned away from responsibilities and interests 'East of Suez'. The June 2016 vote to leave the European Union brings some of these past decisions back into focus as the country re-examines its role in the world.

I have often heard it said that if Britain did not have nuclear weapons, then it would never make a decision now to acquire such a capability. While that might be true, it does not alter the fact that we are where we are. Britain is a nuclear weapons state and with that comes risks, responsibilities, and arguably benefits. It is the balance between these factors, together with the fundamental ethics inherent in possessing the only true weapon of mass destruction – a nuclear weapon – that combine to motivate a range of strongly held opinions concerning the steps that Britain is taking.

Despite being written to help my readers understand early 21st-century decision making, this book tells a historical story. Our story centres on the mid-1960s, another point in history when the UK made its important decisions about the Bomb. The UK has made crucial decisions about nuclear weapons at four points in its history. There was the late 1940s decision to develop plutonium-based atom bombs similar to the Fat Man weapon dropped by the Americans on Nagasaki, Japan, which helped bring the Second World War to a close a bit sooner than might otherwise have been the case. The next decision came in the 1960s. It was to transition the British nuclear deterrent from primarily a Royal Air Force-delivered capability to a Royal Navy submarine-based approach, deploying US Polaris missile technology. The third decision concerned the upgrading of that system through the 1970s with the Chevaline upgrade – a uniquely British idea. A fourth decision came in the early 1980s with the shift to the Trident submarine-launched nuclear weapons system (as in use at the time of writing). A fifth major decision is at the time of writing being implemented – via the construction of a successor system to the original Trident capability.

One might take the view that in order to understand Trident replacement one can gain greatest insight by seeking to understand the original decision to adopt the Trident nuclear missile system in the 1980s – a decision that actually had its roots in policy developments initiated by the Labour government of the late 1970s. Importantly, however, Trident is a deployed nuclear weapons system, and furthermore is likely to have significant similarities to the planned successor system. These realities inevitably mean that Trident technology is highly classified: the secrecy is so all-encompassing that it is hard to present even an overview of the central issues at play in the decision making of 1979 and 1980.

The most studied and accessible British nuclear weapons decision is the first that was taken: a process initiated by Labour prime minister Clement Attlee in the late 1940s for the construction of Blue Danube, the first British nuclear weapon. While there are some constitutional and political issues that are still relevant today, the technology issues of the 1940s and early 1950s are so different from the technicalities of the 21st century that they can provide no significant insight into the 21st-century British experience.

Having eliminated the first and fourth cases of British nuclear weapons decision making, in seeking to gain insight we are left with the stories from the 1960s, and these lie at the heart of this book: the changing role for the Royal Air Force in connection with nuclear weapons, and the new responsibilities given to the Royal Navy with submarine-launched nuclear weapons, which in turn led to the development and later upgrade of the Polaris missile system needed to sustain delivery of the naval option. In considering those stories we can hope to gain some insight into the issues that face us today.

In the years after the fall of the Berlin Wall, advocates of a British nuclear deterrent stressed that that the existence of such a capability helped prevent an attack by an enemy capable of causing existential harm to the United Kingdom. In the Cold War, that enemy had been clear – it was the Soviet Union. But by the close of the 20th century the Russian Federation no longer felt like an enemy and questions were asked: can this system deter our new enemies? Such concerns grew after the New York World Trade Center attacks of September 11, 2001, and the growing awareness of the threat posed by Islamist militants. Could suicidal jihadists ever be deterred by an expensive nuclear weapons system? Probably not – but the reason for having an infrastructure of nuclear deterrence is not to deter all the enemies we might have today. The aim is merely to deter some of the dangerous enemies we might have in the future. The nuclear deterrent should not be regarded as the only component of British defence policy, but rather it is better seen as an element in a portfolio of capabilities.

In this book we consider stories from the 1950s and 1960s in order to understand the present better. One observation from those years is how for Britain the threat-space moved from a global set of confrontation points, particularly including the Middle East and the Far East, to become a more narrowly European, North Atlantic and Arctic story. Since the end of the Cold War, however, Britain's areas of defence emphasis have broadened once again, particularly to the Middle East and central Asia, but also to include west Africa.

The global reach of British power is an area where ambition and obligation collide with the realities of tight budgets.

President Obama memorably declared in a 2009 speech in Prague: 'Today, the Cold War has disappeared but thousands of those weapons have not. In a strange turn of history, the threat of global nuclear war has gone down, but the risk of a nuclear attack has gone up.'[2]

While there have been notable, although perhaps not enduring, successes in nuclear non-proliferation and security such as the 2015 Iran nuclear deal, there have also been failures and difficulties, such as the apparently incorrect allegations of an ongoing Iraqi nuclear programme leading up to the war in 2003, and also the violent toppling of President Ghadaffi of Libya, assisted by British and French military power, only a few years after the British had successfully persuaded him to abandon a nuclear weapons programme. What signals does such history send to a dictator close to developing nuclear weapons? Succumb to international pressure, but face execution at the hands of local enemies within a few years? One must not be complacent about the risks of nuclear proliferation and regional nuclear conflict.

While President Obama was right to stress the real risk of a nuclear attack, the risks of an extended, even global, nuclear conflict have not entirely gone away.

The post-Cold War era has not been an era of peace: 21st-century Middle Eastern and African conflicts have been joined in recent years by renewed concerns for European security and the relationship between the west and Russia. Conflicts in Georgia and subsequently Ukraine point to a resurgent risk. There is at the time of writing much talk as to whether we are once again in a Cold War with Russia. In this regard one must be careful to avoid that one's hopes cloud one's assessment of reality. The Cold War involved 'spheres of influence' with clearly defined and defended borders. There was the western notion of a 'tripwire', which if crossed would prompt rapid escalation to full-scale and mutually devastating conflict. Today Russia appears to have a Cold War outlook, and arguably it only takes one side to see the world in such terms for such a polarised state to exist. Western hopes to the contrary can cloud an appreciation of reality.

Over the last decade there has been a marked worsening of relations between NATO member states and the Russian Federation. President Donald Trump has spoken of the opportunity to build a new more positive relationship with Russia, but controversy concerning possible attempts by Russia to manipulate his election has arguably made things even worse.

In the decade after the fall of the Berlin Wall, NATO had sought collaboration with Russia via a programme known as the Partnership for Peace. Russia initially engaged with that process. However other events were generating a sense of humiliation in the country. For example, President Boris Yeltsin was a heavy drinker, and he embarrassed the Russian people through a series of very public drunken incidents, such as when in 1994 he grabbed the baton from a German band master and proceeded to conduct the musicians enthusiastically. His presidency was followed at the beginning of 2000 by a very different character, a former state security officer, Vladimir Putin. Putin projected sobriety, strength and a seriousness of purpose. The Russian people were desperate for a renewed sense of strength and confidence.

Over recent years Russia has expressed concern as the eastern extent of the North Atlantic Treaty Organisation has come closer to its borders. The Russian leadership has asserted that a promise made at the time of German reunification has been broken by the west.[3] The Russian government argues that Russia was assured that following reunification NATO would not move east from its original positions in Western Germany. Clearly no treaty was signed concerning such issues, but the Russians are clear in asserting their view that promises were made and that they were broken. While many western commentators assert that no promises were made, it is clear that related ideas were discussed at the time including the idea that, concerning the future of the eastern part of Germany, no American, British or French troops would be deployed and no NATO nuclear weapons would be sited there. There are indications that the Russians were led to believe that such ideas related to more than just eastern Germany, but rather included all of eastern Europe, including members of the former Warsaw Pact of nations aligned to the Soviet Union, or indeed parts of the Soviet Union itself such as Ukraine, Georgia and the Baltic States. For example, it is reported that a conversation took place between West German foreign minister Hans-Dietrich Genscher and Soviet minister of foreign affairs, the Georgian, Eduard Shevardnadze:[4]

On Feb. 10, 1990, between 4 and 6:30 p.m., Genscher spoke with Shevardnadze. According to the German record of the conversation, which was only recently declassified, Genscher said: 'We are aware that NATO membership for a unified Germany raises complicated questions. For us, however, one thing is certain: NATO will not expand to the east.' And because the conversion revolved mainly around East Germany, Genscher added explicitly: 'As far as the non-expansion of NATO is concerned, this also applies in general.' Shevardnadze replied that he believed 'everything the minister (Genscher) said.'

Even western voices arguing that Russia is incorrect to assert that promises have been broken concede that a misleading impression may have been created. Furthermore, any such spirit in the discussions of 1990 has now clearly evaporated: the context in Europe has changed and the context of the 1990 discussions has been superseded by events unanticipated, by the west at least, at the time. Proponents of the western case can invoke former Soviet Premier Mikhail Gorbachev. He is reported by Steven Pifer of the Brookings Institution to have said:[5]

> The agreement on a final settlement with Germany said that no new military structures would be created in the eastern part of the country; no additional troops would be deployed; no weapons of mass destruction would be placed there. It has been obeyed all these years.

But Pifer acknowledges that Gorbachev considered later western actions to be a violation of the spirit of the assurances given Moscow in 1990, despite not constituting a broken promise. Notwithstanding such observations, the Kremlin continues to assert that a trust has been breached by the west. Such considerations appear to have parallels with the resolution of the Cuban Missile Crisis of October 1962. That crisis, which features later in this book, was resolved not by a formal treaty but by an informal deal under which the Soviet Union would remove its missiles from the island, while the United States would undertake never again to attempt an invasion, and also to withdraw its nuclear missiles deployed in Turkey. Indeed the latter part of the deal was held secret at the time. The Cuba settlement has been respected over more than 50 years; might, therefore, the Russians have had reasonable cause to believe that a similar understanding had been reached in 1990 concerning the eastern border of NATO?

It is interesting to observe that while the conflict in eastern Ukraine remained dangerous and unresolved, President Barack Obama worked hard in 2015 to move US–Cuban relations forward; arguably so far forward that the 1962 Cuba Crisis settlement might itself be able to move into history.

The current worsened relationship with Russia raises the prospect that we are once again in a Cold War stand-off, or at least the Russian leadership seemingly perceives that to be the new reality. The Cuba crisis came at the height of the true Cold War, and was the point at which the Cold War came closest to becoming a 'Hot War', although the autumn of 1983 is also widely believed to have been extremely dangerous.[6] It is easy to think that the Cold War was a story of a war prevented and avoided, but in this book I take the view that the Cold War was itself a war in the truest sense. Indeed, for the British at least, any transition to a hot war was expected by all concerned to represent a rapid descent into total destruction. Therefore any hot war would merely represent the end of the true conflict – the Cold War.

Although I take the view that the Cold War was a true war, I must concede that it was a war unlike any other. Although, of course, similar claims to uniqueness apply to both the First and Second World Wars. Perhaps most simply: the Cold War was the least violent and most intellectual of these major conflicts. Later in this book we shall draw analogies between the Cold War and a chess game. It was a conflict framed in strategy and tactics, but unsurprisingly there were miscalculations and mistakes.

This book describes Britain during a period of perceived international decline, retreating from Empire and losing independence of action in defence and security. It was also a time of renewed prosperity at home, social change and post-war optimism. I hope that you will gain insight into a Britain of the past, one that is many ways so very different from the Britain of today, but one which can give us insights into, and perspectives on, contemporary choices.

The issues surrounding Trident replacement are often presented in the British press as a choice concerning Britain's 'independent nuclear deterrent' – and indeed it is. Arguably, however, that is not its *raison d'*être. It is also a contribution to NATO strategic security and, perhaps most importantly of all, a British investment sustaining and strengthening security guarantees from the United States. Would the United States really risk its very existence to defend interests on the other side of the Atlantic? The existence of British nuclear weapons arguably affects that calculus, to the benefit of Britain. Such connections and linkages emerged during the Cold War, and in particular the years described in the pages that follow.

It is not the purpose of this book to present a dry history of the Cold War – such things can be found elsewhere. Nor is this book a forensic dissection of nuclear weapons strategy and tactics. This book is a story from the past, one that has resonances for the present. It is not a book stressing Cold War fears. It does not focus on the early 1980s, remembered by many as a frightening and indeed a dangerous time. The 1980s gave us movies such as *The Day After* and *Threads*, which prompted widespread anxiety. This book focuses on a different, earlier, period. Yes, it was a dangerous time – but it was also a fun, exciting time for many people. It is the story of a generation emerging from the dismal rigours of the Second World War into a new and optimistic high-technology future.

Interestingly one of the bleakest movies depicting the horror of nuclear war was made in the pivotal year of our story, 1965: Peter Watkins' film *The War Game*. Intended for BBC television, the film was judged too shocking at the time and was not shown on TV until 1985, when it sat well in a new era of fear. But while this book concerns itself with nuclear weapons, their ethics and destructive potential are not our focus. Rather the intention is to evoke a lost Britain and to reflect on what we might learn from it.

Much of my story pivots on a single military project: the TSR2 aircraft. The label 'TSR2' stood for 'Tactical Strike and Reconnaissance 2', and this was the most ambitious military aviation project ever conceived by the British. It was wonderfully, and recklessly, ambitious. It represented national aspiration verging on hubris, and in early 1965 it was cancelled. Only one aircraft ever flew – and that aircraft, XR219, went supersonic only once.

It is clear that this book tells a rather British tale. I try to explain the TSR2 story to my many American friends by saying that you should imagine that Neil Armstrong and Buzz Aldrin were the only Apollo astronauts ever to have walked on the moon. Imagine if President Nixon had cancelled that programme soon after their return, in a desire to save money. Imagine that America had thus never been given the opportunity to grow bored with its astronauts. Today, how might America look back on those days? Amazement, disbelief and regret would replace the actual emotions of amazement, pride and satisfaction. In Britain, TRS2 continues to resonate. It was not just part of the Cold War chess game; it was much more than that.

I have spent my life in a pragmatic, even cynical, Britain, which makes less and less and which, in the good years at least, seems to get rich by simply pushing money around. For me a counterfactual Britain bold enough to have persisted with the TSR2 would have been a Britain of which Stephenson and Brunel would have been proud. It would have been a Britain built on the shoulders of Barnes Wallis and Reginald Mitchell; a Dan Dare Britain straight out of the pages of the *Eagle*. In contrast, the Britain in which I grew up celebrated heroic failures such as Robert Falcon Scott and Charles Babbage.

When I was a child the Second World War was ancient history. There were lots of people who had fought in it and all the grown-ups seemed to have something to say about it, but for me it was simply part of the past, along with the Roman conquest and the Battle of Hastings. How wrong I was. The Second World War had ended only 20 years before my birth – the year of the cancellation of the TSR2. For all those concerned with TSR2 and wider Cold War defence planning the Second World War was a very clear memory. It shaped attitudes and thinking in very many ways. The story of technology is a story of people, and as we shall see some remarkable people figured in British Cold War planning and the TSR2 story. I suggest that the stories of the people of the Cold War are every bit as interesting as those from the Second World War. In some ways the stories are more interesting – sons sought to outdo their fathers, based on a propagandised version of what their father's generation had achieved.

There have been numerous books on TSR2 and several of them are excellent, but most have been written for the narrow community of aviation enthusiasts. Most previous books on TSR2 have sought to locate the story in the history of post-war British aviation rather than the wider contexts of Britain's role in the Cold War and the changing nature of Britain in the years after the Second World War.

One friend reading an early manuscript commented that my TSR2 story is a tale for Cavaliers, not Roundheads, in that TSR2 gives us a romantic glimpse of what might have been had puritanical realism not intervened. But my cold-hearted Cromwellian opinion is that the TSR2 cancellation was a wise and carefully handled step. It was a sensible decision in Cold War defence policy. It was a correct and timely move in the Cold War game. This book will help explain the choices made, and perhaps reassure those that see error and even conspiracy. The defence decision makers, however, did not fully realise that the choices they were making would start a redefinition of Britain in the spring of 1965, and in those, more romantic, terms it was a very sad decision indeed. The emotion of the story is important. The TSR2 cancellation was a decision that becomes sadder as time passes. It appears to affirm national weakness and a retreat from ambition. It suggests that Great Britain has become Britain. Looking at the story in such terms, it appears to represent a mistake of long-term significance made for narrow, short-term motives. On such matters, however, I will leave you to judge.

In Chapter 2 we will explore the cultural scene in Britain in the years after the Second World War. Technology and modernisation figured prominently at that time. In Chapter 3 we will remind ourselves that the main protagonists concerning the TSR2 story had their formative experiences in the Second World War. That war did much to shape attitudes and thinking in the Cold War. Then our attention will turn to TSR2 itself and the difficult choices facing British defence planners in the late 1950s and early 1960s. By Chapter 10 we are looking beyond the TSR2 to a wider set of nuclear defence issues including the difficulties associated with moving the bulk of the British nuclear deterrent to the Royal Navy in the late 1960s and early 1970s. It is here that we consider the Chevaline upgrade to the Polaris submarine-based deterrent. As we shall see, Chevaline was a technological challenge similar in ambition to the TSR2. It was not cancelled. It was developed, and deployed, but in complete secrecy. So Chevaline never had the chance to capture the public imagination as TSR2 had done. TSR2 had been all over the newspapers and newsreels, but Chevaline was invisible. The public could not see the science and engineering success. In this book we examine the Chevaline decision. As with the earlier Royal Air Force issues, these naval developments have certain parallels that resonate today as we face decisions around the successor to the first generation of Trident capable submarines. We develop such ideas further in Chapter 11.

Above all I hope to share with you an insight into a Cold War story that is insufficiently widely known and which has important parallels for today.

CHAPTER TWO – THIS IS TOMORROW

Britain has changed much over the last 50 years and yet today, in the early part of the 21st century, the people of Britain find themselves faced with choices remarkably similar to those they encountered at the time of a rather special aircraft: the Tactical Strike and Reconnaissance 2 or TSR2.[7] There are strong parallels with the choices concerning nuclear weapons and strategic interests. In addition, however, there are wider parallels concerning the national economy and national identity. It is these aspects that touch the lives of the general population. It is perhaps for such reasons that TSR2 continues to be of great interest today.

It is a British story, arguably a very British story, but it is a story for the world. It involves heroes and villains, good fortune and error. It is about paths not taken and dreams unfulfilled. It is about death and dreams and hopes and fears. Britain, through its history, has given many great stories to the world and those stories did not stop in the Middle Ages, or with Shakespeare or at the D-Day Landings. The story of the TSR2 and what followed is a Cold War story. It is a story of the 1960s. It is a story remembered well by those of advancing years and it is a story that deserves to be told in full before all those who remember are gone.

The TSR2 story is also a tale with contemporary resonance. In the early decades of the 21st century Britain is faced with a fork in the road. We have been at similar junctions before: in the mid-1960s during the government of Harold Wilson and later, and perhaps most clearly, in the 1980s under Margaret Thatcher. Wilson and Thatcher put Britain on course away from large-scale manufacturing and towards an economy built around computer-based financial services. While it is commonplace to attribute the reconstruction of modern Britain to Margaret Thatcher's governments of the 1980s, the redefinition of Britain started earlier than that; Harold Wilson had had a vision for it, as Dominic Sandbrook makes clear in *White Heat,* his history of 1960s Britain:[8]

> The old [Labour party] image of cloth-capped trade unionists bickering with slightly deranged Hampstead intellectuals was no more; instead, commented *The Economist* in June 1964, it had been superseded by 'Mr Wilson's capture of the more positive

image of the white laboratory coat'. Indeed Wilson himself was widely seen as the living embodiment of science and efficiency. Again and again in interviews he talked about 'cutting edges', 'hard facts', and 'tough decisions' while promising a 'dynamic', 'purposive' and 'thrusting' administration fit for the 'jet age'.

Wilson's interest in technology was, however, not simply an enthusiasm for technology. His was a government that set out to understand technology and in so doing to make tough decisions about it. The choice faced by Britain today is once again between a future more dependent upon financial services or one built on a more diverse economy including a re-emphasis on what has now become known as High Value Manufacturing.[9]

In many respects the cancellation of the TSR2 represents a key decision point in that history; arguably that cancellation was the point when Britain started its journey away from world-leading manufacturing excellence and towards Thatcher's Britain, the consequences of which continue to concern the country today.

The path Britain chose during the Wilson years represented a redefinition of modernity in British eyes. These were not just years of technological choices – these were also times of social change. The technological modernism of the 1920s had at its heart notions of aesthetics and utility. These had led to streamlining and by logical extension to the supersonic era. Many enduring elements of the 1920s conception of modernism were captured by Fritz Lang in his 1927 science fiction movie *Metropolis*. Lang and his writer Thea von Harbou imagined a future based upon oppressive social stratification – a worker class toiling at great machines in order to provide a comfortable life for those living above in a gleaming city of towers and skyscrapers. But as it turned out sixties Britain, after TSR2, would see a complete rejection of such futures. For the social reformers of the sixties the future would be characterised by a desire to eliminate social rigidity and all notions of class, racial and gender constraints. In this revolution power would be given to the young – those with the strongest stake in the future.

Part of Britain's social modernisation related to the disempowering of an initially progressive force – the trades unions. These unions, mostly founded in the late 19th century and key to the maintenance of Wilson's Labour party, had been built to improve the position of the working man in a Marxist class conflict between the providers of labour and the ownership of capital. By the 1960s, however, it was becoming clear that these previously progressive forces now stood in opposition to truly progressive social and technological modernisation. The Wilson government resolved to take the first steps to tackle this problem. The path was bumpy at first, and in several key respects little initial progress was made. Barbara Castle's 1969 White Paper *In Place of Strife* did not deliver the changes to working practices that Britain's social modernisation needed. These had to wait for Margaret Thatcher's election ten years later. However what Barbara Castle and Harold Wilson did in the 1960s was to plant the seed of an idea that slowly germinated during through 1970s despite a lack of interest in the topic from weak successive Conservative and Labour governments. James Callaghan, the prime minister defeated by Margaret Thatcher in 1979, was the person who, as home secretary, had actively killed Barbara Castle's reforming proposals of 1969.

Given the ossified state of British industrial relations in the early 1960s, it was perhaps inevitable that if Britain was to have a prosperous future it had to pass through the painful steps on the journey towards the situation we found ourselves in in the middle of the first decade of the 21st century. By 2005 London's Canary Wharf employed roughly 100,000 people on a site which less than 50 years earlier had been the busiest docks in the world. A working-class bastion had become the symbolic vanguard of a high-wage, high-bonus world of deals and arbitrage. In 2005 Canary Wharf lay at the heart of a financial services industry that was widely believed to be the engine of the entire British economy. In 2008, however, things started to change. The once mighty Lehman Brothers collapsed, revealing itself as a bank Too Big to Fail as it nearly dragged the whole global financial system down with it. The autumn of 2008 was a tumultuous time. It was a crisis in the true sense of the word. In some senses the world came as close to the brink as in the Cuban Missile Crisis 46 years earlier. Just as the Cuba crisis confirmed to the world the need for détente, the financial crisis of 2008 revealed the need for systemic change. These changes are not yet complete but, as with the changes of the 1960s, they will not simply be economic: they will also be political, technological and social.

In the closing decades of the 20th century Britain was the most purposeful of all the major economies in seeking a transition from manufacturing to financial services. Now it is, I believe, the country that most clearly sees the fork in the road ahead: either Britain can press ahead resolutely in a belief in markets and unbridled global capitalism, or it can seek to return to the seemingly lost arts of manufacturing; in some senses back towards a Britain as it existed in 1964 prior to the cancellation of TSR2.

In 1964 the more obvious future was the future that never materialised. It was a world built upon ever more sophisticated technologies developed by British engineering businesses in plucky and valiant competition against better funded, but less imaginative competitors. While European competitors were still emerging from the rubble of war, it was the United States that represented the greatest technological challenge. In every way the UK was outmatched by the USA, but despite this it continued somehow to innovate and stay ahead in key, but ever more niche, areas.

The status of technology in the early 1960s Britain is a complex amalgam of reality and perceived reality. There is a clear reality of post-war British innovation in electronics, computing, nuclear energy, nuclear weapons, medicine, telecommunications, radar and aviation. What is even clearer, however, is that such technological innovation was unsustainable. Research and development costs were increasingly unaffordable and, as the Wilson government realised, a high level of selectivity was going to be required to restrict the broad front of British innovation and ideally to pick some winners. A key aspect of the thinking in Wilson's government was that too much emphasis was still being placed on military technologies and not enough on the needs of the civilian economy.

In order to understand how by the mid-1960s Britain found herself in such an unsustainable and militarised reality, it is necessary to go back at least as far as the Second

World War. Arguably that the six years of conflict against Nazi Germany and Imperial Japan represents the most unsustainable, and yet most worthy, period of the entire history of the country. In the sixties the entire adult population of Britain had been shaped by their wartime experience.

THE PSYCHOLOGICAL LEGACY OF TOTAL WAR

In 2010 *The Economist* magazine commented: 'it matters greatly that, almost uniquely in Europe, the second world war is a positive memory in Britain'.[10] There is something special about Britain and its collective memory of a terrible time.

During the 1940–1941 blitz bombing by Hitler's Luftwaffe, Britain and its dominion Canada fought alone to resist the Nazi threat. As the dust settled on the bombed cities the voices of appeasement fell silent, and it became clear that Britain was in a fight to the death. Britain would now strive to throw everything possible against Germany. The Second World War had become a conflict to be fought by means that everyone knew could not be sustained. The sense of foreboding that such awareness must have generated is given voice by George Orwell in his dystopian novel *Nineteen Eighty-Four*, the essential idea for which he first sketched out on the Scottish island of Jura in 1944.[11]

The manifestly unsustainable realities of the war were countered by skilful domestic propaganda which included the 'Mightier Yet!' poster series. These stressed Britain's mechanical strengths, and held within them elements of a propagandised future free from truth. The temptation to apply psychology where engineering truth was insufficient was part of a world which Orwell would later warn against.

The wartime teenage boys who saw these images on their way to school were susceptible to such messages. They did not want to grow up to be bankers or accountants – they wanted to be engineers. They would build even better aircraft than their fathers had. Their planes would fly even higher, even faster and be even more beautiful. The state would pay to build their dreams, and everyone would know their place and get on with it. In the words of a propaganda poster from the start of the war, which interestingly has only entered the popular imagination in the post-crunch realities of the 21st century, everyone would Keep Calm and Carry On.[12]

The novelist J.G. Ballard returned to Britain from the Far East in 1946. He recalled the exhaustion of the British at the end of the war in his autobiography:[13]

> Looking at the English people around me, it was impossible to believe that they had won the war. They behaved like a defeated population. I wrote in *The Kindness of Women* that the English talked as if they had won the war, but acted as if they had lost it. They were clearly exhausted by the war, and expected little of the future. Everything was rationed – food, clothing, petrol – or simply unobtainable … Everything was poorly designed.

Hope would be key if the country was to recover its greatness. The spotty youths of 1943 would go on to become the professional engineers of 1963. They would be, to use a phrase brought back into use by Francis Spufford, the backroom boys.[14] They would build us a better future, not just a streamlined future, but indeed a supersonic future.

Of course, not everyone could be an engineer; most would watch the efforts from afar. J.G. Ballard observed of the 1950s that it took a long time for the mood of exhausted Britain to lift:[15]

> Audiences sat in their damp raincoats in smoke-filled cinemas as they watched newsreels that showed the immense pomp of the royal family, the aggressively cheerful crowds at a new holiday camp, and the triumph of some new air-speed or land-speed record, as if Britain led the world in technology. It is hard to imagine how conditions could have been worse if we had lost the war.

HISTORY AND MEMORY

It wasn't just children that wanted to read about science, technology and the future in mid-1950s Britain. On 22 November 1956 the British weekly science magazine *New Scientist* was launched.

> The original idea for the magazine came to Maxwell Raison upon reading a press report of a speech in which Sir Winston Churchill pointed out the importance of science and technology to the future of Britain. Raison knew all about starting magazines, with experience of *Picture Post*, *Farmers' Weekly* and other successes behind him. When he canvassed his idea among the leading scientists, industrialists and educationalists, he met with a generally enthusiastic response.[16]

J.G. Ballard deftly summarises the changing cultural scene in London in 1956 when he comments:[17]

> I visited a remarkable exhibition at the Whitechapel Art Gallery, 'This is Tomorrow'. Recently I told Nicholas Serota, director of the Tate and a former director of the Whitechapel, that I thought 'This is Tomorrow' was the most important event in the visual arts in Britain until the opening of Tate Modern, and he did not disagree.

> Among its many achievements, 'This is Tomorrow' is generally thought of as the birthplace of pop art. A dozen teams, involving an architect, a painter and sculptor, each designed and built an installation that would embody their vision of the future. The participants included the artist Richard Hamilton, who displayed his collage, 'Just what is it that makes today's homes so different, so appealing?', in my judgement the greatest ever work of pop art.

My late uncle, Richard Hamilton, had an important role in post-war British art and culture. Trained as a fine artist and experienced as an industrial designer in the Second World War, Hamilton is perhaps best remembered as the pioneer of pop art; 'Just what is it that makes today's homes so different, so appealing?' is arguably the first example of the genre.

While Ballard naturally associates the 'This is Tomorrow' show with the future. Richard Hamilton recalls the birth of pop art in somewhat different terms. When asked whether pop art has at its heart a world of industrial products and technology, he replied:

Poster for the 'This is Tomorrow' exhibition 1956, featuring the collage 'Just what is it that makes today's homes so different, so appealing?' by Richard Hamilton (by permission of the artist).

> 'This is Tomorrow' precedes Pop Art, in the sense that we now use that term, by a few years. It did not occur to me that my involvement with the 1956 exhibition was making art, it was a visual commentary on life at that historic moment. Bill Haley's 1954 success 'Rock Around the Clock' was Pop, and the word 'Pop' is an abbreviation of 'Popular Culture'.

> The outcome for me was to paint a work of art called Homage à Chrysler Corp., in 1957, to express the idea that there was little cultural difference between Rock Around the Clock and an Eames lounge chair; they are both consumer products. When an art movement of the early sixties was labelled 'Pop Art' by the critics, I saw an affinity with what I had been doing.

In highlighting the cultural importance of the 'This is Tomorrow' exhibition, Ballard reflects one of the orthodoxies of late 20th-century art history – that pop art was first created for that exhibition. Hamilton, however, reminds us that Popular Art is banal and ubiquitous – it existed before pop art was known. If one is to find explicit linkages between technology and art in Hamilton's work, then one should look elsewhere.

The year before 'This is Tomorrow' Hamilton had mounted a show called 'Man, Machine and Motion', first in Newcastle upon Tyne, where he taught fine art at what was then a satellite campus of Durham University, and later in London at the Institute of Contemporary

Art. 'Man, Machine and Motion' reflected Hamilton's fascination with marine technology, vehicles, aircraft and (two years before Sputnik) space travel. His consideration of flight contrasted the exposure to the elements of the early pioneers with their contraptions built of little more than wood and doped cloth with the conditions faced by the pilots of the 1950s, such as Wing Commander Roland Beamont in his English Electric Canberra. (As was so often the case for Roland 'Bee' Beamont, his name was reported incorrectly in the exhibition catalogue prepared by Reyner Banham and Richard Hamilton.)

The catalogue reports on two contrasting images of flight:

> These two images from the end and the beginning of aviation's first phase contrast the qualities of exposure and protection to which late & early pilots have been subjected. Wing Commander Beaumont (sic) is sheltered from the elements under the plastic bubble of his heated cockpit, whereas the rider of La (sic) Sauteral – one of a number of unsuccessful attempts to give wings to the bicycle – was completely exposed to the outer air. But on the other hand La Sauteral's pilot was at the heart of things, mechanically, being completely unwrapped in flying surfaces and supporting frameworks, while the pilot of the jet-driven Canberra is bracketed out into space at one of the aircraft's extremities, in psychological isolation, from the elements of support and power.[18]

Richard Hamilton's 'Man, Machine and Motion' exhibition, 1955, showing the juxtaposition of Roland Beamont flying his English Electric Canberra (centre left) with Le Sauteral's 1923 pedal-powered aircraft (top right) (by permission of the artist).

Hamilton's celebration of technology reminds us that not only was Roland Beamont's career a central component of Britain's military history in the 20th century, but also it had also found a role in society's attempts to understand itself and the future that lay ahead. It had even found a place in contemporary art.

Elsewhere in the 'Man, Machine and Motion' catalogue, Hamilton and Banham sum up the societal importance of technology most eloquently when they say:

> There is something fabulous in this aspect of modern history; the men are acclaimed heroes and the machines, as they quickly become obsolete, are consecrated not only in museums but in the affections of the public.

This book seeks to explore some of the reasons that TSR2 has become more than a mere technological artefact in museums, but has assumed elements of myth and allegorical power. In an interview conducted for this book, Richard Hamilton offers his own insights into why certain technologies manage to strike a chord with society far beyond what utility or aesthetics alone would suggest is appropriate.

Hamilton makes his point not with reference to an aircraft, but rather with reference to a car. Cars have always held a special fascination for Hamilton.

> One of the last pictures in *Man, Machine and Motion* showed a car with a rocket engine designed by Harley Earl, I think for General Motors. It was one of those dream cars produced solely for promotional purposes, now called concept cars, fantasies having nothing to do with production cars. The rocket engine was a styling motif rather than a likely automobile engine but it made its impact. The reason I know it so well is that I used the rocket's air intake in the painting called *Homage à Chrysler Corporation*.
>
> I know of no earlier picture of a motor car, no work of art which features a motor car. It doesn't mean they don't exist, only that I have never seen or heard of one.

IT'S NOT JUST THE CURVES

Hamilton suggests that in order to understand the nexus of technology, myth and aesthetics one must understand that beauty by itself is insufficient. Both technological excellence and aesthetic beauty are needed if a technology is to help redefine the world around it. He cites the example of the Citroën DS, which Roland Barthes rechristened the 'Citroën Déesse' or 'Citroën Goddess'. Hamilton observes:

> My interest in the DS was its form and the aesthetic qualities, but its engineering was equally beautiful. … The DS is not only the most beautiful automobile ever, but it developed the most sophisticated technology available at the time. – it's the whole – it's not just the curves.[19]

Through the 1950s Hamilton had been fascinated with the inter-relationship of form and function. His breakthrough exhibition had been held at the ICA in London as part of the 1951 Festival of Britain. His exhibit, entitled 'Growth and Form', had been inspired by the work of naturalist D'Arcy Thompson and in particular by his book *On Growth and Form*. Hamilton sees a clear link between his own interest in the structure of plants and animals in 'Growth and Form' and his interest in technology in 'Man, Machine and Motion':

> In my mind it was an extension of Darwin. Away from natural evolution towards the evolution that man had invented for himself. That seemed to me to be an important idea, which nobody took to heart at all. Someone could write a book on the subject, I'm not going to, but it is a good idea.[20]

Arguably the TSR2 possessed the same powerful combination of technological advancement and aesthetic beauty as its contemporary, the Citroën DS. There have been plenty of beautiful aircraft and there have been many technologically advanced aircraft, but there have been few that combined these attributes as well as did the TSR2.

In the mid-1960s Britain would change much and change fast. The TSR2 story is located in the early sixties in the years before the 'Summer of Love' initiated in Britain by the release of the Beatles' Sergeant Pepper album and arguably culminating with the birth of the Isle of Wight Festival in August 1968. TSR2 dates from the years when the Beatles wore Nehru jackets and still had a tidy style. These were the years of the mods on their Vespas and Lambrettas, celebrating a new European modernism.

Britain was in a psychologically dissonant situation, in that the propaganda of the war had described a reality at odds with the daily experience of the population. Britain was not yet ready to hear officially that so many of its technological wartime strengths were merely the imaginings of the propagandists. So the country was struggling to reconcile its memories, with the propaganda messages of the past and the growing need for history. It was easy for elements of propaganda to linger as part of memory or even as parts of history.[21] A vaguely generalised perception of engineering excellence was being built from rare and specific genuine successes, such as the Rolls-Royce Merlin engine and the Chain Home radar system. More generally, however, the British engineering experience in the war had been far less successful. Britain's engineering excellence had elements of myth – but this was a powerful and enduring myth, especially for those young men who would go on to become the engineers of the late 1950s and early 1960s. They would work to make sure that in the post-war era, Britons would be the fastest, the highest, and the most gentlemanly. For them the challenge, above all else, was to beat the Americans.

The minds of children and (what would become known as) teenagers would continue to be moulded by some strategically placed fiction, but this time not from the pens of civil servants in the Ministry of Information: the power over young minds would shift to pop culture and comic books. The *Eagle* comic was launched in the spring of 1950 at the initiative of the Reverend Marcus Morris of Lancashire. He had become increasingly concerned that

British youth were being damaged by imported American comic books, and what was thought to be needed was a wholesome British, Christian antidote. The *Eagle* in particular is remembered as a key element of the pop culture of 1950s and 1960s Britain. In the second decade of the 21st century the *Eagle*'s messages from those decades still resonate strongly with nostalgic middle-aged men, many of whom today occupy positions of influence in modern British society, and it is in part to help such people interpret issues of memory and history that this book has been written. It is clear that the futures foretold in the pages of the *Eagle* and on the TSR2 drawing boards of the British Aircraft Corporation were similarly unrealisable – but for some (now grown-up) teenage boys they gave a sense of a future in which we would be proud and bold; a future that never happened.

Within the pages of the *Eagle* could be found its famous cutaway drawings of cars, ships, planes and all manner of machines. The cutaway of TSR2 is shown in Chapter 6. The *Eagle* also created an iconic and very British hero for the boys of post-war Britain – 'Dan Dare, Pilot of the Future'. Created by illustrator Frank Hampson, Colonel Daniel McGregor Dare was imagined to have been born in Manchester, England, in 1967 and to have been educated at private school. By the early part of the 21st century he had become chief pilot of the Interplanetary Space Fleet, ably supported by his rotund, accident-prone, but utterly loyal batman, Digby. Digby and Dare were of different social classes – each knew his place and was happy with it.

The divergence between the realities of modern Britain and the portrayal of the same period in the frames of the Dan Dare comic strip could not be greater. The differences are technological and social. A British officer does not lead the Interplanetary Space Fleet, and he does not say, when in a bind, 'You brute! Some day – some how (*sic*) – you'll pay for this crime!' while thinking 'Why didn't I listen to old Digby? I wonder if he's still in play?'[22]

In 2009 the Science Museum in London's South Kensington district mounted an exhibit examining technology in Britain in the 1950s and 1960s. It entitled its exhibition 'Dan Dare and the Birth of Hi-Tech Britain'. The publicity showed Dan Dare holding a Bristol Bloodhound guided missile. Elsewhere in the exhibition was presented a WE.177 nuclear weapon (see Chapter 10).

If the TSR2 represented an image of the future for Dan Dare Britain, it is interesting to note that Dan Dare's personal spaceship and jet plane could not have looked more different from the TSR2. His craft, named *Anastasia*, after batman Digby's aunt, featured two stubby wings and a pair of side-by-side bubble canopies for Dare and Digby. It did not reflect the supersonic aesthetic of the times.

In the image, note the British Overseas Airways Corporation commercial supersonic jet liner in the background. In the event, the name BOAC was lost in 1974 when it merged with British European Airways to form British Airways.

MODS AND ROCKERS

The story of Britain's 'mod' or 'Modernist' youth sub-culture parallels the fortunes of TSR2 almost exactly. Emerging from the coffee shops and modern jazz clubs of late 1950s London this youth movement stressed style and sophistication – in strong contrast to the rockers, who by this time had started to appear, to some, as a macho manifestation of the past. The rockers were the ton-up working-class boys of the fifties, with their big rumbling motorcycles. For them the key points of reference were American – rock'n'roll and Harley Davidson. The mods however were new, and they were different. They were clean, they were youthful and they had little interest in America. For them America – or at least white, mainstream, corporate America – was gauche and lacking in class.

Dominic Sandbrook captures the essence of the mod well when he says:[23] 'The whole point was to cultivate a look of 'effortless' Continental sophistication, like an idealised vision of Italian elegance somehow transported to suburban England.'

The *Anastasia* was a super spaceship, named after Digby's Aunt, and presented to Dan Dare by the grateful Venusians when he had brought peace to their troubled planet. The *Anastasia*, with its four methods of propulsion, incorporated the foremost scientific advances of both the Treens and the Therons, the once warring inhabitants of Earth's sister world!

Credit: Image reproduced with kind permission of the Dan Dare Corporation Limited www.dandare.com

The social class and background of the mods is also somewhat unusual as it brought together a fashionable and middle class Art School aesthetic of the late 1950s with the aspirational desires of post-war working-class London youth. In the summer of 1964 the rockers and the mods clashed at various British seaside resorts including Brighton and Margate, although the real significance of these events lies not in what happened on the beach on bank holiday weekends but rather in the media reaction to such things. The process of exaggeration and scaremongering by Britain's tabloid press led Stanley Cohen to cite the perceived phenomenon of mod–rocker conflict as a Moral Panic in his 1972 book *Folk Devils and Moral Panics*.[24]

Arguably the resonance of small skirmishes between groups of mods and rockers acted as some form of allegory for the tensions within Britain at the time. On the one hand there was the almost rustic machismo of the Rockers influenced by American rock and roll music, while on the other was a new cleaner, more explicitly European, aesthetic represented by the mods. The mods loved fine design, and for some aviation had a special appeal.

Don Hughes, self-described 'scooter boy, Mod, soul boy and pill head' has recorded his experiences as a mod in the 1960s in a series of books under the title Friday on My Mind. He was intensely proud of his Vespa SS scooter: it was clean, aerodynamic and modern, so much so that he rode specially to the airport, just so that his picture could be taken there.[25] The resulting image has taken on a rather iconic status, having been widely republished in magazines and books celebrating mod culture.[26]

In June 1969 Paramount Pictures released *The Italian Job* starring Michael Caine. The film was a commercial failure in the United States, but in Britain it has entered popular consciousness as an amusing celebration of certain kind of lost Britishness. A Britishness associated, I would suggest, with the mods, Dan Dare, *Man, Machine and Motion* and the TSR2. To quote the strapline of Terry Rawlings' *Mod: A very British phenomenon*: it was a Britain of 'clean living in difficult times'. Yet arguably British mod culture achieved its commercial zenith just as its roots were in decline under an onslaught of flowers, love and psychedelia.

By the time the Swinging Sixties started in April 1966 with *Time* magazine's cover feature, 'London: The Swinging City', the modernist world of the TSR2 had already become part of history.

Don Hughes captures the moment well:

Spring 1966. It's official, America's most influential magazine, *Time*, declares London is the place to be – switched-on and where it's at. It's Swinging! A city seized by change and liberated by a new affluence. A vitality that is attracting the jet set from Europe and beyond. Back in war-torn Europe the focus in the fifties was on New York, followed by Paris then Rome. Now it's right here on my bloody doorstep … London. The future has arisen around me![27]

CHAPTER THREE – 'THE FEW': THE 1940S

We've no comfort, food or clothing
We've no Hurricanes or spares
We've no Chance light, beacons, wireless sets or flares
Though it's cold and bleak and dreary and it's pouring down with rain
87 Squadron are at Readiness again

Second World War RAF Squadron Song (chorus)[28]

In May 1955 the artist Richard Hamilton had hung his first major exhibit as a new faculty member at Durham University's campus in the proud industrial city of Newcastle upon Tyne in the north-east of England. His 'Man, Machine and Motion' at the Hatton Gallery was a 'control the context' exhibit – almost an installation – and it focused on the relationship between modernism and humanity through a consideration of transport. As noted in the previous chapter, the exhibit featured a picture of Roland Beaumont (*sic*) seated in his English Electric Canberra.

A helmeted pilot, a supersonic jet in an art exhibit – who *is* this figure, seated in his Canberra? It is not, as the exhibition catalogue described, Roland 'Beaumont', nor is it the Second World War ace 'Bob' Beamont as celebrated by the *Evening Standard*. During the war the evening paper had described Beamont as the man 'chiefly responsible for beating the Nazis' flying-bomb in the daytime'.[29] Although Roland Beamont's name was so frequently corrupted, he is correctly remembered as one of the foremost British aviators of the 20th century.

Roland 'Bee' Beamont's career ranged from the 1940 Battle of France through the Battle of Britain, in which he flew Hurricanes. His career would close with the Panavia Tornado project of the 1970s.[30] But it is for something in between that he is perhaps best known – he was director of flight operations for the TSR2 programme, and was one of the projects' key test pilots.

In his later life Roland Beamont became a prolific and accomplished author on technical aviation matters, and in reflection on his own life and career. His memoirs provide the best first-hand accounts of his remarkable career, and especially his outstanding success as a fighter pilot in the Royal Air Force during the Second World War. Let us start our story back in those dark days when Britain faced the Nazi menace almost alone. Beamont wrote of one night-time patrol during the Battle of Britain:

> The guns of Bristol opened fire and though the shell bursts around were somewhat disturbing, I felt sure that I must soon see the Hun who was so obviously just ahead somewhere; but nothing was visible in the glare.

> We eventually passed out of the searchlight zone and as the beams swung off after fresh targets I was forced to return to the patrol line. This was not difficult as there at least six searchlight intersections, some containing up to twenty lights, illuminating the Bristol area. I was climbing up towards the apex of the nearest group with the intention of trying again, when right over the heart of the city intersected in so many lights that the glare reflected faintly on the ground itself, was a Hun; a glittering fly in the centre of a giant iridescent web.

> At full throttle and shouting 'Tally-ho' down the wireless, I dived all out in an attempt to close the range, for I knew that if I did not get him before he got to the edge of the searchlight zone I should lose him … I managed to get the gunsight back on the target and let fly a number of bursts at him.

> It is difficult to put into words the picture I shall always retain of that moment: the dark outline of the hood frame, the glimmer of the instruments and the glowing red bead of the gunsight in the centre of the windscreen, and outside nothing but a confused jumble of brilliant beams of light. In the centre an aeroplane, light grey in the glare with little white flashes appearing all over it and apparently connected to my aircraft by slightly curving lines of red and white tracer bullets looking like tramlines on a wet night. The whole, seen through the glare of flame from the gun muzzles in the wings at each burst, gave the mounting impression that there was no earth and sky.[31]

The old English fox-hunting cry 'Tally-ho!' became a personal battle cry for Beamont, and by November 1942 it had become the motto on the badge of 609 Squadron, based at Manston and by then under Beamont's command. Beamont's 609 flew Hawker Typhoons and later Tempests. Mightier and faster than the more famous Hurricanes and Spitfires, these were two of Beamont's favourite aircraft – even though they generally had a bad reputation, largely as a result of the poor reliability of their 2000hp Napier Sabre engines. For Beamont's pilots undertaking patrols over the English Channel there was also the knowledge that it was almost impossible to ditch the aircraft successfully in the sea.[32]

Beamont was never a Spitfire man, but during the war he did manage to fly the famous aircraft on two occasions. Quite remarkably on only the second time he had flown a Supermarine Spitfire, and for his very first time in a Mark V, he participated in a combat patrol. Such curiosity, bravery and opportunism were characteristic of Bee Beamont. They were attributes that were to serve him well.

War was a dangerous business for the young men of Fighter Command in particular. Death was commonplace, and Beamont provides a lasting insight into those times. By early 1944 he was wing commander responsible for forming and training the first three squadrons to fly Hawker Tempest Vs.

> It was a jolt to us all when Flying Sergeant Mannion and Flying Officer Zurakowski failed to return from a reconnaissance of the channel ports one afternoon in late May [1944]. ... The two Poles, both very capable and experienced pilots, had, with their usual enthusiasm, run out to their aircraft, started up and thundered away in the direction of Belgium within five minutes of the first order. ... [Two hours later Beamont phoned operations command] 'Hallo Ops? Controller please. Yes it's urgent. Wing Commander Flying, Newchurch, speaking. Oh hello old boy. Know anything about these bods of mine? You haven't heard from them since they reported from Boulogne – not a word? Oh well, let me know if you do get anything, won't you. How about a search? ... Air Sea Rescue on the job already. Good show.'

> Alan Dredge, their Squadron commander, had come in while I was talking. 'Do they know anything about the Poles sir?'

> 'Afraid not, old boy. Looks as though they've had it. Probably those bloody heavies [guns] at Boulogne.'

> A further half hour passed by and as I walked out to my aircraft to check it for the evening show, a small and grimy 'erk' [ground engineer] approached self-consciously saluted and said: ''Scuse me Sir, could you tell me any news of Flight Sergeant M? He's been away over two hours Sir, and he's me pilot, an' I should 'ate anything to 'appen to 'im.' There was often a very close bond of friendship and confidence between groundcrews and their particular pilots.

> 'Yes, I'm afraid that we shan't see them again. They would have run out of fuel at least thirty minutes ago, so they can't still be flying. There's no other news. By the way what's your name?'

> 'Anderson Sir, 'B' flight.'

> 'Right Anderson, I'll let you know if any news comes through.' But I knew very well that there would most likely be no further news. It was just another of those incidents which passed almost unnoticed in this strange active service life.[33]

Perhaps sadder still than these tales of friends that disappeared on cloudless sunny spring afternoons was the all too common experience of the pilots coming out as replacements during the Battle of Britain and dying, as Beamont recalled, 'almost before we knew their names'.[34]

Another fighter pilot of the war who would later feature in the TSR2 story is Tom Pike, or as he would later be known, Sir Thomas Pike, GCB, CBE, DFC and Bar. Tom Pike was already an experienced Royal Air Force officer by the time war broke out; he had first joined the RAF in January 1924 as a flight cadet at RAF Cranwell. His wartime service is best remembered for the period after the Battle of Britain: in February 1941 he became commanding officer of 219 Squadron before, in September of the same year, assuming command of all the

Roland 'Bee' Beamont at Newark, Lincolnshire

night fighters of Number 11 Group. His son, Richard Pike, has recorded his father's wartime experiences as a pilot of twin-engined Bristol Beaufighters in the book *Beaufighter Ace*.[35] Tom Pike's wartime experience saw him awarded the Distinguished Flying Cross and Bar (both in May 1941). Much later in life, in January 1960, Tom Pike would be made chief of the air staff, the professional head of the Royal Air Force. In April 1962 he would rise to be a marshal of the Royal Air Force, the highest rank in the RAF. In addition he was at that time NATO deputy supreme commander allied powers Europe. As would be true of so many defence policy makers of the 1960s, in the 1940s Tom Pike was serving his country in the war against Germany.

THREE RAF COMMUNITIES

The Royal Air Force in the Second World War comprised three near-separate communities: the fighter pilots, such as Roland Beamont and Tom Pike; the men of Bomber Command flying repeated missions to the heart of the German Reich; and the sometimes overlooked community that fought the critical Battle of the Atlantic ensuring Britain's connections to far-flung allies and trade partners. All three wartime communities would produce individuals who were to shape the future of British defence policy in the 1950s and 1960s. One such figure, later to play a central role in the TSR2 story, is Douglas Lowe – later Sir Douglas Lowe, GCB, DFC, AFC – a modest man despite his impressive military achievements in the bombing offensive against Nazi Germany and great service to UK defence policy. In an interview and correspondence for this book he was keen to stress that many of his actions were merely those of a young man shaped by circumstance.

In February 1943 Douglas Lowe arrived in Newmarket as a newly commissioned officer with his wings, fresh from training. He described the Newmarket arrangements:

We were actually on the racecourse itself, … The track was on the outside, there was the grass in the middle, and there was the airfield – that was it. The operations were all conducted from the grandstand, and we were billeted in the town. Sergeants, the NCOs, were all in the old jockey club, and the officers' mess was a commandeered house, [a] trainer's house, up on the heath. That was great fun, because I was commissioned the day I arrived on the squadron.[36]

He records the exuberance of the young men based at Newmarket racecourse in his memoirs:

We were all in it together and when not on the serious business of Operations, the dangers of which were appreciated but never dwelt upon, we got up to all sorts of high jinks. These were assisted by the fact that Newmarket town has a very liberal supply of pubs and, if ops were cancelled or not on that night, the thing to do was to go on foot from the racecourse to the billet and call in on as many of these as possible. After a few glasses, bawdy songs became the order of the day and if the local feminine talent could be enticed to join (which they did readily) so much the better. Much later, on the way to the house, we would remove road signs, put up diversions and send traffic the wrong way around a roundabout. The next day the Squadron Adjutant, a fatherly figure, would telephone the police and invite them to collect a lot of road signs from our front lawn. Which they did and took no further action. …

We travelled between the house and the racecourse in 'aircrew' buses, which for some reason, had bars across the sliding windows. Going through the town we would look terrified, cling on to the bars and shout through the windows to the amazed people going by that we didn't want to but THEY were making us do it and were taking us away. All very thoughtless but not harmful and a good release of tension.[37]

Such high spirits reflected the very real dangers faced by the air crew of Bomber Command. Douglas Lowe records:

The target area was a busy place and twice members of my crew were injured by pieces of shrapnel. There were also the night fighters to worry about. Coming away from the target area, they would get into the homecoming bomber stream and have a field day. My rear gunner once spotted one and we escaped by diving into cloud. On another occasion we survived an attack by two Ju 88's but with cannon shell damage and the 2nd pilot injured. The first I knew of the attack was seeing a very bright stream of tracer flying past. The odd thing was that it looked to be coming from dead ahead and my instant worry was of a collision. I pulled back violently on the control column and shot up in the air. I am sure that was what saved us from being shot down for although there were hits and damage, it was not fatal and I must have jerked the aircraft out of the line of fire.[38]

Douglas Lowe was flying the Stirling heavy bomber which, partly as a consequence of its limited operational ceiling, suffered disproportionate losses.[39] Lowe's bravery was recognised with the award of the Distinguished Flying Cross. The award was reported back at Miles Aircraft in the pages of the *Miles Magazine* with the words:

> Mr Lowe in our Plant Department, and young Douglas, his son, was in our laboratory before volunteering for the R.A.F. Now Douglas has been awarded the D.F.C.! Stout Fellow![40]

Douglas Lowe's crew was the first in his squadron to have successfully survived its tour in quite some time; after 25 operations they were done. Normally a full tour would have been 30, but for some reason Group Captain Wasse decided that Lowe's talents should not be risked any further.[41] Douglas Lowe had a bright future ahead of him elsewhere in the RAF.

Meanwhile Denis Healey, as a young British Army officer, was at the heart of key beach landings in the Italian campaign, first facing severe adversity near Pizzo, and later easier success at Anzio Beach until tactical errors by more senior officers later squandered the early advantage gained there.[42] Healey learned many lessons from his time in the Army, ranging from a scepticism of statistics to a belief in the importance of good planning. These skills would help him greatly later in life.

The difficult defence policy decisions that Britain faced in the early 1960s were made by middle-aged men who during the Second World War had been young men. Many of those concerned with our story, such as Bee Beamont, Douglas Lowe and Denis Healey, had been brave young men tested by conflict. Others, such as Jimmy Dell, had been too young to see combat and as a consequence, perhaps, they lived in the shadows of the older boys throughout their careers.[43]

Chapter Four – New Elizabethan Age: 1955–1959

I remember our teacher really focusing on this business of the New Elizabethan
Age … Because of jet travel, climbing Everest, because of all kinds of developments
associated with full employment, the health service, there was this idea that there
was a parallel between the days of John Hawkins and Walter Raleigh.

Neil Kinnock, former Labour party leader and European commissioner[44]

THE SUN NEVER SETS

Writing in the early 21st century and looking back at Britain's defence challenges of the late
1950s it is easy to assume that the whole story revolves around a Cold War stand-off with
the Soviet Union, accompanied by the ever-present threat of a European nuclear war. While
the European context is most definitely a major part of our story, it is by no means the only
part – and perhaps for the story of the aircraft that would become known as TSR2, it is not
even the most important part.

As Britain confronted the emerging challenges of the Cold War and the prospect of
renewed conflict in Europe, it was also coming to terms with an even greater geopolitical
shift – the retreat from Empire. Harold Macmillan caught the mood of the times in 1960
when he spoke in Africa: 'The wind of change is blowing through this continent. Whether
we like it or not, this growth of national consciousness is a political fact.'[45]

This speech is widely regarded as British governmental recognition that the days of
Empire were over. If that is the case, it is perhaps even more interesting to note just how late
this reality dawned.

In the late 1950s Britain was indeed committed to the 1949 NATO Treaty, but the North
Atlantic and Europe had not yet assumed a central position in British strategic thinking.
For instance, Britain perceived itself to have strong strategic interests in Southeast Asia,
defending colonies, territories and allies as diverse as Malaya and Australia. While Australia
was peaceful and prosperous, Malaya was subject to a low-intensity war known as the Malaya

Emergency, and was on its way to independence and subsequent expansion into what is today Malaysia. Noting the NATO model, Britain was a founding member of SEATO, the Southeast Asia Treaty Organization. In the Middle East, Britain also established the Central Treaty Organization, comprising Turkey, Iran, Iraq, Pakistan and the United Kingdom. How different the world might have been today if CENTO had been a success. History clearly reveals it was not. In the late 1950s, however, it was not to be known that CENTO and SEATO would fail[46] while NATO would succeed. The Britain of 1957, conceiving a tactical strike and reconnaissance aircraft, was a Britain with firm treaty commitments all around the globe.

In 1943 Australian prime minister John Curtin had referred to his country's future relationship with Britain as part of a 'Fourth Empire'. Wayne Reynolds, a professor of history at the University of Newcastle, NSW, considered the period 1943–1957 in *Whatever Happened to the Fourth British Empire?*[47] Reynolds' focus of concern is the suggestion that: 'Empire planning was of central importance to British, Australian and South African leaders after the Second World War' and that 'such planning was largely based on the use of nuclear deterrent weapons, not on conventional weapons'.

The extent of the difference between more recent thinking and that of the mid-20th century is revealed by the opinion of Leo Amery who in the mid-1940s was secretary of state for India. He suggested that, as Reynolds observes:

> The Empire would allow Britain to disperse her population and industries so that in future the defence potential would not be destroyed in the event of an air attack on the British Isles. He also envisaged the construction of overseas bases which would provide munitions standardised with those of Britain. These support areas, in Amery's view, would be responsible for Empire defence 'zones'. Australia and New Zealand would form the nucleus in the Pacific. South Africa would be a base for an area stretching as far north as Kenya.[48]

The construction of the English Electric Canberra had been motivated by concerns for Empire defence, as even its name indicates. It became a 'mainstay of the Australian and South African air forces'.[49]

Reynolds argues, in essence, that in 1957 Britain faced a profound choice, and the determinant of the choice would be nuclear weapons capability. One choice would have been the Fourth British Empire choice of partnership with the major southern dominions, which would involve building a military–industrial complex with them, including nuclear weapons technology. The alternative – and this was the one that won the day – was to focus on the UK's strategic relationship with the United States under which much atomic cooperation might become possible. From 1945 through to 1957 Britain had effectively developed its nuclear weapons without the assistance of post-war America. This despite the agreements obtained during the war when Britain's atomic bomb programme – the Tube Alloys project – was sent to the United States. Britain was subject to the constraints of the 1946 US McMahon Act, which forbad US assistance to any foreign power in nuclear weapons matters. While it was to prove possible to release the UK from such constraints, it would not have been possible to share US technology with Australia, New Zealand or South Africa. Britain faced a choice between its Empire and America, and it chose America; and in 1957 the Fourth British Empire died.

Minister of Defence Duncan Sandys (pronounced 'Sands') had lobbied hard on the losing side of this debate. As for the British arguments that civilisation might be rebuilt after a nuclear attack on the homeland, the Eisenhower Administration gave such ideas short shrift. One of its reports observed:

> The United States should not provide assistance to any foreign country (including Australia and New Zealand) for the purpose of developing a base for the rehabilitation of the Free World after a massive nuclear destruction of the United States.'[50]

Avro Vulcan first prototype in flight
[Photograph: Cyril Peckham (1905–1984)]

As we shall see later, Australia was to have a pivotal role in the history of the project which would become TSR2. Australia saw ongoing defence challenges in the same part of the world as did the UK. Britain in the late 1950s had significant ongoing defence commitments in the Far East, with interests in places such as Hong Kong, Singapore, Malaya, Brunei. For Australia the region of concern was the 'Near North'– essentially the same part of the world.

Guy Finch has persuasively argued that the original operational requirement for what became the TSR2 was focused not on British defence needs in Europe but rather for needs further afield, especially in the Far East and the Middle East.[51] He points out that any thinking of the aircraft as a Canberra replacement for European operations was misguided at best. However, Britain's global responsibilities suggested the need for a highly capable tactical strike aircraft. In the 1950s the British were considering the flexible use of tactical nuclear weapons to defend increasingly hard-to-protect global interests. The thinking held that the use of a relatively small number of nuclear weapons could project suitable force without raising the risk of an escalation that would threaten the United Kingdom itself. Furthermore the ability of new aircraft to operate over very long distances, move to the battle space very quickly, and if need be operate from poorly equipped airfields and the other diverse operational capabilities of TSR2 were all perfectly suited to conflict in, for instance, Southeast Asia. It must be remembered, for instance, that in the mid-1950s Vietnam was in transition from a French colonial conflict to a Cold War conflict involving the United States and its allies. The Korean War, to which Britain had contributed significant resources, was also a very recent memory.

A GOLDEN AGE

The Farnborough Air Show in the 1950s was the showcase of British aviation in its Golden Age. The 1955 show opened in autumn drizzle, and the Fairey Delta 2 supersonic test aircraft was on display.[52] So were all three of the V-bombers – the Vickers Valiant, the Handley Page Victor and the A.V. Roe and Company, or 'Avro', Vulcan. The Vulcan and the Victor had been produced in response to the Air Ministry's 1947 request B.35/46,[53] whereas the Valiant had been prompted by the somewhat less ambitious B.9/48 specification. These mighty aircraft were the response of Britain's strongest aircraft companies to a common call – for a deep penetration bomber capable of hitting the heart of the Soviet Union with British nuclear weapons. The V-bomber force would go on to form the backbone of Britain's strategic nuclear defence up until the late 1960s.

Although the Avro Vulcan first flew at Farnborough in 1953, its appearance on the first day of the 1955 show is more widely remembered. This is because shortly after take-off Avro's chief test pilot, Wing Commander Roly Falk, took the second production aircraft, XA 890, into a 30-degree climbing barrel roll.[54] With these bomber aerobatics Falk revealed the surprising manoeuvrability of the giant delta-winged aircraft.

While Britain proudly showcased its new strategic bombers, elsewhere plans were under way to develop an alternative delivery system for the British atomic bomb. De Havilland Propellers Ltd is understood to have received in 1955 the first contract to be prime contractor for Blue Streak, Britain's kerosene- and liquid oxygen-fuelled medium-range ballistic missile. Blue Streak was to be the UK contribution to a ten-year British–American agreement to share knowledge gained from work on intercontinental and medium-range ballistic missiles;[55] known as the Wilson-Sandys agreement on guided ballistic missiles, it was finalised on 12 June 1954. A key figure on the British side of the deal was Duncan Sandys.

Roland Beamont had first met Duncan Sandys in the summer of 1944 when Sandys visited Roland Beamont's Tempest Wing, which was having much success in bringing down the V-1 flying bombs aimed at London in daytime. Sandys was member of parliament for Norwood, but his importance and influence were more than this implies. He was at the time married to Diana Churchill, daughter of the prime minister. Beamont records:

> Sandys arrived to the accompaniment of the, by then quite normal in the area, sounds of Tempests diving at full power, cannon fire and exploding V1s. I gave him a general picture of tactics, training standards, details of the aircraft performance and aircraft and armament servicing under these intensive operating conditions; and also of the methods employed to coordinate the battle and improve interception and success rates. … Mr Sandys listened attentively but without noticeable enthusiasm, and after interruptions on some occasions to watch Tempests intercepting V1s overhead (and shooting one down just beyond 56 Squadron's dispersal), he said that he had seen all he needed to and was ready to leave. After a short silence he suddenly went on to say that we were wasting our time in this flying business – in a few years all this sort of thing would be done by rockets.[56]

Blue Streak at Spadeadam Test Site [Keystone Pictures USA / Alamy Stock Photo]

Hence it is arguable that Sandys had formed a view during the Second World War that the future of air power rested in unmanned aircraft. He is known to have indicated his preference for ballistic missiles when speaking as UK minister of supply in 1953.[57] This opinion would do much to shape the direction of the British aircraft industry in the late 1950s and early 1960s.

BLUE STREAK

As C.N. Hill records in *A Vertical Empire,* the story of the Blue Streak medium-range ballistic missile starts with a March 1952 report entitled *Long Range Project* by L.H. Bedford of English Electric.[58] Bedford observed that in missiles guided by integrating accelerometers and gyroscopes, accuracy decreased with increasing time of flight. The most accurate way to hit a target 2,000 miles away with an unmanned missile would be to use ballistic technology so that the time of flight would be minimised. Through the 1950s, thinking moved forward concerning propellants – liquid oxygen and kerosene being selected – and the principle that once outside the atmosphere the rocket would separate from the warhead which would fall to Earth in a specially designed re-entry vehicle capable of withstanding the stresses and temperatures associated with re-entering the atmosphere at high speed. To consider those specific issues a subsidiary research project was created – the Black Knight rocket programme, which later morphed into the short-lived civilian Black Arrow satellite launcher.

One remarkable feature of Blue Streak and other liquid-fuelled rockets of the time was the extremely thin walls of the cryogenic propellant tanks. Blue Streak's tanks were made of stainless steel a mere 19 thousands of an inch thick.[59] In the absence of pressurisation these huge tanks would wobble and shimmy if gently touched.

BLUE STEEL

Missiles generally were a major pre-occupation for military R&D laboratories in the 1950s. Not only was the UK busily working on Blue Streak, but also much effort was being devoted to Blue Steel Mark I, an 80 km stand-off weapon designed to improve the nuclear strike capabilities of the V-bomber force. Blue Steel deserves special mention as it played an important, albeit brief, part in the history of the British nuclear deterrent. It was not a ground-launched ballistic missile. Rather it was a rocket-powered stand-off weapon released from an aircraft. The context of Blue Steel is that in the 1950s British defence planners needed to cope with the emerging reality that by the 1960s the V-bomber force would be unable to fly over Moscow. As we shall see later, Moscow as a specific target held a special status in British Cold War planning. In the late 1950s Moscow was already emerging as arguably the best defended place on Earth, and it could no longer be assumed that British heavy bombers could get past the ever-improving Soviet air defences. The high-speed stand-off weapon was the solution.

Victor take-off with Blue Steel [Photographer: Stephen P. Peltz]

Despite the lack of experience in guided weapons, the task of developing Blue Steel was given to the A.V. Roe company, developer of the Vulcan bomber. The Blue Steel weapon was delivered to a distance originally hoped to be hundreds of miles from the actual target and released. The Vulcan and Victor bombers needed to be specially adapted to cope with the large Blue Steel missile, flying from a semi-recessed bay below the aircraft fuselage.[60] As the project moved forward the workable range of Blue Steel eroded, especially after the re-purposing of the Vulcan and Victor bombers for low-level attack.

The Blue Steel missile used as fuel a mix of kerosene and high-test peroxide or 'HTP'. HTP is a most unpleasant substance. It can quickly burn the skin or cause blindness, and hence those working with Blue Steel needed special suits and safety procedures. The British regarded HTP as something of a wonder fuel, and they did more to develop it for use than any other country. The British had discovered that a silver-plated nickel gauze catalyst could be used spontaneously to decompose high concentration HTP into steam and oxygen. The oxygen could in turn be combusted with the kerosene fuel for greater thrust.[61]

Blue Steel was in active service as part of the UK strategic nuclear deterrent from late 1962 until 1970. While Blue Steel-equipped bombers were taken to alert during the Cuba Crisis of October 1962, it is believed that at that time the weapons were not cleared for independent flight and hence would have functioned as little more than conventional gravity bombs.[62]

In the late 1950s, as British engineers worked on stand-off (Blue Steel) and ballistic (Blue Streak) missile designs, the world for Britain was changing. A key part of that transition would be the Suez Crisis of 1956.

1956: THE SUEZ CRISIS

The proximate cause of the Suez Crisis was the 26 July 1956 decision by Egyptian President Gamal Abdel Nasser to nationalise the Suez Canal. This came against a backdrop of his repositioning Egyptian allegiances away from the west and into a more non-aligned role, with friendly relations with the Soviet Union and the People's Republic of China. The canal had been constructed on French initiative in the late 19th century and had played a vitally strategic role for the British Empire in the late 19th and early 20th centuries. In 1956 it still represented an enormously important strategic resource for both France and Britain. The nationalisation decision caused much anger and disquiet in London and Paris, and a secret plan was hatched with Israel.

On 29 October 1956 Israel launched Operation Kadesh – an invasion of the Sinai Peninsula and the Gaza Strip. The British and French, who had positioned naval and air assets in the eastern Mediterranean, feigned outrage at the conflict and issued an ultimatum to both sides. On 31 October, they initiated bombing campaigns. Their purpose was to secure the canal under their control. While largely successful militarily, the British, French and Israeli adventure was a geopolitical disaster for the British and French. Not only was their subterfuge increasingly clear for all to see, but both the Soviet Union and the United States were aligned in their hostility to the intervention. The strength of American government opposition was somewhat unforeseen, and in the face of it the British and French had to withdraw speedily. For many, this was the clearest sign of a transfer of geopolitical power across the Atlantic from the old European colonial powers to the United States.

Indeed the late 1950s were the years of grave errors by European Great Powers, applying as they did misguided thinking and outdated mindsets to post-war problems. The British diplomat Robert Cooper observed:

> Suez was a mistake, at least for Britain: it was fought on the basis that Nasser was a new Hitler and a threat to order, but neither the threat nor the order really existed. Algeria was a mistake: France was fighting for a concept of state (Algeria remaining a part of metropolitan France) that was no longer sustainable. Vietnam was a mistake: the United States thought it was fighting the Cold War when in reality it was continuing a French colonial campaign. These conceptual errors had heavy costs. Clarity of thought is a contribution to peace.[63]

The subterfuge and cynicism of the Israeli–French–British actions in the Suez campaign led to a massive worsening of UK–US relations. The Eisenhower Administration did not, as British prime minister Anthony Eden had hoped, regard the events as an action by the west against a Soviet-leaning Egyptian regime, but rather regarded the whole sorry affair as a dishonest threat to regional, and even global, security. Eisenhower wrote to Eden:

> All of this development, with its possible consequences, including the possible involvement of you and the French in a general Arab war, seems to me to leave your

Government and ours in a very sad state of confusion, so far as any possibility of unified understanding and action are concerned. It is true that Egypt has not yet formally asked this Government for aid but the fact is that if the United Nations finds Israel to be an aggressor, Egypt could very well ask the Soviets for help – and then the Middle East fat would really be in the fire. It is this latter possibility that has led us to insist that the West must ask for a United Nations examination and possible intervention, for we may shortly find ourselves not only at odds concerning what we should do, but confronted with a de-facto situation that would make all our present troubles look puny indeed.[64]

Suez was to cast a long shadow across British foreign policy and defence thinking. For the British government, the years and decades that followed were shaped by the desire to rebuild the much vaunted, but never really extant 'special relationship' with America. For military types in particular Suez was not a happy memory: Sir Dermot Boyle, chief of the air staff in 1956, is reported to have remarked in 1987:

When you compare it with the Second World War, one was proud of everything that happened in the Second World War, and one wasn't proud of everything that happened at Suez. I think that's about the summing up of the situation.[65]

Many, however, held negative impressions not because of the dishonesty and neo-colonialism of the Suez debacle but because more simply it represented a failure.

Evelyn Shuckburgh at the Imperial Defence College (IDC) noted in his diary:

Now that our withdrawal 'without delay' from Suez has been announced by Selwyn Lloyd, everyone at the IDC has become suddenly very gloomy and all the services feel that they have been betrayed, and that we will never be able to show any independence as a nation again. A long letter from Admiral 'Lofty' [Sir Arthur] Power, who has been on the operation, and who describes it as 'conceived in deceit and arrested pusillanimity'. Petrol is up by one and sixpence.[66]

The RAF tried to use the Suez Crisis to demonstrate the capability of the V-bomber by deploying Valiants from four squadrons to the RAF's air base at Luqa in Malta. As with the rest of the Suez campaign, this demonstration of Franco-British power did not go well: the Valiants faced no resistance and were presented with only the easiest of targets.[67] It was not a combat test of the V-force in any sense whatsoever.

A BOMB WITH A UNION JACK ON IT

The early 1950s were a busy time for British nuclear engineers. The first nuclear power stations were under construction in Cumberland (part of what would later become Cumbria). Meanwhile in facilities across the country, work was under way on a British atomic bomb, to be known as Blue Danube. It was a similar design to the American Fat Man dropped on

Nagasaki at the end of the Second World War, but the British design incorporated various improvements, notably relating to safer transport, and was undertaken without access to previous American collaborators and their files, as that had been blocked by the US McMahon Act of 1946. It would not be until 1958 that the British would regain access to American secrets, despite having worked collaboratively during the war on the Manhattan Project. It was the remembered knowledge of the British scientists that allowed Blue Danube to emerge. Britain not only needed knowledge; it needed plutonium – and that was being hurriedly produced up in Cumberland, at the Windscale facility. Windscale was a name that would become infamous when in October 1957 one of the plutonium-producing reactors or 'piles', as they were then known, caught fire, causing one of the world's worst nuclear accidents.

One young scientist involved in Blue Danube was Colin Hughes. He had taken a job at Fort Halstead in Kent without knowing what the work would be. His work involved him in the early phase of bomb development, and led him to travel to Australia as part of the team involved in Britain's second nuclear weapons test in the desert, near the middle of Australia, at a camp known as Emu. The precise location is in northern South Australia, not far from a small community called Mabel Creek. Getting from Aldermaston, to which operations had moved in late 1952, to central Australia in 1953 was no easy task, and Colin Hughes recalls it well. One part of his story is especially evocative of the times and of the importance given to the task in hand. He writes of his four-day journey to Sydney on a Lockheed Constellation, the airliner developed at the initiative of American aviator and businessman Howard Hughes:

> The Constellation was an elegant, four engined, propeller driven aircraft large in size but carrying just 40 passengers in style. The aisle was wide to accommodate a restaurant-style serving trolley, from which three or four course meals were served. We had china dishes and plates, real cutlery and linen napkins. There was opportunity to stretch legs during the flight and on the ground. There were many stops: short stops to set-down and pick-up passengers at Frankfurt and Java, allowing ongoing passengers to take coffee in the terminal building; longer stops for refuelling and refreshments at Rome, Karachi, Calcutta and Darwin; and overnight stays in hotels at Beirut and Singapore, the costs included in the fare.[68]

That trip for a young man from the valleys of South Wales was a step into another world; a world more familiar to Hollywood movie stars and captains of colonial industries. It was clear to the small team from Aldermaston, travelling in style, that the atomic bomb was important.

As the Suez Crisis dominated British and French concerns, a significant event occurred in Europe. In Hungary, a student protest on 23 October 1956 became one of the most significant challenges to Communist power in post-war central and eastern Europe. Protests by students snowballed into full-scale revolution such that one week later one might have achieved the impression that Hungary had liberated itself from Soviet control. Any such optimism, however, was very short lived; on 4 November the Soviet military struck back, and within one week the country was firmly under Moscow's control. The events in Hungary are remembered for the lack of a strong response from the west. Western radio broadcasts had played an important role in building the protest, but were no match for Soviet guns. America's Radio Free Europe analysed its influence via a 1957 survey of 315 newly arrived refugees.[69] Claiming such people to be representative of the population as a whole, the RFE researchers observed that a remarkable 97 per cent listened to western broadcasts, and of these 96 per cent listened to RFE, although not exclusively. Of the various types of programmes on offer, news was that most eagerly sought by the listeners.

LOWE AND HAYHURST

In 1956 former Bomber Command pilot Douglas Lowe was in his early thirties, and he found himself involved in a most interesting task. Together with the similarly young and dynamic John Hayhurst from the Future Projects Office of the Ministry of Supply, Lowe was tasked with developing a new operational requirement, number 339, for an aircraft system capable of meeting an emergent idea – the Islands Strategy – and likely advances in Eastern European air defences.

Lowe and Hayhurst together developed the specification which was to start the TSR2 story. Lowe describes the requirement:

> We devised a concept of target approach at very low level to get under radar cover and delay detection until the last possible moment. (Radar had difficulty in dealing with ground clutter and the Moving Target Information technique was a long way in the future). We also proposed that the speed of attack should be the highest possible subsonic Mach number. Because of the range needed between islands we proposed a 1000nms radius of action with 700nms at altitude and the final 300nms at 50 feet and speed increasing to Mach 0.9. Also, having in mind the high engine power needed for the high speed, low level requirement, we thought it should be possible to ask for short take off and landing as well. It was clearly going to be expensive and when presented to the DPC [Defence Policy Committee] was not well received.[70]

While Lowe and Hayhurst were not the first to propose low and fast attack, the combination with the other operational capabilities yielded a formidable and novel technological challenge.

Lowe further provides an insight into the later controversy as to whether the Buccaneer might have been a better bet. He continues:

> We were told to consider [presumably by the DPC] other aircraft already in service or being developed such as the Naval Strike aircraft the NA 39 (later named Buccaneer), or even a so called thin wing Javelin. We laboured at papers rejecting these alternatives, mainly because of inadequate range, but still failed to get official blessing for OR339.

Our new project had become stalled at TDC, an abbreviation normally standing for 'Top Dead Centre' but to John and me it now meant 'Top Dead Central Committee'

The British aircraft industry was becoming desperate for work and Lowe and Hayhurst were regularly visited by industry designers keen to learn something about the planned Operational Requirement (OR) 339. Without official approval, which the relevant committees would not give, it was not possible to issue the industry with a firm requirement in the form of an OR. Lowe and Hayhurst came up with the idea of issuing a General Operational Requirement: GOR 339.[71] This would indicate the general idea under consideration, but place the responsibility and the cost for design squarely with the aircraft companies. The only thing Lowe and Hayhurst had changed in their paper was the title – but now they had sidestepped the problematic requirement of committee approval.

Sir Douglas recalls:

> Six months later John asked me to go and see him. He took me into a spare office and there stacked to the ceiling were the brochures from most, if not all, the major firms giving solutions to GOR 339. There was so much detail and paper and firms were so anxious to ensure safe arrival that vans had been hired for the delivery. Moreover for the Government it was something for nothing, for industry had done the work as a Private Venture.[72]

As the weeks passed Lowe recalls that political interest in the ideas started to grow and some started to see the GOR339 project as a means to reduce the size of the British aircraft industry through forced amalgamations.[73] Taking these ideas on board, the two young men chose the more attractive elements of several design proposals, looked to the track records of the companies behind the ideas, and put together a hybrid.[74] That hybrid would go on to become the TSR2, but before it flew Douglas Lowe had moved on, posted to RAF Manby for a flying college course. He was to have no further direct contact with the TSR2. When interviewed in May 2011 he remembered the days of GOR339 happily. He commented:

> I'm looking at it through the eyes of a very junior officer, Squadron Leader, in this vast Air Ministry, completely unused to it. … Having gone through the variants of the Canberra, the PR7, PR9, and got those under way, I was then faced with this request to write a requirement for the replacement, which … at first, I gazed at my blank sheet of paper with awe, and wasn't quite sure what to do. … You see, the difficulty for the Air Force, at that stage, is, the Navy had its dockyards, and the Army had its various depots, and they were totally responsible for not only saying what they wanted, but getting it. Aircraft production became of key importance, and Churchill had brought in Beaverbrook to do that, and that had resulted in a new Ministry, a Ministry of Supply, with Beaverbrook at the head, and it had absorbed all the aircraft industry and organised it, and very successfully. It produced all the aeroplanes that were required. But, after the War, the Air Force was then straining at the bit, by comparison with the

Army and the Navy, not really having control of its procurement. It was in another Ministry, which in fact was at the other end of St Martin's Lane, up in St Giles Court. And when I arrived in the Operational Requirements Division, dealing with the Canberra, … every time there was a problem and there was a complaint from the frontline or anywhere in the Air Force, you were writing minutes to these people … and then days went by, and the delay was absolutely appalling! I just got fed up with it, and decided that it's no good writing minutes. I'm afraid I'm a person who doesn't write a great deal. … I got on my legs and walked up, and bashed my way into this Ministry. … It took me an hour, on the first day, to actually get through the door and get a pass and … I had to say who I was meeting, and why I was meeting and so on. When I eventually broke into the door of this chap I'd been corresponding [with], he turned out to be somebody as old as my father and five times more doddery … So it was no wonder we weren't getting anywhere. So, at that stage, I thought, well, we're not going to get very far with the Canberra replacement in this organisation.

But, luckily, the future requirements were dealt with under Handel Davies – now, he's another very important chap, and he was Future Aircraft Requirements or Future Aircraft Technology, and that's when I met this chap John Hayhurst, who was an enormous influence on me, and TSR-2 and everything else. … There was literally no money – the defence budget was under enormous pressure. The Navy were after new carriers, we were after this Canberra replacement, the Army was after a new tank, and, you know, the whole thing was in great difficulty.[75]

Over the years much has been written about the TSR2 and its eventual cancellation. Numerous aviation experts have commented on the relative merits of the Blackburn Buccaneer, the General Dynamics F-111 and BAC TSR2. Sir Douglas Lowe's remarks relating to the very earliest days of the TSR2 project make clear that the choices facing the UK in times of great austerity were not between aircraft for a contract with the Royal Air Force, the contest was much bigger than that; it was between the services themselves. The UK simply could not afford the TSR2, new aircraft carriers and a new main battle tank for the Army. The TSR2 story lies at the heart of UK Cold War defence policy. It is not merely a footnote in the history of the Royal Air Force.

1957 'NEVER HAD IT SO GOOD'

During 1957 and early 1958 four Valiants from 49 Squadron were used in the British 'Grapple' hydrogen bomb tests conducted from Christmas Island in the South Pacific. The Grapple tests comprised four series: Grapple, followed by Grapple X, Y and Z. It was during the single test firing of Grapple Y on 28 April 1958 that a Vickers Valiant dropped Britain's biggest hydrogen bomb, with a yield of 3 megatons (i.e. equivalent to 3 million tons of TNT). In demonstrating a true hydrogen bomb with a megaton yield developed under its own resources, the United Kingdom was to open the door to the fullest nuclear collaboration with the United States. This would be cemented via the Mutual Defence Agreement of the following year. These issues are discussed more fully in Chapter 10.

1957 is the year in which the figure of Duncan Sandys re-enters our story, via the publication of the Defence White Paper which to this day is associated with his name.[76] The White Paper is remembered most strongly for a perceived assertion that in future, combat in the air would be conducted via missiles rather than using piloted aircraft. Such a bold position might have merit in the early 21st century, but in the middle of the 20th it was far too premature an idea. In fact the White Paper does not make the famous claim explicitly. The White Paper is noteworthy for its brevity, at only ten pages, in contrast to the voluminous defence policy documents of today. It emphasises a simple set of key messages. First, that Britain cannot afford its bloated defence system, with costs running at 10 per cent of gross national product, employing 7 per cent of the workforce and with 690,000 men in uniform. It is repeatedly stated that too much national effort and technical capability is being devoted to defence which could more beneficially be employed in civilian industry. Second, and most profoundly, the Sandys White Paper points to the importance of nuclear deterrence, stating: 'the overriding consideration in all military planning must be to prevent war rather than to prepare for it'. Given the British combat experience in Suez, Malaya and Korea, it is this notion of a nuclear weapons-determined strategy that jumps off the page. It is in such a context that the RAF would shift away from fighter interceptors and towards guided missiles. The Sandys White Paper restricted its *missiles in preference to manned aircraft* message to the RAF, as it noted that for the Royal Navy 'the role of the aircraft carrier, which is in effect a mobile air station, becomes increasingly significant.'

Although the White Paper cancelled the Avro-730 large supersonic bomber project, it held open the prospect of Air Force aircraft for nuclear strike – this is the aircraft that would become known as TSR2.

The third major idea of the White Paper is perhaps the one that resonated deepest in British society. A generation of young men, which included my father, were relieved to learn that National Service would be abolished by the end of 1960 and that they would hence be spared that particular experience.

Whatever the words of the White Paper, it is the case that it proposed a radically different future for the Royal Air Force; and for those concerned with new RAF manned aircraft there was the prospect of only one major show in town going forward – it would be TSR2.

For his book *Nuclear Illusion, Nuclear Reality*, Richard Moore uncovered an amusing entry in the *Sunday Express* of 11 May 1958 concerning Duncan Sandys. That newspaper observed of the man behind the notion that the future would have no more need for pilots:

> Picture the drama that swirls about this rugged, red-haired, remarkable figure. Every morning at 9.30 sharp he walks hatless up the steps into the Ministry of Defence building overlooking St James's Park. Every morning he sits himself firmly behind his desk and gazes with his cool, unblinking eyes at the procession of service chiefs

and other officials who come to see him. Most of them gaze back with equal coolness. For in their minds is but a single thought. *How on earth can we get rid of this fellow?*[77] (Emphasis original.)

The architecture of British government relating military planning to defence procurement in the late 1950s was completely different from that of today. The Whitehall landscape was cluttered with the Ministry of Supply, the War Office, the Admiralty and the Air Ministry, and from 1959 the Ministry of Aviation as well, with responsibilities for technology R&D. Richard Moore notes:

> The MOD ... was not the huge organisation it has become today; on the contrary, its powers were limited and its staff numbered in the hundreds rather than in the thousands. Until 1958, the minister's authority derived chiefly from his responsibility to allocate resources between the three single service ministries; he 'had no powers of initiative either in the field of strategic planning or of weapons procurement'.[78]

In the early 1950s it was clear to the British government that there were simply too many aircraft companies; a structure that had served the country's needs in wartime was no longer appropriate to the high-technology demands of the Cold War. Gone were the nightly bombing raids of the Luftwaffe; gone was the need to run hidden shadow factories; and gone was the need to ensure progress without the possibility of national coordination. The new realities would demand focus, communication and economies of scale.

On 16 September 1957 Sir Cyril Musgrave, the permanent secretary of the Ministry of Supply, summoned the leadership of the 11 largest companies in the British aircraft industry to the ministry's offices in Shell-Mex House, London. There he told them that following the Sandys White Paper only one manned military aircraft project would be commissioned, and that would be for Lowe and Hayhurst's GOR339 – the project that would become the TSR2. Even more shocking than the news of the scaling back of military orders was the announcement that it was the intention of government to award the GOR339 project to a consortium. Sir Cyril made it clear that the future for the British aircraft industry lay with no more than four grouped units. For the 11 company bosses present, the instruction was clear: 'amalgamate or die'.[79] As it turned out, by the end of the sixties there would not be four groups – only two. Lowe and Hayhurst's GOR339 would profoundly reshape the British aircraft industry.

The double challenge of industrial reorganisation and world-beating technology development lay at the heart of the ministry's plan. The aircraft industry understood and did not underestimate the challenge ahead. Prominent among the industrial leaders present at the Shell-Mex House meeting was George Edwards, head of Vickers-Armstrongs (Aircraft) Ltd. Vickers was already a mighty aircraft company when a young George Edwards joined the company in 1935 as a design draughtsman.[80] Revealing his design talents early on, he was soon promoted. By the time of the 1957 meeting, Edwards was a towering figure in the industry, but he knew that his Weybridge design team did not have the experience necessary to deliver such an advanced supersonic project. From the days of the Edwards-designed Wellington bomber with its advanced geodesic airframe through to the success of the Vickers Viscount passenger aircraft, the company had become known for large aircraft increasingly catering to civil markets.

Seeing the need for fast jet experience and focused on winning the GOR339 project, Edwards turned Vickers' attention to Supermarine – most famous for designing the iconic fighter, the Spitfire, for the RAF. The Supermarine project of greatest interest to Edwards was the Scimitar. This carrier-based aircraft was just entering service with the Royal Navy at the point that the terms of GOR339 were being announced.

Despite the success of the Scimitar, Supermarine knew that the future would be difficult for their design team. George Edwards proposed that key Supermarine designers such as George Henson and Alan Clifton should move to Vickers to head up a new design group at Weybridge dedicated to the challenge of GOR339.[81]

Despite Edwards' gambit of partnering with Supermarine, once the various competing teams had lodged their designs with the air staff it was clear that a rival bidder had the preferred airframe design. The winning ideas had come from English Electric in the form of their P.17 proposal. This was to be a delta wing design with pilot and observer seated in tandem and powered by twin RB.142/3 engines with reheat.[82]

What the government really wanted, however, was the Vickers integrated systems approach and project management capability matched with the supersonic know-how of English Electric. The government morphed GOR339 into GOR343 so as to suit the needs and demands of Vickers and English Electric, and a collaboration was born.

As Vickers faced the prospect of merger with English Electric, George Edwards recalled:[83]

> The Vickers Directors emerged with the job of convincing blokes like me that it was a fate worse than death on the one hand, but sooner or later we would have to get on with English Electric on the other.

Robert Gardner comments on the culture shock between Vickers and English Electric when he wrote:

> Whereas Vickers had traditionally been led by its chief designers – Pierson, Wallis and now Edwards – English Electric Aviation was ruled by those at its manufacturing power base at Preston, presided over by the dominating figure of Arthur Sheffield. Designers such as Petter and party were given short shrift by Sheffield who reported directly to Lord Nelson. The aviation company was merely a subsidiary and was treated as such.[84]

Richard 'Dick' Evans, later a leading figure in the aerospace industry, recalled those days at English Electric with the words:

Sheffield was a tyrant. ... 'The design company was totally separate from the manufacturing company run by Sheffield. Sheffield had run the whole of the Hampden programme during the war and built up expertise in building aircraft. He treated Petter and his guys as a bunch of complete amateurs, and they were certainly never taken seriously ... . So there was a very unusual coexistence between the two organisations.[85]

Vickers' George Edwards recalled what faced him as the head of the new BAC:

I had got to face up to designing a pretty difficult aeroplane and coping with a very difficult production problem in one ball of wax. The timescale really didn't allow for a lot of farting about between two big companies that had got themselves into one. As far as I remember, I was bloody anxious as to how I was to overcome the law of the jungle between the two, and at the same time design and make an aeroplane of the performance and general quality of the TSR2.[86]

Vickers and its new partner, English Electric, could not have been more different. While Vickers was a company steeped in tradition and capable of designing and building some of the largest aircraft flying, it was a broad-based aviation company with an increasing emphasis on the rapidly growing field of civil aviation. English Electric, in contrast, was not a cohesive entity. The main company was a sprawling, diversified conglomerate responsible for producing all manner of electrical equipment from power distribution equipment to trolley buses and trams. Within it, however, was a most remarkable aircraft company, which had been formed to serve the needs of wartime aircraft production producing other companies' designs under licence in hidden shadow factories. After the war English Electric aircraft designers had produced some of the most beautiful and successful military aircraft of the era. For example, the Canberra light bomber and reconnaissance aircraft had been so successful that it was even built under licence in the United States. The last British Canberra aircraft only left RAF service in 2006. Another English Electric success was the remarkable English Electric Lightning interceptor, perhaps the fastest jet the RAF has ever, or will ever, fly. This shiny, unpainted aircraft consists of little more than a pilot astride two massive Rolls-Royce Avon supersonic jet engines. With little or no space inside the fuselage and with the wings used as fuel tanks, any munitions were slung under the low-profile swept-back wings. While by the late 1950s Vickers had become safe, or even dull, English Electric Aircraft was a creative place of vision and success, perhaps in part as a consequence of the difficulties it faced in dealing with its parent company, headed by the oppressive presence of Arthur Sheffield.

In the late 1940s the newly formed design team of the English Electric Company was housed in a wartime-requisitioned garage in Corporation Street in Preston. The team was led by the enormously creative but diffident William 'Teddy' Petter.[87] Only a few yards away in Strand Road stood the Dick-Kerr engineering works of English Electric, managed by Arthur Sheffield, a man described as 'crusty' by Roland Beamont.[88] It was Sheffield's empire that had so successfully produced the aircraft for the RAF during the war. As we have already seen, the relationship between Sheffield's vast enterprise and Petter's new upstart team was not good. Roland Beamont, who joined Petter's team in 1947, described the relationship between the two outfits in Preston as one of 'mistrust and antagonism'.[89]

Roland Beamont was the first man to fly the magnificent Lightning. He flew the P1B prototype to Mach 2.0 in 1958, and observed wryly: 'Britain now has a potential Mach 2.0 fighter as a result of the determination of Teddy Petter, Freddy (*sic*) Page and the English Electric team not to be diverted by the government edict of 1947 that manned supersonic flight was too dangerous for the British.'[90]

Air Commodore (ret'd) Neil Taylor described his first contact with the English Electric Lightning as a 25-year-old RAF officer arriving at RAF Coltishall in 1971:

> We were pretty awestruck by looking at this beast, which was sitting on the flight-line there. Day one was arrival. Day two we had a familiarisation trip, where we got ourselves in our flying kit and we jumped in the aeroplane. Sat in the left hand seat, which is the captain's seat and the instructor sat in the right hand seat and he said 'OK this is just air experience you don't have to do anything at all except press the stopwatch, and I'll say 'now' when I let the brakes off – press the stopwatch, and stop it when I get … say 'now' at 40,000 feet. And the rest was a bit of a blur I have to say; in that it accelerated like a rocket … It climbs really incredibly quickly. From ground level to 40,000 feet took two minutes and 15 seconds. This was in the training version which was called the 'T-bird' which was pretty sluggish by single-seat standards. And there we were at 40,000 feet doing Mach .9 cruising along and that was about the time to start the recovery– we had nearly burned all the fuel. So it was a turn around the Norfolk coast at what became the Bacton terminal and the technique in the Lightning for descending was, from what was now about 36,000 feet you looked at the distance from the runway that you were going to land on and you halved it and added two. So at 36,000 feet we needed to descend at eighteen miles plus two – so twenty miles from the airfield, you selected idle and fast idle on the engines. Fast idle was to keep the a.c. power on-line. That maintains 65% on one engine and 34% on the other… and then just lower the nose, accelerate to .95 down the hill which was about a 30-degree dive … and then I seem to remember it was 2,000 feet above the height you wanted to level at… Now still not touching the throttles you break into the circuit. A 6G break into the circuit and you are pulling down all the way and I can still remember vividly to this day the final turn. Now most aeroplanes in the final turn you have to be careful not to stall it and the sure-fire indication that you're stalling, of course, in-stall-buffet, getting buffet across the wings. The Lightning flies into buffet all the time when you are in a turn. I was sitting in the left hand seat in a left-hand turn I am sitting at the bottom and my instructor is sitting up here above me and we are going round the corner looking for the runway, which is over here somewhere and you are travelling at this stage at about … 200 knots going around the final turn and it gets to 300 feet. Roll the wheels level, start to ease the power up, to cushion the landing… brake action and then stop. And I think that was a 23 minute sortie from

grey tar to grey tar. And I can recall the next vivid memory is thinking there is no way in the world that I'll hack this. And indeed... the loss rate on the course, it was called the 'chop rate', was pretty high... It was a very, very demanding aeroplane, and indeed one of the people on the course with me was chopped at the end of that air experience ride, never having touched the controls.[91]

Taylor describes his experience of the Lightning's infamous thirst for fuel:

Again another trip that sticks in my memory is one night in December, coming up to Christmas when the weather was absolutely foul. And we got airborne. I was dual with one of the weapons instructors to do some intercepts. And again, as the student, you sit in the left-hand seat, which is the Captain's seat. [The instructor] has got a very limited display and he has got to look across you to see yours – so the prospects of him doing much ... are very limited. He's got a stick, a stick with throttles, but that's about it. And we came back from this particular sortie and there was a thick snowstorm. We made a first approach into Coltishall and didn't see the runway, so you overshoot. Now when you are recovering on fuel in the Lightning the basic rule was: if you were cruising in at 36,000 feet, which is the normal recovery height, once you started your descent you no longer had sufficient fuel to get to your weather diversion. So there was a decision made there: do I elect to go down? If I go down, I know I can't make the weather diversion, but I can make the crash diversion. On this particular night Coltishall was Base, weather diversion I think was Binbrook, might even have been Leuchars, crash diversion was Marham and we went down the hill. Didn't see the runway at all; it was a thick snowstorm. So you either go straight to the crash diversion or you do what the guy who was the captain decided we were going to do was overshoot and have another attempt, which I thought hmmm ... that's going to make it a bit tight if we end up going to the crash diversion by missing again. So, again, you can save a bit of fuel by shutting one engine down. So we flew the overshoot and the close-pattern VCA approach single engine. So you put yourself in an emergency situation already and tried a PAR – a Precision Approach Radar approach monitored instrument landing system – so you are flying two systems, hmmm, and [we] actually made it. You know – we saw the runway in the snowstorm. Putting down with probably a bit less fuel than we needed to get to our crash diversion. We would have been landing with less than minimums. You know, another lesson about the Lightning – it was always short of fuel and it could be desperately short of fuel very quickly and your options were pretty limited.[92]

But despite these concerns Taylor shares a widespread view among RAF interceptor pilots lucky enough to fly the Lightning:

It was a beautiful aeroplane. Sometimes you fall in love with aeroplanes and this was a very easy one to fall in love with. It looked nice, it flew like a dream. Anybody that can design an aeroplane that can go from zero to, well I flew it at Mach 2.3, up to 78,000 feet with the engines working, with the air flow over the wings perfectly reasoned. I mean it says an awful lot for the design; particularly when you have got the engines staggered as they were to fit them in the fuselage. It wasn't one directly above the other. It was one lower one and the upper one set back on the lower one. So in profile you had about one and a half engines' worth in the shape of the fuselage. But, actually to get the air-flow through that nose, and … split to go down the engines and come out the back without coughing and interrupting each other was absolutely unbelievable.[93]

Despite lacking the scale and breadth of experience of Vickers, English Electric would have much to contribute to the GOR339 project, or as it would later become known, TSR2.

SPUTNIK SHOCK

Friday 4 October 1957 started like any other day, but by the time it ended a wave of fear was spreading across America. The Soviet Union had launched the world's first artificial satellite, Sputnik I. About the size of a beach ball, it was a space-based radio transmitter, optimised not for reception by advanced space laboratories but by as many people as possible, the radio frequency used for transmitting the characteristic Sputnik 'beeps' having been chosen to suit amateur radio operators. The first official announcement of the launch was a small front-page story in the Soviet newspaper, *Pravda*, headed simply 'TASS report', a reference to the state news agency.[94] The world already knew, however, as the haunting beeps had already been heard by many thousands of radio hams, and Sputnik could even be seen in the night sky over America – America felt violated. Former US Congresswoman Clare Boothe Luce quipped that each beep from Sputnik was an 'intercontinental outer-space raspberry to a decade of American pretensions that the American way of life was a gilt-edged guarantee of our national superiority'.[95]

The extent of the shock is perhaps surprising given that the Soviets had been stating their intentions for months and had declared their plans to transmit on a widely accessible frequency and had described in the 1 June issue of *Radio* magazine how to pick up the signal. The only exception to the widespread sense of shock was the Japanese Radio Operators' League who had successfully monitored Sputnik from the moment it first went into orbit.[96]

Much of the fear of Sputnik related to the notion that if the Soviets could launch a radio transmitter into space then they could launch a nuclear weapon. While the truth of that initial logic was somewhat flawed, the idea soon strengthened when one month later, on 3 November, the Soviets launched Laika, the space dog, into orbit. The American response was dramatic – a massive increase in federal defence and space-related research. America had lost the first lap of the space race, and this would not be allowed to happen again.

1957 also saw the publication of a novel that was to shape attitudes to nuclear war and nuclear weapons. *On the Beach* by Nevil Shute, an engineer who had worked on the inter-war British airship programme, deals with events around Melbourne, Australia, in the months after a devastating nuclear war in the northern hemisphere.[97] A deeply fatalistic book, it arguably presented the right ideas but for the wrong reasons. In Shute's book the nuclear war has shifted to the use of weapons designed to kill by radioactive fallout rather than by blast and fire. The use of these weapons is so extensive that all human life on Earth is doomed. For those in Melbourne and the state of Victoria death is inevitable, but for much of the book it lies a few months away. The stoicism and relative normality of civilisation under such circumstances makes the book all the more frightening.

The premise of the book relies upon the notion of radiological warfare made possible by weapons capable of generating cataclysmic levels of fallout. A similar theme, the doomsday weapon, underpins another key component of Cold War popular culture, the 1964 movie *Dr Strangelove*. The weapons involved are sometimes termed 'salted bombs' – an allusion to the notion of fertile land being rendered useless when covered by salt. It appears that while in principle possible, such weapons have never been developed; their importance lies in popular culture and the public imagination.

The notion of a radiation war based on devastation by fallout may have had no basis in military thinking, and furthermore the consequences of such conflict may have been exaggerated, but the central notion of global catastrophe from a nuclear conflict is important. In the early 1980s concerns emerged that a nuclear conflict could generate sufficient smoke to alter the climate – the scenario was termed a 'nuclear winter'. This provided compelling evidence that the impacts of a nuclear war would not be restricted to the combatants, but could even harm the whole world. As the young and vibrant character Moira Davidson says in *On the Beach*: 'There never was a bomb dropped in the southern hemisphere, … Why must it come to us? Can't anything be done to stop it?'[98]

1958

The 1957 Sandys Defence White Paper had come as a blow to both the aircraft industry and to the Royal Air Force. The RAF of the late 1950s was led by officers whose formative experiences had been in the Second World War, either in the Battle of Britain or the later massed bombing raids on Germany. One such leader, the future air chief marshal, Wallace H. Kyle, had served Bomber Command at RAF Marham during the war. In 1958 he publicly challenged Duncan Sandys' views when, as assistant chief of the air staff and an air vice-marshal, he strongly supported a continued role for manned aircraft in a speech to a Royal Air Force conference. He later wrote up his ideas for the *Royal Air Force Flying Review* under the title 'Why The RAF Needs These Aircraft'.[99] Concerning the future of the V-bombers, he pointed to the coming introduction of the 'powered guided bomb' (Blue Steel Mark I) and to a range of electronic countermeasures for the aircraft which is 'in effect a form of defensive armament'. His only direct reference to the Sandys White Paper was carefully phrased: 'It is the manned fighter which provides the most difficult conundrum. A year ago it was officially announced that we would not develop another fighter, but circumstances change fairly rapidly'. He was, of course, to be proved right, although not because of ballistic missile countermeasures, as he went on to predict.

In fact since 1958 Britain has had a continuous role in the development of manned fighter aircraft, right up until the Eurofighter Typhoon of today. While today one can indeed see a future based upon unmanned aerial vehicles (UAVs) and missiles, in the 1950s Duncan Sandys' vision for an RAF future without pilots was premature at best. While the future was to see a long sequence of manned aircraft projects, the years immediately following the Sandys' report did indeed see a strong attempt by politicians of all parties to implement his radical vision. It is arguable that the role of reconnaissance is the thing that helped the GOR339 (TSR2) survive the Sandys White Paper as the only manned aircraft project whose development was recommended for continuation. Wallace Kyle was strongly supportive of the need for a Canberra replacement when he said:

> This aircraft must have the greatest possible flexibility. It must combine very high performance with the ability to operate from restricted airfields. We must exploit the latest developments in navigation, bombing and reconnaissance equipment to give it an all-embracing capability as a strike/reconnaissance aircraft in all weather conditions.[100]

In the years that followed, the pages of the magazine RAF Flying Review would continue to reverberate with opposition to government policy and the 1957 Sandys' White Paper. William Green penned an article called 'Supersonic Scrapheap!' for the September 1961 issue, in which he wrote:

> The fault is not that of the British aircraft manufacturers but that of short-sighted politicians who failed to see the need for consistent planning; whose withdrawal of backing from so many promising British combat aircraft which, for the most part, had been brought to the threshold of flight testing, culminated in the disastrous 1957 White Paper on Defence declaring an end to manned fighter development and the supplanting of the aeroplane by the missile![101]

Those that knew about military flying were not happy with Duncan Sandys and his bleak pilotless vision of the future. For them the only significant source of hope was GOR339 (TSR2).

It is only fair at this point to acknowledge, however, that the UK did have one other major aircraft project under way in the years after Sandys, one that was to turn out to be a global success story. It was the Harrier jump jet developed by Hawker Siddeley, of which more than 800 have been produced in one variant or another. The Harrier project survived the Sandys White Paper because it was built without British government money. While it did benefit from some NATO funding, the financial risk was shouldered by Hawker Siddeley in a remarkable example of leadership by the company board. An even more ambitious aircraft, Hawker Siddeley's vertical take-off and supersonic P.1154, required government support –and, like the TSR2, that project would end in cancellation in early 1965.

US-UK MUTUAL DEFENCE AGREEMENT

As we have seen, in the late 1950s Britain made a choice between on the one hand an evolution of imperial defence of, and with, far-flung dominions, and on the other hand a renewed and close defensive alignment with the United States. The Suez Crisis had made clear that British-led action would be impossible in the face of active American displeasure. It would not be until the Falklands conflict 26 years later that Britain would again develop a sense of national independent capability in a context of formal American neutrality, albeit with much behind-the-scenes American help. But in the late 1950s, British unilateral capability appeared unsustainable, and notions of imperial grandeur an anachronism. Britain's choice was clear – partnership with the United States.

The most substantial consequence of this new national re-alignment came with the signing on 3 July 1958 in Washington DC of a treaty entitled: *Agreement Between the Government of the United Kingdom of Great Britain and Northern Ireland and the Government of the United States of America for Cooperation on the Uses of Atomic Energy for Mutual Defense Purposes.*[102] The power relationships underlying this partnership are revealed by the rather unusual sight of American spellings and date formats in a British official document. The agreement, which has been repeatedly extended via treaty amendment, gave Britain access to the US W28 nuclear weapon design so that it might be modified for deployment on the Blue Steel Mark I missile. The related story of Britain's copying and tweaking of an American nuclear weapon design is discussed in Chapter 10.

A 1959 amendment to the Mutual Defense Agreement established the principle of nuclear barter under which the UK would provide the United States with 5.37 tonnes of plutonium in return for 6.7 kg of tritium and 7.5 tonnes of highly enriched uranium.[103] In addition the UK would provide the US with 470 kg of plutonium.[104] The US had an acute shortage of plutonium at this time, and Britain was able to assist. Britain, in contrast, was short of highly enriched uranium.

It is important to stress that the agreement does not cover just know-how and materials relating to nuclear weapons, but also, importantly, technology relating to the nuclear propulsion systems of submarines. One of the agreement's first measures was to transfer an entire nuclear propulsion system for Britain's first nuclear-powered submarine, HMS *Dreadnought*. After the success of bringing in American naval reactor technology, the UK commenced on a programme of British nuclear submarine propulsion led by Rolls-Royce, based in Derby. That national capacity exists to this day, and in recent years Rolls-Royce has started to stress the contribution that the company could make to developments in civil nuclear power. That said, in 2019 the company indicated a desire to sell off a large part of the capabilities it had built up in the civil domain.

Meanwhile the journey to develop Britain's new strike bomber was proving complicated. During 1958 the original GOR339 was revised four times each time making the task ahead more difficult and demanding for the engineers at Vickers and English Electric.[105]

The ever more demanding requirements were inevitably to have a consequence in increasing project costs. Concerns for cost have been a near-continuous theme in UK nuclear defence planning, and indeed they remain to the fore today as the UK contemplates the future of the nuclear deterrent.

Cost concerns were so intense in 1958 that in part they prompted the chancellor of the exchequer, Peter Thorneycroft, to resign in January of that year. He observed:

> For 12 years we have been attempting to do more than our resources could manage, and in the process we have been gravely weakening ourselves ... First, we have sought to be a nuclear power, matching missile with missile and anti-missile with anti-missile ... At the same time, we have sought to maintain a welfare state ... We have been trying to do those things against a background of having to repay debt abroad during the next eight years of a total equivalent to the whole of our existing reserves; against the background of having to meet maturing debt in this country ... against a background of seeking to conduct a great international banking business and against a background of sustaining our positions of one of the world's major overseas investors. In those circumstances, it is small wonder that we find some difficulties.[106]

1958 flowed into 1959, and the dream of Britain's Canberra replacement aircraft needed to shift from an aspiration to a tangible exercise in engineering design. This design could no longer be known as simply an operational requirement number – so, despite the fact that no order had been placed, it needed a name. It was decided that the name should not imply that that the plane was to be a bomber in the traditional RAF sense, as it was too soon after the very public cancellation of the large supersonic bomber project, the Avro-730. On 1 January 1959 the name was announced – it was TSR/2, along with a D-Notice to the media telling them to say nothing about the aircraft's actual capabilities beyond the words: 'this aircraft will be a strike reconnaissance aircraft which will be supersonic and capable of operating from small airfields with rudimentary surfaces'.[107] (Over the years of the TSR2 almost every possible presentation of the of the name was used by those involved. While TSR.2 featured more prominently than most (including TSR/2) we here adopt the simplest form, TSR2, except when quoting contemporary materials, in which case the presentation used in that original source is maintained.)

So by early 1959 in Weybridge, Surrey, the two formerly rival teams sat down together to plan a joint enterprise whose scale and ambition would test them like nothing before or since. That enterprise was TSR2. The supersonic pioneers of English Electric found themselves opposite the imposing delegation from Vickers-Armstrongs (Aircraft) Ltd led by the formidable George Edwards.[108] Unlike the exploratory policy-focused meetings at Shell-Mex House in 1957 the agenda now was clear – the TSR2 had to be built – and two very different companies, Vickers and English Electric, would need to learn how to work together as the new British Aircraft Corporation.

EAST OF SUEZ

It is easy from the perspective of the 21st century to forget that in the early 1950s Britain retained global defence responsibilities. The military needs of far-flung commitments increasingly came into tension with more European, NATO-oriented, concerns. The prospect of another major war in Europe loomed ever larger, becoming an existential threat to the UK. By 1958 a change was under way, but it would take many years to percolate through national thinking. Britain would increasingly orient her concerns towards North America and Europe and turn away from her southern dominions, and retreat from colonial thinking. In 1958 those still concerned about defence threats 'East of Suez' appreciated other risks and threats than those being considered by their colleagues oriented to issues in the North Atlantic, Europe and the Arctic Ocean.

There were numerous threats to consider East of Suez; the 1960s would see significant conflict in the Aden Crown Colony and the Aden Protectorate – and, of course, there was ever-increasing violence and conflict in Vietnam and across Southeast Asia. British military thinking for East of Suez contained a set of competing ideas and proposals. It should be stressed that for military planners experienced with global conventional conflict in the Second World War, these East of Suez challenges were intellectually more attractive than the apocalyptic scenarios of conflict in Europe. The concerns of these military thinkers were not as lofty as notions of a Fourth British Empire, but they would highlight the need for change as pre-war colonial structures became increasingly unsustainable. Previous plans based upon a network of globally connected bases were vulnerable to growing anti-colonial sentiment. Military historian Ian Speller has highlighted that these fixed bases, lacking expeditionary capability, were too inflexible and also represented a focus for local resentment.[109] The Abadan crisis of 1951 and the Suez Crisis of 1956 would reveal the shortcomings most starkly: too many British bases were leased from foreign countries, rendering them vulnerable to deteriorating relations with the host country. This was when the Royal Air Force came up with the idea of the Islands Strategy; it would allow the UK, if equipped with suitably advanced aircraft, to maintain a credible position from a limited number of sovereign bases, some of which – for example Cyprus – would literally be on islands. In addition, it was possible to imagine the use of nuclear weapons in such regional conflicts such that the British homeland itself would not be put at risk. Increasingly in Europe nuclear weaponry would be seen as a deterrent to conflict rather than as part of an actual conflict.

Needless to say, the Royal Navy, looking ahead, saw an alternative future to the Islands Strategy; it was pushing for a new fleet aircraft carrier, designated as 'CVA'. This would be the biggest British carrier thus far (53,000 tons[110]), and work designing the first example, CVA-01, would start in 1962.[111] The Navy's grand project, however, would fall victim to defence budget cuts in February 1966, not unlike those that had ended the TSR2 dream a few months earlier. Part of the thinking behind the cancellation of the CVA-01 was the need to keep open the option of the American F-111 as a replacement for the cancelled TSR2.

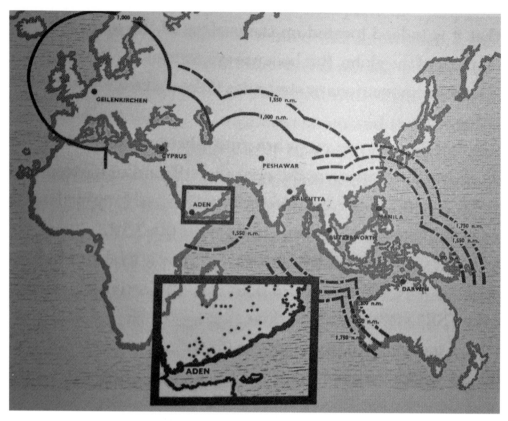

*The RAF Islands Strategy would allow UK power to be projected in protection of
its core interests from a limited number of stable bases [Brooklands Museum]*

Arguably the RAF Islands Strategy outlived the Royal Navy's fleet carrier vision, but it too
would die in January 1968 with the cancellation of the British F-111 order.

It is interesting to note that in 2014 and 2017 the Royal Navy has launched two new
Queen Elizabeth class aircraft carriers. At 65,000 tonnes, these are the largest ships the Royal
Navy has ever possessed. What role will they have for post-Brexit Britain?

CHAPTER FIVE - COLD WAR KIT: 1960-1963

It is not the purpose of this book to provide a comprehensive history of Britain's post-war aircraft industry. Keith Hayward has already done that with his two books, *Government and British Civil Aerospace* (1983) and *The British Aircraft Industry* (1989).[112] Our purposes can be better served by focusing on the period between two major government documents: the Sandys Defence White Paper of 1957 and the December 1965 Report of the Committee of Inquiry into the Aircraft Industry, named for its chairman, Lord Plowden.[113] These two documents bracket in time our particular focus: the tactical strike and reconnaissance aircraft TSR2. They also shape the development, the cancellation and the legacy of this important aircraft. More than any other project, the story of the TSR2 provides an insight into the state of the British military aircraft industry and defence technology policy during changing times.

Early 1960s Bristol Siddeley drawing office – note the lack of computers [Author's collection / Bristol Siddeley]

As the 1960s opened Britain was well on its way to building national champions in the aircraft sector. The front runners were the the British Aircraft Corporation busily developing the TSR2, and the Hawker Siddeley Group, pressing ahead with the Harrier.

One of the earliest decisions for the combined BAC team developing the TSR2 was the choice of engines. The decision was made to go with Olympus engines, as developed by Bristol for the V-bomber force. Even this aspect of the story includes inducements for industrial convergence: the engines were chosen because Bristol Aero Engines had agreed to merge with Armstrong Siddeley to form Bristol Siddeley.

THE ENGINEERS

In his 1948 novel *No Highway*, Nevil Shute had captured the essence of the British aircraft designer:

> All really first-class designers, for this reason, are both artists, engineers, and men of a powerful and an intolerant temper, quick to resist the least modification of their plans, energetic in fighting the least infringement upon what they regard as their own sphere of action. If they were not so, they could not produce good aeroplanes.[114]

In engineering terms, what was TSR2? Lowe and Hayhurst's 1959 specification required:

> A general-purpose aircraft, the TSR.2, is being developed for the support of the Army and for other tactical operations. It will have a supersonic, low-flying, all weather capability and will, in its strike and reconnaissance role, provide a suitable replacement for the Canberra. At the same time it will meet the need for a versatile fighter-bomber to co-operate with troops in the field. The TSR.2 will be capable of carrying nuclear bombs and air-to-air guided missiles. Its ability to use airfields of moderate length and light construction in forward areas will be of especial value in limited war operations.[115]

The TSR2 included a range of highly advanced aircraft technologies. These included:

- Ducted air for extra lift
- Line scanning camera for reconnaissance
- Stowable undercarriage suitable for soft field operations
- Supersonic Olympus engines
- Terrain-following radar and avionics
- Pilot 'Head up' display
- Blackburn Cumulus starter turbine to permit independent start of the aircraft.[116]

Another innovation for the RAF concerned the aircraft paintwork. The early aircraft were developed with all-over anti-flash white paint. Today's visitors seeing either of the two remaining aircraft on museum display – one (XR220) at the RAF Museum, Cosford, and the other (XR222) at the Imperial War Museum, Duxford – often ask why the paintwork is not finished. They say this because the white paintwork and the light, pastel-coloured RAF roundels look like an undercoat. In fact they were the finished form, and the RAF roundel had been adjusted into a light pastel palette to reduce the heat deposited into the aircraft from the flash of a nuclear detonation. As such the beauty of the TSR2 is directly linked to its role as a delivery platform for weapons of mass destruction. TSR2's gleaming beauty and its dark purpose are intimately linked. In fact it is highly unlikely that the TSR2 would ever have entered RAF service in full anti-flash white, because by the mid-1960s it was already becoming clear that the best way to observe incoming low-flying strike aircraft was from above, with radars or even visually. As a consequence, the planned paint schemes for RAF TSR2 deployment were to shift to camouflage of the aircraft's top surfaces.

For Bristol Siddeley the TSR2 engine requirements proved particularly challenging.[117] The designers of the Olympus B.01.22R engines were required to cope with:

- Extremely high intake ram air temperatures (higher even than Concorde)
- The development of an infinitely variable reheat system
- Very high fluid temperatures (air, oil and fuel) requiring new types of seal
- A novel low-pressure turbine shaft with unusual bearing layout.

However, the innovation was by no means restricted to the engine developments at Bristol Siddeley. The airframe engineers, for instance, used large integrally machined parts for the first time.[118] Bob Fairclough has noted that such components widely deployed in the wings could give the aircraft a long life in hostile fatigue environments while also being structurally efficient. The innovation would also save significant weight.

Another innovation, in this case very British, was the use of boundary layer spill ducts to improve lift at low speeds. These ensured that at take-off the speed of the air flow over the top surfaces of the wings would be significantly faster than the speed of the aircraft alone would imply. This technology had been developed by Supermarine (of Spitfire fame) for the Scimitar.[119] As discussed earlier, Vickers had recruited Supermarine to work up their original bid under requirement GOR339, and the newly formed BAC consortium was to benefit from that earlier Vickers decision.

Brian Mann was a Cranfield-educated electronics engineer tasked with developing the flight simulator of the TSR2. That role led him to have a very good overview of the anticipated capabilities of the aircraft and its key technology systems, especially in navigation, weapons and radar. In a 2009 lecture for the Institute of Engineering and Technology, he recalled the take-off and landing specifications of the TSR2: rotate at 120–130 knots,[120] lift at 160 knots, cross threshold at 175 knots and touch at 160 knots.[121] Mann observed that the core mechanical aspects of the aircraft were to push the technological frontier. For instance, military aircraft hydraulics of the time typically worked at a pressure of 3,000 psi, whereas TSR2 worked at 4,000 psi. He recalled an adage from working on the TSR2: 'one of the characteristics of this particular project was that nobody, but nobody, would say "no".

One of the most important innovations of the TSR2 was the proposed first use of a digital flight computer in a British aircraft. This held out the prospect of greatly improved navigational accuracy, but required the computer to hold 40 geographical checkpoints in its memory. The US had the technological edge in militarily deployable computers with the Verdan machine, which took its name from Versatile Digital Analysis. The Verdan computer had first been deployed in US Navy submarines, but by the time that the TSR2 was under development the Verdan was already in service with US aircraft such as the North American A-5 Vigilante, which first flew in August 1958 and entered service in 1961. Mann observed in 2009 that no British computers of the era were up to the tasks required by the TSR2.[122] Two Verdan computers would be needed. In fact, even two Verdan machines would have been insufficient for all the simultaneous tasks required of a real TSR2 combat mission, and the TSR2 was cancelled before the difficult computer challenges were fully resolved. Clearly, however, the rapid improvements in digital electronics from the late 1960s onwards would have ensured that if TSR2 had been deployed, extensive upgrades for both reconnaissance and attack would have been easily possible throughout its operational life. It also seems probable that with electronics miniaturisation the TSR2 would have acquired capability in-service in the specialist areas of electronic countermeasures (ECM) warfare and electronic intelligence (ELINT) gathering. These roles were an important part of the Cold War. ECM capability had, for instance, been fitted to the V-bombers; for the Victor it had been relatively straightforward, but for the Vulcan the rear fuselage required significant modification.[123] At the 'TSR2 with Hindsight' seminar organised by the RAF Historical Society in April 1997, Wing Commander Jimmy Dell endorsed the view that the electronics capabilities of the TSR2 would have been highly upgradable, as the later experience with the Panavia Tornado aircraft demonstrated.[124] He pointed in particular to the very large avionics bay behind the rear cockpit, designed for early 1960s avionics; that space alone permitted huge opportunity for mid-life upgrades.

From the perspective of the 21st century, with in-car satellite navigation and smart mobile phones capable of powerful computations, it is easy to fail to appreciate the effort and creativity that went into addressing the digital needs of advanced 1960s military aircraft such as the TSR2. As was typical of the TSR2, the computing and avionics challenges were at, or even perhaps beyond, the state of the art at the time. While the digital computer challenges were causing concern to Elliot Automation Ltd, other important technical aspects were being approached in electromechanical ways. John Forbat has filled an important gap in national memory of the TSR2 in outlining its planned and achieved avionics capabilities.[125] One such area was the inertial navigation stable platform and the highly sensitive accelerometers and gyroscopes supported by it.[126] These hugely impressive little machines provided data to be processed by the overstretched Verdan computers which, when added to radar-observed contact with the frequent fixed checkpoints on the ground, could accurately get the aircraft to its target. To enable such checkpoint fixes the TSR2 was to be fitted with sideways-looking radars. Help for this difficult task of navigation was given by forward and backward Doppler radars able to support the assessment of the aircraft velocity provided by the accelerometers and associated computer processing. Part of the technical attraction of the navigation challenge was that it combined ambitious engineering hardware with sophisticated theoretical considerations. For instance, as Forbat explains, the system even needed to take proper account of the fact that the Earth is not a perfect sphere, as well as including the more obvious effect of the Earth slowly rotating under the moving aircraft. The combination of all these aspects into a system that could allow the aircraft to reach its target in all weathers and at night represented a key technological challenge at the time. The use of electromechanical solutions was not restricted to the avionics kit, but was also applied more directly to the work of the crew, especially the observer. The observer, sitting directly behind the pilot, would spend his time facing a bank of instruments; he would not be looking out of the window. While focusing on his instruments and entering data he would be being buffeted by the extreme forces of a high-performance aircraft.

One of the observer's many tasks was to record the avionics inputs needed to ensure the aircraft achieved its target. One key tool was a Moving Map Display, made by Ferranti.[127] On this the observer would follow the progress of the aircraft, comparing ground features with those observed visually or, more likely, picked up by the sideways-looking radars. As each check point was approached the aircraft was automatically brought level and put on a constant heading to match the moving map expectations and to avoid radar image distortion.[128] As the checkpoint was passed, the observer would enter the data into the computer.

As specified, TSR2 was to be a nuclear-capable strike aircraft with reconnaissance capability. The reconnaissance task was to be achieved by means of a special pack fitted into the bomb bay.[129] This was to include very high resolution and all weather capable sideways-looking radars and advanced photographic techniques.[130] The reconnaissance pack included long-focus lens still photography and video recording, but the most impressive capability was the line-scan apparatus. In daylight this could operate passively. Through the use of a rotating mirror a 100-mile-long stripe of terrain could be scanned by the moving aircraft. The line scanner would sweep left and right, allowing the image formed to be a stripe typically one mile wide. At night the device would operate in an active mode emitting a swept beam of light below the aircraft. The sweep of this beam would be so fast that no observer on the ground would be aware that the process was under way.

TSR2 stretched technological capability in avionics, airframe and engines, and even the undercarriage. As the project developed through the first years of the 1960s all were conscious that the project was falling behind and going over budget – but amazing technological progress was being made. The stresses on the engineers involved were considerable. Looking back from the perspective of later cancellation, Roland Beamont recalled the efforts of the TSR2 workforce:

MACH2 MAPMAKER

WITH NEW EMI RECONNAISSANCE SYSTEMS. At height, the TSR2 strike reconnaissance aircraft flies at Mach 2— [gr]ound level it is faster than any other machine. To match this performance, EMI has developed the most advance[d] [el]ectronic aids to navigation and reconnaissance in the world. SIDEWAYS LOOKING RADARS which perform the dual task [of na]vigation and reconnaissance and provide an accurate map of the ground over which the aircraft is flying, look o[ut] [si]deways instead of ahead to avoid alerting enemy counter measures. Equally advanced is LINE SCAN an optical scann[er] [us]ed for mapping at low levels. Pictorial information stored in the aircraft can be transmitted back to base where [a ph]otograph of the ground over which the aircraft is flying is instantaneously produced. Even if the aircraft does n[ot] [re]turn, vital reconnaissance information is obtained. Airborne radar and reconnaissance systems are just some of th[e ad]vanced military equipment produced by EMI. From the depths of the oceans to the vastness of space, EMI is playir[g a] [v]ital part in the defence of Britain, the Commonwealth and our allies.

EMI ELECTRONICS LTD

MILITARY PROJECTS DIVISION · HAYES · MIDDX · ENGL[AND]
TEL: HAYES 3888 · TELEX 22417 · CABLES: EMIDATA LOND[ON]

In 1964 EMI celebrated its role in providing the TSR2 with
reconnaissance capability [Author's collection / EMI]

The whole workforce: the engineers, the ground staff, the aircrew of course, the flight developers the air worthiness people, the administrators backing it all up had been working on an all-hours basis. There was no knock-off time – you worked on through the night. Leave was cancelled. Family arrangements were disrupted. Tensions developed in families because husbands were overworked – overstretched. This had been going on for years.[131]

Some of the stress associated with the TSR2 project was a consequence of the coming together of Vickers and English Electric to design and build the aircraft. There was significant mutual distrust between the engineers at the different sites. Jeff Daniels, a BAC engineer at Warton Military Aircraft Division, recalled of the Weybridge (Vickers) and Warton (English Electric) difficulties:

The result was a good deal of unhappy rivalry, amounting at times to downright unhelpfulness, between the Warton engineers – responsible for the rear fuselage, the engine installation, the wings and the tail – and the Weybridge people who were in charge of the forward fuselage and all it contained, including the cockpits and all the electronics.[132]

CONSOLIDATION OF THE BRITISH AIRCRAFT INDUSTRY[133]

In the early 20th century the UK aircraft industry was characterised by the emergence of a plethora of small- to medium-sized producers spread across most of the country. These companies were frequently led by technologically enthusiastic entrepreneurs; some names, such as Geoffrey de Havilland and Thomas Sopwith, have passed into popular history. Numerous other names and firms are recorded only in specialist histories or as part of local social history in town archives. For the case of aircraft manufacturing, Günter Endres has recorded 74 different firms in his 1995 book *British Aircraft Manufacturers since 1908*.[134] The firms listed by Endres exclude those devoted solely to airships, microlights, gliders and gyrocopters as well as those that have produced only foreign designs under licence.

Although for the TSR2 story our period of interest starts at least ten years after the end of the Second World War, it is clear that the legacies of that conflict provide much of the context for 1960s aircraft industrial policy. During the war, 60 per cent of all engineering factories took on some aircraft work.[135] This redirection of activity resulted in various degrees of success. Corelli Barnet notes that, for instance, in 1943 the development of the Whittle W2B jet engine had to be removed from a Rover motor vehicle 'shadow factory' and given to Rolls-Royce, because production at Rover had been found by officials to be 'chaotic'.[136]

The war years are widely acknowledged to have provided an enormous impetus to UK military aircraft design and production, although some, such as Corelli Barnett, insist that the real period of creativity lay not during the war, but in the mid-1930s.[137] These disagreements apply even at the level of individual aircraft. Some, such as Peter Lewis, argue that the Vickers Windsor four piston-engine heavy bomber represented the high water mark of Second World War British aircraft manufacturing, while others such as Barnett argue that it was one of the 'most spectacular failures of all'.[138] History cannot tell us about the performance of the Vickers Windsor in the Second World War, as the Windsor project was cancelled just as it became clear that the war was won.

Generally the UK aircraft industry, across a spread of small entrepreneurial firms, is regarded as having had a good war. Corelli Barnett notes:[139]

> The reasons why the wartime British aircraft industry failed to achieve a better comparative record in design, development and productivity are twofold: despite its now formidable size and central place in the war effort, the industry still suffered from profound defects inherited from the nature of its small-time origins in 1935, while further weaknesses had resulted from the scrambling haste of its expansion ever since – a corner shop that suddenly found itself a Harrods.

While the Second World War provides an important contextual backstop, it in no way represents a period of turmoil before stability. Many would take the view that it represents a period of turmoil set against a more general backdrop of national decline. George L. Bernstein has robustly argued against the prevailing orthodoxy of British decline, but even he confirms the severe reduction of the global importance of British manufacturing during our period of interest.[140]

Share of world manufactured exports, 1950–1979 [Source: George L Bernstein, The Myth of Decline – the Rise of Britain since 1945][141]

	1950 (%)	1960 (%)	1970 (%)	1979 (%)
France	9.9	9.6	8.7	10.5
Japan	3.4	6.9	11.7	13.7
UK	22.5	16.5	10.8	9.1
USA	27.3	21.6	18.5	16.0
West Germany	7.3	19.3	19.8	20.9

In 1946 there were 27 different British airframe design companies and 8 separate British aircraft engine companies.[142] The need for consolidation into fewer larger industrial concerns was clear. British policymakers, impressed by the war-winning industrial capacity of the United States, were keen to construct manufacturing firms to rival Boeing. Of course from a 21st-century perspective such ambitions can appear to be hubristic verging on deluded, but back in the 1950s the relative power balance between the UK and USA had not yet become clear to all.

Although some beneficial restructuring had been achieved prior to the Sandys White Paper, there were still 20 airframe companies and 6 engine companies in 1958. The TSR2-

mediated restructuring ensured that by 1960 these were integrated into two airframe groups, one helicopter group, and two engine groups.[143] The new industry consisted of: Hawker Siddeley Group and British Aircraft Corporation as airframe groups; Westland Aircraft as a helicopter group; and Bristol Siddeley and Rolls-Royce as the main engine companies. As we have already seen, government coordination and review had led the venerable Vickers Armstrong, with its heavy bomber piston-engined pre-war heritage, and English Electric Company, the new upstart high-technology supersonic specialists, to come together to form the British Aircraft Corporation. (Similar industrial consolidation was under way in several industries, most notably the automotive sector.) In October 1960 the newly amalgamated entity, BAC, was finally awarded the contract for nine pre-production TSR2 aircraft,[144] the contract having been announced in January 1959.

TSR2 test pilot Roland Beaumont said of English Electric: 'a new design team was formed in 1945 specifically to design and build for the RAF its first jet bomber – the Canberra. English Electric were regarded as newcomers by the rest of the industry, and I think slightly resented for that'.[145]

The Vickers team was the prime contractor responsible for the front fuselage section including the cockpit, weapons systems – and, all-importantly, budget control. English Electric was to concentrate on the aerodynamics, wings, tail and rear fuselage.[146] The institutional integration of these radically different firms would be achieved via systems integration on one of the most challenging high-technology projects attempted up to that point.

The firms involved in these mergers had been bitter rivals with quite different histories, philosophies and sources of institutional pride. These differences also operated at the level of individuals. George Edwards of Vickers is quoted as saying: 'never had it been less likely that such personalities [the founders and the 'hero aircraft designers'] would willingly have become subservient to each other – certainly not while business remained to be done'.[147]

The post Sandys White Paper threat from government that business could only be done if egos were compromised and firms successfully amalgamated makes clear that there was indeed a metaphorical gun to the industry's head.

The institutional and engineering integration was, however, far from straightforward. Government and project subcontractors both represented points of difficulty, especially as many of the subcontractors were communicating directly with government without going via the BAC project team.[148] This and other problems led to severe difficulties with project management, as Roland Beamont recalled:

> … one of the committees that I attended of industry and the ministry officials and civil servants from the establishments and elsewhere. The Chairman took a look round the room, when we started in St Giles Court, Long Room – full of cigarette smoke and battered cups of tea. He took a look around the room and he said 'I want a count taken' and there was a head count taken at this meeting and there were fifty-eight people in the room; and the Chairman quite reasonably said 'this is quite

ridiculous nobody could control a programme with meetings this size. I want you all to go away and the next meeting is convened for such-and-such a date, and I want to see a significant reduction in the numbers at that meeting', and in due course we all came back to the reconvened meeting and there were sixty-one in the room.[149]

The final years of the Conservative government were far from stable. The difficulties peaked in the summer 1963 with the Profumo scandal.[150] John Profumo was secretary of state for war in the Conservative government. On 5 June 1963 he resigned, admitting that he had lied to Parliament about his relationship with a call girl, Christine Keeler.[151] One aspect of the scandal was that Keeler was also believed to be in a relationship with a defence official from the Soviet Embassy. An important figure in these developments was the Labour MP George Wigg.

George Wigg, later Baron Wigg of the Borough of Dudley, was born in Ealing on 28 November 1900.[152] He grew up in a family destroyed by drink.[153] His father was a drunk, and his mother was a pillar of strength. He enlisted in the Army as the First World War came to an end, and then spent much of the 1920s in Turkey and the Middle East. During the Second World War he was a colonel in the Army Education Corps. Wigg was encouraged by A.D. 'Sandie' Lindsay, later Lord Lindsay, who was a figure of enormous influence in further and higher education: in the Army, as master of Balliol College, Oxford, and as founder of Keele University in Staffordshire – the first of Britain's new universities established after the Second World War.

George Wigg's driving enthusiasms were for the Army, education, the Labour party and horses. To this was added an intense interest in gossip, rumour and state security. Cambridge University history professor Christopher Andrew, in his authorised history of MI5, is rather dismissive of Wigg at several levels, noting that while Wigg most definitely had the ear of the prime minister, Harold Wilson, he was not especially well trusted by either MI5 or his colleagues on the Labour benches in Parliament.[154] Indeed Andrew goes on to emphasise the hypocrisy of a man seeking out sexual gossip on others while himself being later associated by the press with significant behavioural weaknesses of a sexual nature.

Daily Mirror columnist William Connor, writing under the pseudonym Cassandra, is reported to have said of George Wigg:

He is an odd bird; vigilant, unpredictable, shrewd and solitary. ... He is the chillie pepper in the Parliamentary chutney. Very hot and inclined to burn the mouth. But George Wigg keeps the boys on their toes and when the House gets dull Wigg the Wag shakes 'em good and hard. Which is no bad thing.'[155]

George Wigg is today best known for his role in revealing the scandal and in prompting the parliamentary events that led to Profumo's resignation as secretary of state for war. Even more interesting, however, is the role Wigg played in nuclear defence thinking during the government of Harold Wilson, when he held the title of paymaster general from October 1964 to November 1967. At the time the post of paymaster general was a government appointment with few formal obligations, and such a role gave Wigg space to pursue his security and defence interests on behalf of the prime minister. Wigg was consistently sceptical of the value of nuclear forces, and especially troubled by the high economic costs involved with such systems.

Back in 1962, in the weeks following the Cuba crisis and the arrest of John Vassall, the homosexual spy honey-trapped by the Soviets, George Wigg had received a mysterious phone call. He records the fascinating opening to what would become the Profumo scandal:

> On November 11, 1962 I attended Armistice Services at Stourbridge and Dudley, then went for lunch to the home of our Labour Party Agent, Councillor Tommy Friend, where I found there had been a 'phone call for me. I telephoned my home in Stoke, but my wife had neither called me nor received a message. Soon afterwards the call to Friend's house was repeated. A muffled voice said, 'Forget about the Vassall case. You want to look at Profumo.' Then the 'phone went dead. Driving back to London, the nagging question kept recurring: how did the unknown caller know where I was and how did he get the number?[156]

George Wigg nicely summarises the initial uncertainty around Christine Keeler in the minds of those with security instincts: 'Who was using the call-girl to "milk" whom of information – the War Secretary or the Soviet Military Attaché?'[157] Wigg is clear in his assessment: 'Profumo was not, at any time, a security risk.'[158]

Christine Keeler later remembered George Wigg with clear animus, in some contrast to her ongoing admiration of Profumo: 'Jack Profumo (family motto: Virtue and Work) was under pressure because British military resources were overstretched. That ugly George Wigg, who I always thought looked like a pervert, was Harold Wilson's man on the army and he was after Jack.'[159]

Although Stephen Ward was convicted for crimes relating to prostitution (he committed suicide at the end of his trial) the compelling narrative is that he was assisting Yevgeni Mikhailovitch Ivanov in attempts to extract defence secrets from John Profumo. Ivanov had arrived in London in March 1960. The official British view has long been that these attempts failed and that no secrets were in fact transferred to the Soviet Union. Furthermore, the orthodox view is that Stephen Ward was a relatively minor figure in Cold War affairs.[160] George Wigg tended to be more sympathetic to Ward, believing Ward's repeated assertions that he had made the Security Service (MI5) fully aware of his meetings with Ivanov and Keeler, and about his friendship with Ivanov.[161]

The Americans, however, were more worried than the British about the risks posed by Stephen Ward's activities. At time the British did not know that the Americans were hearing from a KGB double agent that numerous secrets had apparently been successfully obtained and transmitted to the USSR by Ivanov. Following a series of security failures in the UK, the Americans did not trust the British enough to share their intelligence for many years. With hindsight, historian Christopher Andrew tends, however, to the view that the allegations from the Americans' double agent were both improbable and unreliable.[162] It appears that the dominant British view remains that the Profumo scandal involved no actual espionage.

Keeler is direct in her assessment: 'I knew Stephen was a spy but had not allowed myself to think how great his scope was or what his actions could mean.'[163]

It has long been asserted that the secrets that Stephen Ward allegedly sought to obtain from John Profumo related to plans for the Americans to deploy nuclear weapons in Germany, and indeed more specifically the date on which it might be expected to occur. Lord Denning's formal report into the Profumo scandal pointed to a wider motivation for Ivanov's actions – to drive a wedge between the British and the Americans on matters of defence and security by any means necessary.

George Wigg was struck by Ward's assertions that he had played an important and useful role in the October 1962 Cuba Crisis. Wigg records:

> His (Ward's) second venture in Ivanov-directed diplomacy – again as a go-between – occurred during the Cuba crisis. This time, according to Ward, he was the link between Ivanov as peacemaker and the British government, represented by the Foreign Secretary, Lord Home, and the Prime Minister.

The extent of Stephen Ward's actions are hard to judge, and there is no reason not to accept the standard British line on the story, but it is interesting to note that over the years further small details of the lives of Stephen Ward and John Profumo have emerged. For example:

- Duncan Sandys was not only treated osteopathically by Stephen Ward,[164] but also sat for portraiture by him and knew him socially.[165]
- In 2017 it was revealed that from the early 1930s John Profumo had had a relationship with a glamorous Nazi spy, Gisela Winegard. Profumo had himself reported his German friendship to British authorities in 1941.[166]

The growing political turbulence of the Profumo scandal affected the military aircraft programme with a flurry of short-lasting ministers for aviation. Sir Reginald Verdon-Smith, the chairman of BAC, is reported as remarking on a 'mood of growing frustration at this time'.[167]

INDUSTRIAL DISEASE

The TSR2 project broke with established British practice in aircraft development: the project went ahead without a prototype. The decision was to adopt a method used with success in the United States – a development batch procedure in which a set of useful aircraft would be built straight off the drawing board. The contract was for nine development batch aircraft and two structural test airframes.[168] In retrospect the development batch decision was a grave error; it almost certainly delayed the project and it certainly added greatly to the development costs. Perhaps if the design had been finalised before production started the plan might have worked, but with an aircraft as advanced as the TSR2, finalisation of a design without a prototype would appear to have been too ambitious a plan.

In his impassioned 1966 plea to rescue the British aircraft industry, entitled *The Murder of the TSR-2*, Stephen Hastings argues that the UK should develop a source of core research activities applicable to multiple aircraft projects: 'The "building brick" approach to all aerospace research and development should be adopted. The Plowden Committee opine that we cannot afford to employ this method. My contention is that we cannot afford not to do so.'[169]

The Plowden Committee saw such broad-based industrial capacity as an international matter, and decided that for Britain alone it was unaffordable. Indeed, in the years ahead Europe would address such issues via international consortia for military aircraft such as the Panavia Tornado and the Sepecat Jaguar.

While the TSR2 project raised issues about the structure of the development process of an advanced military aircraft, it also revealed that in the future aircraft would be mere elements in a system of assets to be conceived and developed in harmony. One small example is that BAC even found itself in the ground vehicle development business.[170] The required ability to disperse the aircraft to poorly prepared airstrips and to operate for extended periods of several weeks forced BAC to develop a specialist multi-fuel-engined and air-conditioned general servicing vehicle which would help replenish fuel and water to the TSR2, and recharge the aircraft hydraulics. Other vehicles, such as an automatic test equipment trailer and a universal lifting trolley, were also planned, and all were designed to be air transportable in an Argosy freighter aircraft.

The scale of ambition, in the breadth and depth of the technical scope, and the overly ambitious use of a development batch procedure for the TSR2, were causing numerous difficulties, delays and cost escalations, but through the late 1950s and into the early 1960s forward progress was maintained as the staff involved stretched themselves to the limit.

In early 1960 the TSR2 test programme prompted a personal crisis for Roland Beamont. His wife, Pat, was gravely ill and required life-saving surgery. Six years before he had promised Pat that he would give up test flying at the age of 40; now he was to turn 40 in August 1960, and Pat was very far from well. He describes his announcement to Pat that he was to test fly TSR2 as having all the elements of a bad melodrama. He was particularly conscious of the risk at that time that if anything were to happen to him their children might be orphaned.[171] The impression one gets of Roland Beamont is that despite his clear concerns, only one possible outcome would fit with the man – he was going to test fly the TSR2. As his memoirs indicate, despite the eventual failure of the TSR2 he had no real regrets – 'We had been right to try'.[172]

WINDS OF CHANGE

The 1960s was to be the decade of space flight and, as we have seen, rebellious youth. It would reveal remarkable feats of technological organisation, and also deconstruct and disassemble the structures of society. While rock and roll had emerged into mainstream popular culture in the fifties, the decade of the sixties opened with no obvious clues to the social upheaval that was to come, even though some in the African-American community may have been amused to see that their well-established euphemism for sex, rock'n'roll, now being talked about all over the airwaves of middle America. However, the technical prospects for the decade ahead were more apparent. Throughout the 1950s popular culture on both sides of the Atlantic had been swamped with images of manned space flight.

At the end of the 1950s military aviation was dominated by ambitious supersonic projects. In the US North American Aviation was developing the Valkyrie prototype for the planned B70 high-altitude strategic bomber. The B70 would be the latest in a succession of aircraft that each flew faster and higher than those that had gone before.

In Canada the 1950s had seen a story with remarkable parallels to the story that lay ahead for the TSR2. In the early 1950s Canada had sought to construct an advanced delta-winged Mach 2 supersonic interceptor. The result was the Arrow, developed by Avro Canada. The CF-105 Arrow looked remarkably like the TSR2, and it suffered a similar controversial fate when in 1958, during its flight test programme, it was abruptly cancelled by the Canadian government.

Rollout of the Avro Canada CF-105 Arrow, 4 October 1957 [Keystone Pictures USA / Alamy]

On 1 July 1960 the British Aircraft Corporation was formally established, with 40 per cent stakes owned by each of Vickers and English Electric. The remaining 20 per cent share belonged to the newly-formed Bristol Siddeley Engines Ltd, because of the importance of the Olympus engines being developed by what had until recently been the Bristol Aero Engines division of the Bristol Aeroplane Company.[173] Bristol had been a late addition to the BAC plans, having previously been assumed by many interested in rationalising the British aircraft industry to be a better fit with the Hawker Siddeley Group.[174] The name British Aircraft Corporation was chosen by the boss of the new amalgamated company – George Edwards.

For those concerned with military aviation, the sixties opened with a sense of urgent innovation and progress. This progress led towards faster, higher aircraft, but this was all to change when on 1 May 1960 Francis Gary Powers' U2 spy plane was brought down over the Soviet Union near Degtyarsk, in Sverdlovsk Oblast, Russia. The conventional view is that Powers' plane was brought down by a SA2 Guideline surface-to-air missile, although Captain Igor Mentyukov of the Soviet Air Force claimed in a 1996 newspaper article that he had caught Powers' plane in the slipstream of his pared-down Sukhoi Su-9 interceptor.[175] His intention had been to ram the incoming U2.[176] It has been suggested that the order to ram the U2 spy plane, if necessary, came from Lieutenant General of the Air Force Yevgeniy Savitskiy.[177] Mentyukov claims that the SA2 had actually shot down a Mig-19 flown by one of his Soviet colleagues. Mentyukov's 1996 assertion, however, seems unlikely to be credible. In his memoirs former Soviet test pilot Stepan Anastasovich Mikoyan reports:

> When Powers was flying over Soviet territory at an altitude of more than 20,000 metres, several attempts to intercept him with our fighters, including the newly adopted Su-9, were made, but none of them was successful. The combat pilots on those missions failed to climb up to the height at which the U-2 was travelling, even though it was within the capability limits of the Su-9. I was instructed to send a test pilot from the Institute to the combat regiment in question to establish why the altitude had not been reached and to give recommendations for the future. When Leonid Fadeev arrived at the regiment's airfield in Kazakhstan he discovered that the regimental pilots had not quite mastered the Su-9 yet and did not know how to climb up in it correctly. The point is that the ceiling of a supersonic jet is achieved in a certain pattern. First the aircraft must break the sound barrier at 10,000 to 11,000 metres, then speed up to Mach 1.8 or so, and only after that start climbing up to the ceiling at this speed. Trying to reach the ceiling as fast as possible, the pilots had started to climb at an insufficient Mach number, unaware that at that speed the ceiling of the aircraft was much lower.[178]

In recent years fuller accounts of events have emerged from the former Soviet Union including from the son of the Soviet premier, Nikita Khrushchev, casting further doubt on Mentyukov's claim.[179]

Whatever the details, the impact of Powers' plane being brought down at 65,000 feet was profound. That altitude was far higher than the altitudes planned for the next generation of high-altitude bombers. If Powers' U2 was vulnerable, then so would the new bombers, such as the North American Valkyrie. Something was going to have to change, and that was going to be the direction of development, now towards strategies based upon fast and low penetration. TSR2 seemed perfect for such realities.

BLUE STREAK CANCELLED

1960 also saw the cancellation of Blue Streak, Britain's nuclear-armed intermediate-range ballistic missile (IRBM).

As early as 1956 the Treasury had been expressing concerns about the cost of the Blue Streak project. In 1959 the British Nuclear Deterrent Study Group had been set up under the chairmanship of Sir Richard Powell, permanent secretary at the Ministry of Defence.[180] The committee reported to the chiefs of staff on 5 February 1960 and concluded:

> We need a new strategic nuclear weapon system to replace the V-bomber/Blue Steel Mark I in about 1966, but since we regard Blue Streak as a 'fire first' only weapon we do not consider that it meets that need. We therefore recommend the cancellation of its further development as a military weapon. We also recommend the cancellation of the planned deployment.[181]

For some time concerns had been expressed that the Blue Streak system, located at fixed sites in what would today be called underground missile silos, could prompt a pre-emptive strike by the Soviet Union rather than deter it. In his history *A Vertical Empire* C.N. Hill argues that such arguments were flawed.[182] He quotes a 1961 letter from Sir Robert Cockcroft, former controller of guided weapons and electronics at the Ministry of Aviation. Cockcroft wrote to Sir Solly Zuckerman, chief scientific adviser to the Ministry of Defence:

> Blue Streak was cancelled because it was not politically viable rather than because it could be pre-empted. The scale of the pre-emption was admitted to be of the order of 3,000 megatons. Supporters of the system argued that this was so excessive that pre-emption could be ignored in practice. The argument was not accepted and vulnerability was advanced as the main reason for cancellation. The real reasons were more fundamental although still not clearly appreciated. I suggest no British statesman could visualise exploiting a deterrent threat which if mis-handled could only lead to the annihilation of the whole country; nor could he believe that a threat involving such consequences would be taken seriously by an opponent.

Sir Solly was not an engineer; he had risen to his position from a scientific background in zoology. Moreover, he was South African and Jewish. Many in the aviation industry regarded him as an outsider. Frank Barnett-Jones acerbically captures the mood of the aircraft community with the words:

> He was a zoologist and a leading authority on glandular behaviour in monkeys. Although his publications are very few, especially those on defence and aviation, there are a number of papers on the relationship between man and apes. He appeared to have shunned seeking knowledge of Britain's aviation industry, preferring instead, he said, 'to keep an open mind and free from any particular influence'.[183]

Denis Healey also noted Zuckerman's weaknesses. He writes in his autobiography:

> He was intolerant of people he regarded as less clever than himself – a very large group – but could always be relied upon to think outside the ruts in which the rest of us were too often stuck. … Unfortunately, Solly's mercurial nature did not make him an ideal Chief Scientific Adviser for me. He was liable to change his position without warning, and to reject the advice which his own staff had given me weeks earlier.[184]

Whatever the reasons, the advice of Sir Richard Powell's study group was accepted and Blue Streak was duly cancelled. The technology continued to be developed, in the form of a space launcher: Blue Streak formed the basis of the first stage of Europa, as developed by the European Launcher Development Organisation, precursor of today's European Space Agency. The Europa rocket itself was a failure, although not as a consequence of any shortcomings in the Blue Streak technology. Europa was abandoned in 1972.

The cancellation of the Blue Streak and Europa programmes stands in contrast to a great little British success story – the Black Arrow launcher, initially developed by the Saunders Roe Company on the Isle of Wight. Building upon 22 successful launches of its earlier Black Knight rocket, Saunders Roe had been commissioned to develop a three-stage launcher.[185] In a tale which mirrors many of the issues of the TSR2 story, the Black Arrow programme was cancelled for budget reasons despite demonstrated success in flight. In the case of Black Arrow, the success was achieved with the launch of the X-3 Prospero satellite three months after the project had been cancelled in late 1971. One aspect of the Black Arrow story is particularly depressing – the failure of the government to recognise that the ability of the rocket to launch only small payloads would not in fact be an obstacle to future commercial success. During the 1970s the global market for satellite telecommunications exploded and at the same time associated electronics became lighter and more compact. It seems clear that the British government cancelled a major technology programme just as the country had developed a potential world-beater. The Prospero satellite marked Britain as the sixth country in the world to have successfully launched a satellite using its own national resources. It was something Britain did just once – and, it seems, will never do again.[186] Today there are many in the UK who nostalgically take the view that TSR2 was also a potential world-beater cruelly ended by ignorant and short-sighted politicians. I take the view, however, that such perceptions are largely incorrect, as we shall see.

Interestingly there is one point of direct contact between the TSR2 story and that of Black Arrow/Prospero. C.N. Hill has noted that the inertial navigation system deployed in Black Arrow had originally been developed for the TSR2. The team developing the stand-off weapon, Blue Steel, was meanwhile soldiering on with much more primitive and power-hungry guidance equipment.[187]

With the cancellation of Blue Streak in 1960 the long-term future of Britain's nuclear deterrent now relied upon just one advanced missile project – the Skybolt air-launched system, under development in the United States. From early 1959 Britain had helped shape the design of Skybolt, ensuring its compatibility with the UK V-force bombers.[188] During 1959 and 1960 the missile went through several modifications including those allowing it to carry a heavier nuclear warhead. But these modifications restricted its possible UK use to the Vulcan bomber, with its greater ground clearance.[189] Historian Richard Moore has described the capabilities of Skybolt:

> Launch was intended to be from fairly high altitude: 40,000ft and Mach 0.8 for the B-52, or slightly higher and faster for the Vulcan. Launch from as low as 10,000ft was also possible in theory, but true low-level capability for the carrying aircraft was unnecessary given the range of the missile: it would not be necessary for the B-52 or Vulcan to approach within range of Soviet air defence radars. The missile would fall freely for a couple of seconds before first stage ignition and a 30°-40° pull up. The second stage would fire shortly after separation then accelerate to final velocity of 95,000ft/sec and separation of the gently spinning RV.[190]

The term 'RV' refers to a re-entry vehicle: at this point in the weapon's journey the nuclear warhead would be in space, falling back to Earth and its target. Skybolt was to be a highly capable system; it was moving quickly and it was a US project which the UK now relied on.

While those concerned with Skybolt were looking to the United States, many still saw the role of Britain in the world through a lens of Empire. Whatever one's views of Empire, it was clear by 1960 that it was a story from Britain's past and no longer core to Britain's future. In February 1960 Prime Minister Harold Macmillan focused attention on the British situation with an address now known as the 'Winds of Change' speech. Speaking to the South African parliament he said:

> Ever since the break up of the Roman empire one of the constant facts of political life in Europe has been the emergence of independent nations. They have come into existence over the centuries in different forms, different kinds of government, but all have been inspired by a deep, keen feeling of nationalism, which has grown as the nations have grown. In the twentieth century, and especially since the end of the war, the processes which gave birth to the nation states of Europe have been repeated all over the world. We have seen the awakening of national consciousness in peoples who have for centuries lived in dependence upon some other power. Fifteen years

Tomorrow's supersonic engine is flying now!

The Bristol Siddeley supersonic Olympus is now undergoing flight trials in a Vulcan flying test bed. This engine will power the B.A.C. tactical strike/reconnaissance aircraft—TSR 2, which will have a speed in excess of Mach 2 and is due to fly in 1963.

A civil version of the supersonic Olympus is also under development and is ideally suited to the requirements of Mach 2 transport aircraft.

As powerplant of the Avro Vulcan V-bomber force the Olympus has proved to be one of the most reliable large gas turbines in service.

The Olympus 301 has recently completed an official Type Test at a thrust rating of 20,000 lb and a more advanced version of the engine has for some considerable time been achieving thrusts in excess of 30,000 lb with reheat on the test bed.

BRISTOL SIDDELEY ENGINES LIMITED
AERO-ENGINE DIVISION. PO BOX 3, FILTON, BRISTOL, ENGLAND.

TURBOJETS · TURBOPROPS · TURBOFANS · PISTON ENGINES · RAMJETS · ROCKET ENGINES · MARINE AND INDUSTRIAL GAS TURBINES
MARINE, RAIL AND INDUSTRIAL DIESEL ENGINES · PRECISION ENGINEERING PRODUCTS

Vulcan XA894 flying test bed for the TSR2 supersonic engines, early 1962 [Brooklands Museum]

ago this movement spread through Asia. Many countries there, of different races and civilisations, pressed their claim to an independent national life.

Today the same thing is happening in Africa, and the most striking of all the impressions I have formed since I left London a month ago is of the strength of this African national consciousness. In different places it takes different forms, but it is happening everywhere.

The wind of change is blowing through this continent, and whether we like it or not, this growth of national consciousness is a political fact. We must all accept it as a fact, and our national policies must take account of it.[191]

At a political level withdrawal from Empire was increasingly well understood, although much military thinking – including key aspects of the plans for TSR2 were still approached with a 19th-century colonial mindset:

> *We don't want to fight but by jingo if we do,*
> *We've got the ships, we've got the men, and got the money too!*
>
> G. W. Hunt (1878)

1962: CUBA

In August 1962 Blue Steel was given emergency operational status.[192] So fast was Blue Steel pressed into service that it now seems clear that for the first few months of deployment it was not a stand-off weapon at all, but little more than an expensive iron bomb.[193] This was as a consequence of reliability difficulties, and these problems had to be kept secret from the enemy: in deterrence, perceived capability is more important than actual capability. Blue Steel was now part of the British deterrent simply because it might be perceived to be.

1962 has a special place in the history of the fear of nuclear war because of the October crisis surrounding the deployment of Soviet nuclear missiles on the Caribbean island of Cuba. At its closest point, Cuba is only 90 miles from Florida, and the crisis represented nuclear brinkmanship of the highest order. Arguably it represents a triumph of deterrence, but such an assessment is too facile, as it masks some important realities. The first consideration is risk. As Robert Norris and Hans Kristensen explain, clearly a key element of the crisis was the risk of military errors based on misinformation and the risk of uncontrolled escalation of conflict.[194] The central risk was that the US, under the leadership of the charismatic young president John F. Kennedy, would launch a ground invasion of Cuba with US forces. Such an attack is far from unimaginable, especially given that the US had sponsored a failed counter-revolutionary invasion, ostensibly by Cuban ex-patriots, at the Bahía de Cochinos, or Bay of Pigs, in April 1961, only 18 months earlier. By October 1962, unbeknownst to US planners, Cuba's defenders already had a range of nuclear weapons at their disposal. A key risk, in retrospect, was that in the event of an attempt at an invasion by the USA, especially one carried out on a sufficient scale to suggest success, the Soviet nuclear weapons on Cuba would have been used, assuredly prompting catastrophic escalation of the conflict.[195] As Norris and Kristensen explain, key to the risks of nuclear conflict in Cuba was the fact that the Soviets had established nuclear forces which could be used for war fighting, but which were still secret and hence could play no role in deterring US invasion. The Cuban Missile Crisis was a risky time indeed. It is often said that October 1962 is the closest the world has ever come to nuclear war.[196]

The October 1962 Cuba Crisis represented not just a frightening threat to the United States but also to her NATO allies, especially the United Kingdom. The UK was home to much of the core nuclear NATO capability that would have been invoked if the crisis had escalated into a European, and hence a global, conflict.

The UK was home to nuclear-capable US Air Force bombers as well as the British V-force described earlier. The UK was also the location of 60 Thor IRBMs built by the Americans. These forces would prove to be an important addition to NATOs nuclear deterrent in October 1962. Although entirely an American technology requiring American operational support, and with dual key launch control, the Thor missiles, based at four main sites in eastern and northern England, would each have the RAF roundel painted on the side.

John Boyes has provided an excellent overview of the story of the British Thor missiles and the reasoning behind their deployment.[197] Boyes observes that the February 1958, British acceptance of the American proposal for IRBMs in England came as a consequence of a desire by the new British prime minister, Harold Macmillan, to repair the UK–US relationship after the Suez Crisis. Time to deployment was to be tight, and the US technology was not designed for use in underground silos, prompting the use of above-ground bases. Sites at RAF Driffield, Feltwell, Hemswell and North Luffenham were chosen; each RAF Thor base had five satellite stations with a potential three missiles at readiness. The nature of nuclear war with unprotected launch sites meant there would be no opportunity for a second launch from any site. So in principle all 60 missiles had to be simultaneously at readiness.

Boyes explains that there was some concern among UK defence planners when the American ideas were first considered in 1956 and 1957. The worry was that the deployment of Thor would make the UK a more likely Soviet target. The secretary of state for air wrote to Duncan Sandys about Thor:

> their operational value to the United Kingdom is little, while they increase our attractiveness as a target. We must be careful that we do not pay too much for the principal advantage of the deal, i.e. its contribution to the development of Blue Streak in terms of R&D knowledge.[198]

Given that Blue Streak was later cancelled, it would appear that the enduring benefit of the British acceptance of Thor would be solely in the diplomatic domain of the UK–US 'special relationship'.

As the Cuba crisis reached its peak in the third week of October 1962, British Prime Minister Harold Macmillan ordered the V-bombers to alert. The Victors and Vulcans were fuelled up, and their five-man crews readied. [199] I have heard it said that some of the aircraft were held at the end of the runway for an entire day, ready to launch at a moment's notice. The mighty Vulcans were ready to go, but interestingly the prime minister did not order the V-bomber force to be dispersed to 27 diverse bases, as had been developed as standard tactics for a crisis. It seems that the prime minister regarded such a step as escalatory and likely to bring a greater attack on the UK in the event that nuclear war occurred.

Another indication of the severity of the Cuba crisis and the important role played by Britain concerns the Thor force. While Prime Minister Harold Macmillan was keen to avoid sending any escalatory signals to Moscow, military staff acted to ensure the readiness of the Thor missiles. Air Marshal Sir Kenneth Cross of RAF Bomber Command ordered the Thor sites to readiness level 1-5, indicating 15 minutes' preparedness for launch.[200] The sites were also alerted to adopt pre-planned anti-sabotage security measures.[201] In his book *Project Emily*, John Boyes notes that the readiness of the Thor force was facilitated by the recently completed second Micky Finn no-notice dispersal military exercise of 20 and 21 September 1962. Boyes' research indicates that while US military personnel associated with UK Thor operations were indeed, according to one witness, 'all hyped up', the RAF personnel were much more relaxed. By way of illustration he notes that Number 102 squadron went ahead with an open day for 100 visitors, and Number 226 Squadron held its annual Hallowe'en party for staff families. Such actions could indeed have been an indication of relaxed normality, but perhaps they were a consequence of a top-level steer for as much normality as possible, coupled with British stoicism. Across the UK as a whole the fear of nuclear conflict was palpable, and the Thor sites would have ranked among some of the most probable Soviet targets in the whole country. Perhaps stoicism was favoured by the Cold War perception that the best place to be when atomic bombs start falling was under one. Boyes presents much evidence that measures taken by the Thor force during the Cuba crisis were measured and proportionate to the situation. In his book *Launch Pad UK*, Jim Wilson argues, however, that the UK-based Thor missiles were at an alarmingly high state of readiness during the crisis. He cites Alistair Horne, Harold Macmillan's official biographer, when arguing that relatively low-level military official took Britain to the brink of mobilisation almost by mistake.[202] He further cites a *Daily Mail* report of 18 February 1963, headed 'When Britain went to the brink'. He notes that the *Daily Mail* report led to a heated exchange in Parliament between opposition Labour MPs and Prime Minister Macmillan. Macmillan's responses stressed the normality of the Thor force situation during the crisis – he said: 'Certain pre-cautionary steps were taken, but more than this was not necessary'.[203] Macmillan's answers appear consistent with the impression gained by John Boyes in his research into attitudes among Thor personnel. Jim Wilson, in contrast, takes the view that the Thor situation was more alarming than the British government wanted its people to appreciate.

BRITAIN'S ROLE IN THE WORLD

By late 1962 so much had changed for Britain in the 17 years since the end of 'the War'. The country had been humiliated over Suez; it had lost many of its imperial possessions; and it had been brought to the brink of nuclear annihilation because of a crisis between America and Russia over Cuba. It was increasingly clear that British defence needs were changing, to reflect ever more strongly an alignment with the United States and a concern for European defence. Despite this reality, however, official policy had not yet adjusted, as is clear from this part of the 1962 British government's Statement on Defence:[204]

> 3. The basic objectives of Britain's defence policy will remain:
>
>   (a) to maintain the security of this country;
>
>   (b) to carry out our obligations for the protection of British territories overseas and those to whom we owe a special duty by treaty or otherwise;
>
>   (c) to make our contribution to the defence of the free world and the prevention of war in accordance with the arrangements we have with individual countries and under collective security treaties.
>
> 4. … We provide simultaneously contributions to three collective security alliances, NATO, CENTO and SEATO. Thus we must be able at any time to maintain forces in three areas of the world.
>
> 22. … We support NATO and SEATO with land, sea and air forces, and CENTO with our air striking force.

In 1962 all three branches of the British military had their own nuclear weapon capabilities and ambitions. The Royal Navy had carrier-based nuclear strike; the Royal Air Force had the V-bombers and was soon to deploy the Blue Steel stand-off weapon; and the Army had access to the US surface-to-surface nuclear-capable weapons systems Corporal (coded MGM-5) and Honest John (coded MGR-1). In the years that followed there was also dual key access to US atomic demolition munitions and nuclear mines, ready for use in a European war. Starting in the 1950s the British had explored their own nuclear mine concepts, the first of which was known as Blue Peacock, famous (or infamous) for the reported plans to use live chickens to keep the weapon ice-free in cold northern European winters.[205] Luckily, for the chickens at least, such British improvisations were never deployed.

The 1962 Cuba Crisis came not long after the Royal Navy had taken delivery of its latest nuclear strike aircraft, the Blackburn Buccaneer, armed with the small British nuclear weapon Red Beard. The Navy had earlier matched this weapon to its Scimitar and Sea Vixen aircraft.[206]

THE ARMY AND THE BOMB

The British Army had long wanted a domestic equivalent to the US Corporal and Honest John systems. The consequence of that ambition was the development by English Electric of the Blue Water surface-to-surface battlefield nuclear weapon. By 1962 Blue Water had been under development for nearly five years. Even before the Cuban Missile Crisis there was a growing sense that even the smallest nuclear conflict could rapidly escalate into all-out strategic nuclear war. The concept of limited battlefield nuclear war was starting to be questioned, especially by defence planners in Britain and Europe.

Such considerations and a growing awareness of the rapidly rising cost of nuclear weapons development reached the Cabinet at 11 a.m. on 3 August 1962:[207]

> points of such importance as to require the attention of the Cabinet. The most important of these concerned the future of the Army's nuclear weapon BLUE WATER. The original intention behind the development of these so-called tactical nuclear weapons had been to interpose a stage between small-scale military aggression and the outbreak of strategic nuclear war. The British contribution to the Western strategic nuclear deterrent was assured, since the cancellation on military grounds of BLUE STREAK, by the deployment of BLUE STEEL and subsequently SKYBOLT, with the V-bombers of the RAF. The British Army of the Rhine has been equipped with the tactical nuclear weapons HONEST JOHN and CORPORAL, both of United States origin: the next generation of weapons was to consist of the United States SERGEANT and the United Kingdom BLUE WATER, which although it would come into service later than SERGEANT was certainly a better weapon.

The record of the Cabinet's deliberations on 3 August 1962 also reveal the emerging opinion in British military circles that a limited 'tactical' nuclear war in Europe would in all probability be an immediate precursor of national annihilation. If the British Army were ever to fire a Blue Water battlefield nuclear weapon as a means to halt a Warsaw Pact advance into Western Germany then, increasingly, British defence planners believed that conflict escalation would be very likely to lead to the use of medium-range nuclear weapons in Europe. For the Americans such a scenario might have remained something that might be termed 'tactical', but for Britain such ideas could not be more strategic. The Cabinet noted:[208]

> In regard to BLUE WATER, it seemed increasingly doubtful whether the sort of campaign in which BLUE WATER would be used could ever take place. This was not to say that opinion in military circles in the United States and in the North Atlantic Alliance would easily be brought to accept our conclusions.

The early 1960s represented the core of a British understanding of potential European nuclear conflict termed the 'tripwire'. This thinking, which had originated in the United States, held that a Soviet attack on western Europe would most probably not be quelled by NATO conventional forces and that NATO would resort to the defensive use of nuclear weapons.

This would be expected to escalate rapidly, leading to the complete nuclear annihilation of western and central Europe. The goal of policy therefore had to be to deter any conflict with the Soviet Union in Europe. For Britain the tripwire policy had particular strength, as it implied that any conflict in Europe, and especially any use of a nuclear weapon in Europe, must be regarded as an existential threat to the United Kingdom. The UK had little time for extended war-fighting plans or for any 'tactical' nuclear war in Europe. The main thing had to be to deter war. The United States, imagining that conventional forces might actually be effective in shielding Soviet aggression, turned away from tripwire thinking in 1957.[209] The British were less sanguine and the enduring notion of the tripwire was to have profound implications for UK defence prioritisation in the 1960s and 1970s.

While the Blue Water cancellation discussions reveal disquiet about the notion of the British Army initiating a nuclear war in Europe, the aversion to tactical nuclear capability was not so complete that it was felt the capability should be dropped; rather it should be transferred to the Royal Air Force. The TSR2 appeared perfectly placed to assume this responsibility, as the Cabinet itself concluded:[210]

> It was essential to provide a replacement for the Canberra bombers in the shape of the TSR 2. In his [the Minister of Defence's] view and in the view of the Air Staff the TSR 2 would be capable of satisfactorily discharging the role planned for BLUE WATER on the European front. On the other hand the Chief of the Imperial General Staff could not accept this view, which had not been accepted by any other army in the Alliance and would result in depriving the Army of control of what they still regarded as their own heavy artillery.

This discussion also reveals another side to British military thinking at the time. While Britain might not at that point, in 1962, have been able to imagine fighting a limited nuclear war in Europe, such a conflict might have seemed to be a sensible option elsewhere. In 1962 Britain still possessed numerous 'Imperial' defence responsibilities, such as in Southeast Asia. In those contexts Blue Water might have been useful – but as we shall see, TSR2 would be regarded as better.

On 3 August 1962 the Cabinet decided that the Army's Blue Water missile was to be cancelled. The Army was to lose its Bomb.

Derek Wood has noted that the money saved by cancelling Blue Water was pumped into RAF and Royal Navy nuclear weapons development.[211] The Blue Water cancellation represented a first step in the reduction in the scope and power of the individual branches of the British military. The Army was the first branch of the services to lose its own nuclear weapons capability, and eventually the Royal Air Force would have to follow, resulting in the reality of the early 21st century, in which British nuclear weapons capability was restricted to the domain of the Royal Navy.

The compromises and consolidation of British military force in the second half of the 20th century was a major source of tension and friction. The British Army, the Royal Navy and the RAF were each fiercely proud of their traditions and protective of their remits. However, the legacy of imperial ambition was unsustainable, and cuts, mergers and transfers of responsibility were essential. In August 1962 the TSR2 project became embroiled in the process of service capability cuts as the RAF triumphed over the Army in terms of tactical nuclear weapons capability. As we shall see, TSR2 was to figure strongly in similar inter-service rivalries in the years ahead.

While the Army's Blue Water missile could never have been more than a short-range tactical weapon, TSR2 was enormously more flexible. Intermittently throughout the TSR2 story there arises the notion, never officially adopted, that TSR2, or a variant of it, might have a strategic role. What, however, did 'strategic' mean in this context? It was a term associated with policymakers and defence planners. It related to the controversial choices of Sir Arthur 'Bomber' Harris in flattening the cities of Nazi Germany. From the Second World War and into the Cold War it was, arguably the raison d'être of the RAF, but it was not a term heard in the Mess and among the pilots and crew of the Royal Air Force. It was simply not part of their daily lexicon.[212] The RAF had strike capability and it had reconnaissance roles. Now, for those on the planes the notion of something separate called 'strategic' was creeping in from outside. RAF officers would hear MoD people or politicians talking about strategic capabilities. Perhaps air crews were discouraged from thinking too much about their targets beyond being something to hit. While the TSR2 was not officially strategic, any RAF long-range bomber (especially with refuelling capability) was a very strategic weapon, and hence the TSR2 was always a strategic weapon in all but name. For the RAF top brass it represented something special, but they knew – officially at least – that the T stood for tactical. For the ordinary officers and men of the RAF the TSR2 assumed a special status: even they could see that it represented the RAF's only real hope for continued leadership in UK defence.

One key consideration in favour of the continued role of the manned bomber in the 1960s was the greater accuracy that it gave compared to long-range ballistic missiles. The relative inaccuracy of missiles favoured a shift to larger-yield nuclear weapons and hence greater devastation. This cemented the sense that the use of such weapons would form part of a strategic conflict threatening the very existence of the country.

US-led NATO nuclear strategy in the early Cold War had focused on two principles – countervalue and counterforce targeting. The countervalue strategy dominated up to and through the 1960s.[213] Guy Finch has argued that counterforce targeting had been of interest to top-level British military planners in the early 1950s, but at that time technological limitations had made it impossible, a point well understood by those more middle-level military planners concerned with the practicalities of defence policy.[214] The countervalue approach will target retaliation on those things most valued by the enemy, including cities and civilian infrastructure. In the early 1960s the Cuba crisis gave weight to those who said that the option of a more traditionally military, but nevertheless strategic, nuclear conflict should be possible. A counterforce strategy would target nuclear weapons on elements of the enemy's military capability. However any such conflict, especially with low-accuracy ballistic missiles, would inevitably result in a level of destruction similar to that arising from a countervalue attack. For those advocating a continued role for the manned bomber, issues of accuracy and flexibility remained powerful; however, the accuracy of long-range ballistic missiles was improving all the time.

The RAF was not only seeking to protect its individual weapons programmes but also to protect its institutional position in UK defence. Formed in 1918 near the end of the First World War, the Royal Air Force was by far the most junior branch of the UK armed forces. Its importance to the UK was, however, established by the Second World War, and especially by the pivotal role played by RAF Fighter Command in the 1940 Battle of Britain. That success was enabled by the significant boost given to the Air Force by the rearmament programme of the late 1930s. The total expenditure of the RAF overtook that of the Army in 1937 and the Royal Navy in 1938.[215] On the back of this military expansion came an industrial expansion: 26,263 aircraft delivered in 1943 compared to only 2,827 in 1938.[216] The expanded aircraft industry continued to thrive in the ten years after the war. David Edgerton notes that in the first ten months of 1947 the UK exported £10.9 million of complete aircraft while the United States achieved exports of £13.8 million.[217] This rapid growth of military and industrial capability coupled with public affection, and a perceived spirit of adventure led the Royal Air Force into a strong position in the 1950s.

Through the 1950s and 1960s there was intense inter-service rivalry within the UK armed forces. Former air chief marshal, Sir Douglas Lowe, a lifelong RAF man, described it well:

> [An] approach, which is all the time going on in the Air Ministry, and of course I'm now looking back from having been at the top level, all the time, right until I retired, there was this constant back of the mind worry: how can the Air Force resist the Navy, in particular, and to some extent the Army? How can we get our bite of the cake? They're therefore always looking for policies, for strategies, which are going to be better than the alternatives which these people are going to be equally bubbling and pushing.[218]

Sir Douglas speculates that such issues may have impinged on the Defence Policy Committee's reluctance to issue OR339 as originally conceived. He comments:

> John Hayhurst and I had written this OR. We had failed to get it approved by the committee systems, largely I think because these committees were tri-service, and therefore it met total resistance from the Navy and partial resistance from the Army, because they saw it as encroaching on their interests. So it stalled. [Sir Frederick] Brundrett [chairman of the Defence Research Policy Committee] and Mountbatten were not keen on it, Mountbatten because he was dark blue, and they had never totally accepted, in the centre, the... argument about the Island Strategy being a viable option. So there was this terrible in-fighting going on all the time... I'm talking as the desk officer, who, having got the thing up to a point where, having invented this general operational requirement and got the industry to respond, at

no expense to the MOD, or to the Air Ministry, with all this valuable data of how it could be met, and actually, having got them started work on actually cutting metal and doing things about it, … at that point, I was promoted to Wing Commander, which I thought, my God, I'm doing alright here! So I felt that I was really conducting a one-man campaign for this new aeroplane, and I was totally disappointed when I was suddenly posted at the end of my time … I knew that this new aeroplane, the 330, had been cancelled by then, so I knew that this was the only new aeroplane that we were really liable to get, or needed to get if we were going to have an Air Force. So, yes, I was indoctrinated in the importance of Trenchard's moral victory, that there had to be an independent Air Force.[219]

The Cabinet meeting of 3 August 1962 further noted:[220]

The main deterrent to Russian aggression was the strategic nuclear striking force of the United States and the United Kingdom. It was not clear that any supplementary nuclear deterrent was required that could not be provided by the great number of nuclear weapons already deployed in Europe, with the addition of the TSR 2.

Concerning TSR2, the Cabinet concluded that:

It would be better to insist on the capability of the TSR 2 aircraft to discharge whatever role might remain to be performed by nuclear weapons in the front line.

The words 'whatever role might remain' reconfirm that tactical nuclear weapons delivery was falling out of favour inside the Ministry of Defence. As regards nuclear capabilities as a whole, TSR2 had ensured victory for the RAF over the Army, but as we shall see this victory was short lived. A competition would soon emerge between the RAF and the Navy in the area of strategic nuclear capability.

In the months after the Blue Water cancellation, British nuclear strategy evolved further and the Cabinet faced yet more decisions concerning nuclear weapons. These were prompted by unilateral decisions across the Atlantic. The United States had, for domestic defence policy reasons, decided that it would have no use for Skybolt, the new air-launched nuclear missile then under development. Such a decision was of profound importance for the British, whose defence planners had assumed that the British nuclear deterrent would remain an RAF-led activity in the medium term, based on the V-force using longer-range stand-off nuclear weapons, so Skybolt would be perfect for British needs after the Blue Steel system. But now the Americans were putting such plans in jeopardy.

POLARIS

On 3 January 1963 the prime minister, Harold Macmillan, briefed the Cabinet on meetings he had had in the Bahamas before Christmas with the US president, John F. Kennedy. The briefing notes record:[221]

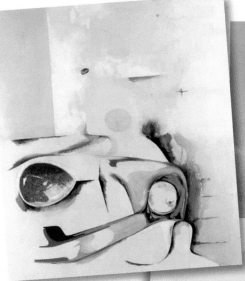

TSR2 in flight, early 1965. [UK Government]

Above: Richard Hamilton Homage à Chrysler Corporation [with permission of the artist]

Right: Mightier Yet! WWII British propaganda poster [Alamy]

MIGHTIER YET!

Every day more PLANES
Every day more PILOTS

Above: Bloodhound Missile at the Dan Dare and the Birth of High Tech Britain exhibition at the Science Museum, London, April 2008 [Alex Lentati/Evening Standard/Shutterstock]

Left: Young MOD Don Hughes astride his Vespa SS at Heathrow Airport 1965 [Source: Don Hughes, Friday on my Mind, Armadillo, 2010]

Right: 609 Squadron Spring 1943. Roland 'Bee' Beamont standing in the doorway centre. The two dogs "Blitz" and "Spit" and all the aircrew are listed in the webpage dedicated to F/Lt Baron Jean de Selys Longchamps at https://www.manstonhistory.org.uk/ [Coloured image: Mark Crame]

Left: Flight magazine cover,
29 August 1958 [Flight]

Right: Painting by John Young (1930-2015) originally
illustrating an article by AC Lovesey entitled Engine
Development for Military Aircraft, as published in the
Battle of Britain Souvenir Book 1964.

ROLLS-ROYCE AVONS POWER THE
ENGLISH ELECTRIC LIGHTNING
THE ONLY MACH—2 AIRCRAFT
OPERATING WITH THE RAF TODAY

TSR2 as it would have appeared in standard
camouflage [Source: Skyraider, ©Ronnie Olsthoorn]

Left: Farnborough Air Show official programme September 1964 [SBAC/ADS]

Below: Much of British industry took pride in its association with the TSR2 project [Brooklands Museum]

TSR2 . . . the Rotax contribution

Solid Rotor Alternators and the co-ordination and environmental testing of the complete generating system. In addition, ignition units, actuators, switchgear and air valves have been designed, developed and manufactured by Rotax.

Rotax—Precision engineers to the aircraft industry.

ROTAX

ENGLAND · AUSTRALIA · CANADA

North American XB-70 Valkyrie [NASA]

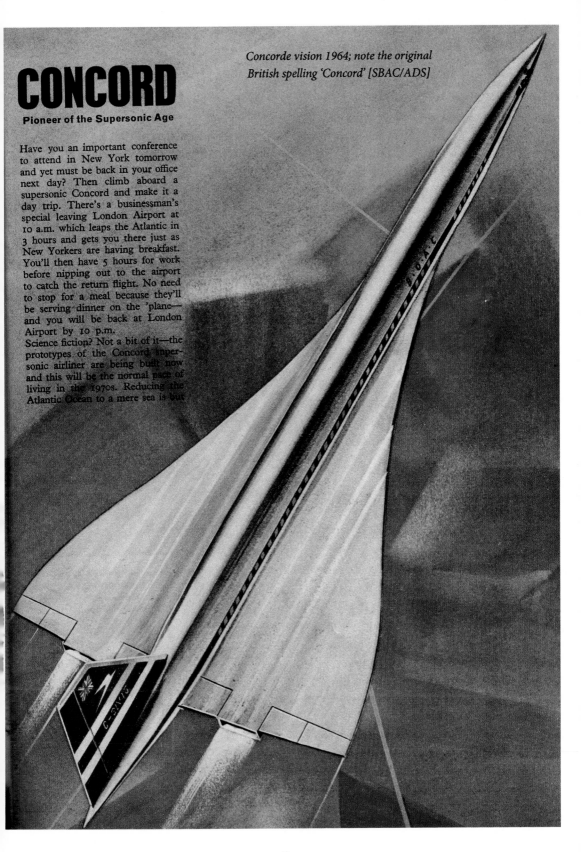

CONCORD
Pioneer of the Supersonic Age

Have you an important conference to attend in New York tomorrow and yet must be back in your office next day? Then climb aboard a supersonic Concord and make it a day trip. There's a businessman's special leaving London Airport at 10 a.m. which leaps the Atlantic in 3 hours and gets you there just as New Yorkers are having breakfast. You'll then have 5 hours for work before nipping out to the airport to catch the return flight. No need to stop for a meal because they'll be serving dinner on the 'plane—and you will be back at London Airport by 10 p.m.

Science fiction? Not a bit of it—the prototypes of the Concord supersonic airliner are being built now and this will be the normal pace of living in the 1970s. Reducing the Atlantic Ocean to a mere sea is but

Concorde vision 1964; note the original British spelling 'Concord' [SBAC/ADS]

5

Above: Avro Vulcan and BAC TSR2 Together [Damien Burke / HandmadeByMachine.com]

Left: Sukhoi T-61 [Source: Yefim Gordon, Sukhoi Su-24, Polygon Press, Moscow, 2003]

Blackburn Buccaneer
[David Gowans / Alamy]

Above: General Dynamics F-111
[US Air Force]

Left: A Polaris missile lifts off after being fired from the submerged British nuclear-powered ballistic missile submarine HMS Revenge (S27) off the coast of Florida (USA) near Cape Canaveral Air Force Station. This was the 10th in a series of Polaris test flights
[US Department of Defense]

Left: RAE Farnborough's Roy Dommett and the Chevaline system on which he worked. One of the two nuclear warheads is represented by the object near his left elbow [© Matt Casswell, British Library (www.bl.uk/voices-of-science)]

Above: James Rosenquist, F-111, first exhibited 1965 [© James Rosenquist/VAGA at ARS, NY and DACS, London 2018]

Airfix model aircraft kit TSR2 [Hornby Hobbies ltd.]

Those discussions, in which he [the prime minister] had been joined by the Foreign Secretary, the Commonwealth Secretary and the Minister of Defence, had covered a wide range of topics; but they had necessarily concentrated mainly on the issues arising from the decision of the United States Government to abandon development of the airborne ballistic missile SKYBOLT for their own forces. ... the decision to discontinue development of SKYBOLT was genuinely based on the fact that the United States Government had available, in POLARIS and MINUTEMAN, alternative deterrent systems of proved reliability, ...

President Kennedy had first suggested that the United States and the United Kingdom should share, on the basis of equality, the cost of continuing the development of the weapon and that we should thereafter place such production orders as we saw fit. But from our own point of view this would have been an open-ended commitment: and we should have found it difficult to exercise effective control over development carried out in the United States. He [the PM] had no doubt that it would have been wrong to accept this proposal. ... He had therefore decided to press the United States Government to supply us with the seaborne ballistic missile POLARIS instead of SKYBOLT.

If Britain were able to acquire the Polaris submarine-launched nuclear missile system for the Royal Navy, this would represent a massive growth in Britain's strategic capability. If the UK could indeed secure such a system from the Americans it would represent a remarkable achievement – but, as the Cabinet noted, sometimes you have to be careful what you wish for:[222]

The introduction of the POLARIS weapon implied heavy additional expenditure in the latter part of the present decade. This would inevitably involve even more drastic curtailment of other defence expenditure than had previously been contemplated, if defence was not to absorb an excessive share of national resources..

Despite such anxieties, Harold Macmillan secured the Polaris strategic nuclear weapons system for Britain. All saw immediately that this was a remarkable achievement: in so doing he had set in motion a process that would lead to the Navy's dominance in UK nuclear defence and which would contribute in a key way to the unravelling of the case for the TSR2.

In the early 1960s, memories of the 1940 Battle of Britain were still very fresh. Each year a souvenir book was published, and in the 1963 edition George Edwards of BAC wrote eloquently about the TSR2 project under development in his company. He saw the context very clearly, and said a surprising amount about what the future might hold:

The ballistic missile has come into being. The original and rather too simple thinking was that there was no obvious means of defence against it. In fact (and realisation of this presumably lead (sic) to the cancellation of the British Blue Streak Missile) the ballistic missile can be destroyed either on (or under) the ground before launch or in the air by anti-missile missiles. We should remember here that even if the Polaris submarine is regarded as undetectable and therefore invulnerable while under the surface of the sea, the Polaris missile warhead is as vulnerable as that of any other land-launched or air-launched missile as it approaches the target.

There are answers even to the anti-missile missile, e.g. the scattering of a considerable number of decoys from the warhead during its trajectory. These decoys can be made virtually indistinguishable from the warhead itself so that the missile will seek out and destroy only one of them, leaving the real warhead to get through.[223]

As we shall see, in those few words Edwards had correctly anticipated British nuclear technology policy for the next 20 years. His intention, however, was to mount a strong defence of another option – the TSR2. He concluded his article with the words:

By virtue of its ability to penetrate to a target at long range through strong defences TSR2 although originally designed for tactical use, can provide this country with an effective nuclear deterrent.

Thus TSR2 will not only give Bomber Command effective striking power and reconnaissance in all non-nuclear wars but will also maintain the nuclear deterrent when the credibility of the high altitude bomber has vanished.

George Edwards had not only seen the future that would happen; he had also seen the potential for TSR2 to provide an alternative.

However, all was not going well for TSR2. By January 1963 the planned TSR2 in-service date had slipped back to 1968, past what would become the expected arrival date for the Royal Navy Polaris system. A system that George Edwards clearly saw as a rival.

In opposition, the Labour party politician and former Second World War army captain Denis Healey was already pointing to the fact that the TSR2 was a tactical weapon developed to support the Army. He said: 'TSR.2 will only drop ordinary high explosive on tanks and bridges.'[224] Such rhetoric would further weaken the RAF's status as the force expected to lead British nuclear weapons capability in the years ahead.

Grammar-school socialist Healey would find an unlikely ally in imperial aristocrat Lord Mountbatten. As a lifelong Royal Navy man and an admiral of the fleet, Mountbatten had good reason to resist the expensive ambitions of the RAF.

A great-grandchild of Queen Victoria, Louis Mountbatten was born on the Windsor Castle estate on 25 June 1900.[225] He was to spend his life occupying an unusual position at the nexus of the Royal Family, the military and government. The high-point of his government service was his role as the last viceroy and the first governor-general of India. He oversaw the controversial partition of British India and the creation of the independent states of India and Pakistan. In 1949 he returned to Europe and his Royal Navy career. In 1956 he was promoted to the rank of admiral of the fleet and in 1959 he became chief of the defence staff. It was in this role that he was to turn his attentions to the issue of the TSR2.

1963 TROUBLE DOWN UNDER

The Royal Australian Air Force faced a challenge very similar to that faced by the RAF; they needed to replace their Canberra bombers. (The very name of that aircraft reveals the importance of the British Commonwealth to Britain's aircraft industry.) Roland Beamont later recalled efforts to sell the TSR2 to Australia:

> I made two visits to Canberra with teams from British Aerospace [*sic*] to make presentations on the TSR2 programme during which we understand that they were planning to acquire thirty airframes – the Royal Air Force was planning to have 150 and this 30 would have made a nice addition and made the production run really stable. During the early part of 1964, [which] was the year in which the aeroplane first flew, we understood that the Australian government had virtually signed up for a contract for TSR2.[226]

In fact the Australians had already – in October 1963 – formally signed up for the American rival F-111 aircraft.[227] Presumably it had taken a few months for the bad news to make it to the flight crews at Boscombe Down. It is widely reported that BAC efforts were being undermined by the chief of the defence staff. Lord Louis Mountbatten, ever the Navy man, was allegedly briefing the Australians against the TSR2, reportedly stressing that in his opinion the aircraft would never be built.[228] He deployed one particular party trick. Derek Wood reports: '[he had the] habit of slapping down five photographs of the Buccaneer and one of the TSR.2 and saying "Five of one or one of the other at the same cost".'[229]

George Edwards apparently held the view that the blame for the Australian decision lay with Lord Mountbatten. Robert Gardner reports Edwards saying: 'The chap who got the credit for Australia cancelling it was Mountbatten.'[230]

Richard Moore has, however, argued persuasively that allegations of mischief on the part of Mountbatten are exaggerated and possibly unwarranted.[231] Moore argues that Australia was well aware of the attributes of the various aircraft under consideration and was aware of British doubts around the future of the TSR2, independent of any lobbying by Mountbatten in support of the Blackburn Buccaneer.

Government archives in both the UK and Australia reveal extensive interactions over many years between the two countries concerning the TSR2 project.[232] The Australian military, and especially the Royal Australian Air Force, appear to have had much enthusiasm for the new British bomber. Derek Wood notes, however, that the RAAF was less than enthusiastic about the interim arrangements proposed by the British to meet Australian needs up until the point that the TSR2 aircraft would arrive. The British would loan Vulcan aircraft, but the opening suggestion that these aircraft must remain under British RAF operational control was not received well.[233]

The Australian government was nervous about the probable cost of TSR2, while being courted by the Americans keen to sell their F111-A. The British understood the Australian government concerns, and as the decision day drew close tried to reassure them. On 4 October 1963 Harold Macmillan wrote to his Australian counterpart, Bob Menzies, indicating that the British would shield the Australians from the R&D risks which were already becoming obvious. Macmillan said:

> I am anxious that you should have my personal assurance that we will be glad to make all the supply arrangements with you on a direct Government-to-Government basis, integrating your requirements with our own and according them equal priority, both in training and in delivery of operational aircraft, and charging you only the actual *extra* cost to the British Government of meeting your requirements. Normally, as you know, the price includes an element for the recovery of our development expenditure. In this case, and as an exceptional measure. I would be prepared to waive this element altogether. This will ensure that you get the aircraft at the lowest practicable price and relieve you of worry on the score of development costs.[234] (Emphasis original.)

The Australians appreciated the importance of this message, and a few days later Prime Minister Menzies replied. However, he did not write to Harold Macmillan, but rather to deputy prime minister Richard Austen Butler, always known as 'Rab'. Macmillan had been taken ill.

Bob Menzies stressed to Rab Butler the long-term importance of getting the TSR2/F-111 decision right. He advised that his defence minister, Athol Townley, was about to leave for discussions in the United States, but he assured the British that no Australian decision had been made. While stressing the importance of cost, he also hinted at a changing sense of geopolitical order in the Australian Near North when he said, of Townley's forthcoming discussions:

> we should arrange a political discussion with the United States. We would hope as a result of this to have a new and close assessment of the strategic requirements in the South East Asian area over the next several years, and of the contribution that we may be able to make towards them. What we are anxious to do within the financial strength that we have is to find the best way to add to our own defensive capacity and to enhance the collective strength of the area. A discussion with the United States will throw better light on priorities and timings than we have at present.[235]

In mid-October 1963 the US Department of Defense very much had its eye on Southeast Asia, and Vietnam in particular; the US was worried about the stability and reliability of South Vietnam under the leadership of Ngo Dinh Diem. But Diem was overthrown and executed on 2 November, and President Kennedy himself was assassinated three weeks later.

Australian Defence Minister Townley, visiting Washington DC in October 1963, would surely have gained a strong impression that the United States was committed to the Southeast Asian theatre. At the time Britain was firmly committed to Malaysia in its confrontation with Indonesia, but this was less globally visible than the difficulties of South Vietnam. Opposition Labour party MP Denis Healey recalled his visit to Saigon, South Vietnam, in April 1964:

> the Americans were everywhere but in the front line. Besides the military 'advisers' there were thousands of Americans from the CIA, the US Information Services, the Aid Programme, and, of course, the Embassy. The US Army, Navy and Air Force were engaged in fighting one another, and all three were at loggerheads with the CIA and the State Department; the latter tended to share the British view that the Vietnamese Government was heading for a disaster from which no amount of military intervention by the United States could rescue it.[236]

Later in his career Healey would ensure that no British soldiers would be deployed to South Vietnam. But Townley, on his October 1963 visit to Washington, had already crossed that Rubicon: on 24 May 1962 he had deployed the first Australian military personnel to South Vietnam – a group of 30 military advisers, one of whom died in an accident in June 1963.[237]

Whatever the prognosis for Southeast Asian security, the Australian TSR2/F-111 decision was always going to hinge on the price tag, and during October 1963 the Americans were also improving their offer. On 22 October, Tonley sent a message from the Australian Embassy in Washington to Prime Minister Menzies. In it he reported on his haggling with US Defense Secretary Robert McNamara and others:

> Sometimes in the dark night watches I wonder if some of my forebears earned their living in the bazaars of Cairo. The end result, however, has I am sure given us an outstanding deal.'[238]

The F-111 (or TFX as it was known in the early days) was the brainchild of US Defense Secretary Robert McNamara. Coming from the Ford Motor Company and bringing a commercial industrial mindset to the US government, he saw great advantage in an aircraft platform common to both the US Navy and the US Air Force. But the US military is famous for its inter-service rivalries and there was little enthusiasm in either the USAF or the USN for McNamara's idea. Nevertheless, two variants were initially envisaged: the F-111A for the air force and the F-111B for the Navy. Consistent with naval norms, the two crew would sit side by side, rather than in the more conventional air force tandem format, as in the TSR2. As it turned out the F-111B was never taken into production and McNamara's vision was not fulfilled, but in October 1963 the F-111 was something of a pet project for the US defense secretary, and the Australian deal must have been a source of comfort, whatever the cost.

The British were aware they were in a bidding war, and the British press reported a last-minute offer was made to cut the cost of each TSR2 by £200,000.[239] The sands of time had run out. The Australians made their decision – announcing it on 24 October. As it turns out the Australian government was unaware of the last-minute British offer. In a letter to Sir Allen Brown dated 22 November 1963, Australian civil servant Ted Bunting notes:

> You asked whether the reduction of £200,000 ever got over to us. The answer to that is no. Judging by the press, there is a good deal of circumstantial evidence that some proposition was about to be put to us, but we have never received it.[240]

If there really was such an offer it came simply too late. The decision had been made. Just before his announcement to the Australian Parliament, Bob Menzies wrote to the new British prime minister, Sir Alec Douglas-Home:

> What I will be saying is that we have undertaken to buy two squadrons of TFX aircraft, now known apparently as F111A, … the United States has engaged to apply certain price and finance arrangements which are very attractive to us, and no less important, for delivery purposes we are to rank equally with the United States Armed Forces. On the available estimates, this means the first aircraft will be available to us in the latter part of 1967, which is something like a two year improvement on what formerly seemed to be in prospect.[241]

As things turned out the Australians did not receive their first operational F-111 aircraft until 1973.

Menzies' message to Douglas-Home closes with a personal insight:

> One thing more, and for your private information. We can't ignore the significance of this with the United States. Although I have no doubt that the excellence of the delivery and price terms owe a great deal to the talents of my colleague [Townley], there is more than an element of US initiative in this transaction. By accepting it we do two things. We strengthen materially our own defensive power, and we add a good deal to the total free world capacity in this area. Further, we do it in a way which undoubtedly greatly satisfies the United States, and sustains their interest in this corner of the world. This is a most important by-product of the decision and one which I hope may contain some merit from your point of view.

The Australian decision was pivotal for the TSR2. Coming in late 1963, it was before British Labour party thinking for TSR2 had become fixed. If the UK had won an export order for 30 TSR2 aircraft to such a close ally, one with whom it had diverse defence, industrial, historical and cultural links, then it is hard to imagine that even a British Labour government would have been able to cancel the project in 1965.

The transition of power in the UK in the autumn of 1963 is an interesting story. Prime Minister Harold Macmillan resigned suddenly on 18 October, as he believed he had a serious and life-threatening prostate illness. In fact he was later to make a full recovery, and he lived on until 1986. The Conservative party had no clear process for choosing its leader, and Alec Douglas-Home, Lord Home, was Macmillan's controversial preferred candidate. Despite no clear constitutional requirement, the Queen accepted Macmillan's recommendation. This was all the more unusual because Home's parliamentary seat was in the (unelected) House of Lords rather than the democratically elected House of Commons. Noting it would be inappropriate to serve as prime minister from the Lords, Douglas-Home used the recently passed Peerage Act 1963 to resign his peerage so that he could fight and win a safe Conservative seat in the Commons. (The Act had been created to permit left-wing Labour MP Sir Anthony Wedgwood Benn to resign his peerage and enter the Commons, where he was known as Tony Benn.) As the October 1963 administrative transition moved forward, for two weeks the UK had a prime minister without a seat in Parliament. He had resigned his seat in the House of Lords and he had not yet won a seat in the House of Commons – constitutionally a rather remarkable situation.

TSR2 – RISING COSTS

The spring of 1963 had passed into summer and summer had passed into autumn, and progress on the TSR2 had remained slow and tortuous. The costs of TSR2 were rising and the production schedule was slipping. George Edwards was most worried by the lack of progress being made by English Electric at its Preston works in the north-west of England. Biographer Robert Gardner quotes George Edwards as saying:

> I had a hell of a job with production of TSR2 because of that [delays primarily at Preston, where Arthur Sheffield ruled supreme] and I moved the assembly of a development aircraft away from them because they just weren't doing it. I could see that they had got it round their necks, and it was no good pretending they hadn't. But it really caused a revolution; compared with that the French Revolution was a tea party![242]

Throughout 1963, worsening delays with English Electric at Preston caused George Edwards, a lifelong Vickers man, much anxiety. Robert Gardner reveals a memorandum written by Edwards on 2 January 1963 to English Electric's lead aviation administrator Lord (Robin) Caldecote:

> I have spent many hours this week going through the position, and am disturbed to find yet another slippage in the Preston programme of a further six to seven weeks. You will recall that, based on the delivery of the complete rear fuselage at the end of December, I promised Julian Amery [the aviation minister] when he was at Weybridge in September, in the presence of the chairman and Freddie Page [TSR2 designer], that we could achieve the first flight in August, although this was a pretty

unpopular statement. We have not given the Ministry any official intimation that we are changing the August date, although I was, of course, told by Shorrock [the works director] shortly after the meeting with Amery, the end of December was in fact becoming mid March [1964].[243]

1963 was not only a year for developments shaping the TSR2. Of more immediate concern was the basis of the nuclear deterrent as managed by the Royal Air Force. While the Blue Steel Mark I stand-off weapon designed by Avro might appear to have been ready during the 1962 Cuba Crisis, the reality was that it entered service properly as the backbone of Britain's strategic nuclear deterrent only in 1963. Designed to operate at Mach 2 at an altitude of 80,000 feet, Blue Steel was fitted with the American-inspired 1 megaton Red Snow warhead.[244] Blue Steel would play this role for five years until the arrival of the Polaris system with the Resolution class submarines, the first of which entered service in 1968.

Blue Steel presented many technical difficulties for those directly concerned with its readiness. In particular the rocket-powered missile used the impressive but difficult high-test peroxide fuel discussed earlier (Chapter 4). This particular fuel came with a set of troubling memories. The British had acquired HTP technology from the German submarine programme at the end of the Second World War.[245] Two experimental HTP powered submarines were developed by the British during the 1950s. These vessels, HMS *Excalibur* and HMS *Explorer*, proved extremely difficult to operate safely, so much so that they were nicknamed HMS *Exploder* and HMS *Excruciator*.[246] While there was never an actual explosion associated with either *Excalibur* or *Explorer*, the Royal Navy had experienced a serious accident with the submarine HMS *Sidon* in June 1955.[247] In that case an HTP-fuelled 'fancy' torpedo motor had started while still on board the submarine, causing a catastrophic accident leading to the loss of 13 lives. The Royal Navy of the 1950s had, unsurprisingly, a very negative impression of HTP fuels, and the RAF experience with Blue Steel ten years later would prove to be almost as troubling.

By the time of the Cabinet meeting on 18 February 1964, Sir Alec Douglas-Home was both an MP and prime minister. He reported on his own recent visit to Washington.[248]

The United States Government were anxious to maintain the momentum of discussion with the Soviet Union in an attempt to promote a further relaxation of international tension. For this purpose they would welcome our support, in the forthcoming deliberations at the Disarmament Conference in Geneva, of President Johnson's proposal to 'freeze' nuclear delivery vehicles. The discussions in Washington had established that the United States Government would not regard a measure of this kind as affecting either our fleet of Polaris submarines or the TSR-2 aircraft and that they would hope that the multilateral nuclear force, if it were created, would be similarly excepted from the scope of the 'freeze'. In other respects, however, the concept was still in the early stages of development and many of its details remained to be settled.

President Lyndon Johnson's Administration would propose two major arms-control measures – a nuclear freeze and a fissile material cut-off agreement or treaty. The latter idea remains under active consideration even now, at the time of writing.

Douglas-Home's Cabinet considered TSR2 at its meeting held on 4 June 1964. They resolved to permit representatives of the Federal German government to conduct a technical examination of the TSR2 aircraft with a view to making a possible purchase. At this time Britain was increasingly taking the view that TSR2 would be a flexible nuclear bomber, but of course that aspect would not play well in still war-ravaged Germany. It was noted that no public emphasis should be given to TSR2 nuclear weapons capabilities in connection with West German interest: for the Germans, TSR2 would be presented in purely conventional battlefield terms. Despite all the British concern to German sensitivities, the German delegation did not place an order.

As can be seen from the Cabinet papers, the government of Sir Alec Douglas-Home was prepared to allow the TSR2 project to move forward under its own momentum and free from close scrutiny of politicians, but the coming autumn of 1964 would be a crucial period for TSR2 and for politicians in Britain.

CHAPTER SIX – WHITE HEAT: 1964

In all our plans for the future, we are re-defining and we are re-stating our
Socialism in terms of the scientific revolution. But that revolution cannot become a
reality unless we are prepared to make far-reaching changes in economic and social
attitudes, which permeate our whole system of society. The Britain that is going
to be forged in the white heat of this revolution will be no place for restrictive
practices or for outdated methods on either side of industry.

*Harold Wilson MP, White Heat speech, Labour
party conference, Scarborough, 1 October 1963.*

1964: TSR2 UNVEILED

Although the TSR2 project had been revealed to Parliament in December 1958 with the
disclosure of GOR 339, the first prototype was not unveiled until 1964. This disclosure
prompted a wave of popular interest in the TSR2 and its beauty. TSR2 entered the popular
imagination and it soon found its place in many a young boy's collections of cutaways from
the pages of the *Eagle*.

Colin Frewin, curator of 2007 exhibition 'Dan Dare and the Birth of Hi-Tech Britain',
writes of the cutaways:

> The *Eagle* Cutaways show an amazing depth of technology and vision, which was
> very much part of every day life in Great Britain after the war, something nowadays
> that is in the 'lost world' of design and innovation. Yet the Cutaways will never be lost.
> They are part of an exciting nostalgic period of time in the technical and engineering
> development of this country.[249]

Leslie Ashwell Wood, who led the drawing of the famous cutaways, drew 617 of the 946
examples,[250] including the TSR2 example shown on the next page. While many were in black
and white, the most memorable are the full colour examples revealing the inner workings
of all types of machines. Jonathan Glancey has captured the essence of the *Eagle* cutaways

TSR2 cutaway from the Eagle, 14 November 1964 [Image reproduced with kind permission of the Dan Dare Corporation Limited, www.dandare.com]

accurately when he writes: 'In the drawings is a vision of an alternative Britain, a country that appeared to be emerging in the 1950s, but one that was to have all but vanished by the late 1960s.'[251]

The Times newspaper featured the newly revealed TSR2 prominently on the first page of its Aviation Supplement of 7 September 1964. The supplement was timed to match to the period of that year's Farnborough Air Show. The air show continues today in even-numbered years, although now the event is held in July. The idea that *The Times* might produce a 24-page broadsheet supplement celebrating the aviation industry is so far removed from 21st-century experience as to be barely credible. In its own way, this simple fact alone reveals just how much Britain has changed in the last 50 years.

Ted Wheeldon, president of the Society of British Aerospace Companies, organisers of the Farnborough show, wrote tellingly in *The Times* supplement:

> Of the eight types of aircraft expected to make their first appearance at a S.B.A.C. Farnborough show this week undoubtedly the star is the much-discussed TSR 2 supersonic low-level strike and reconnaissance aircraft, one of the most advanced machines yet produced in any country. If it is 'cleared' to do so in time, it will fly over from its base at Boscombe Down, Wiltshire, but will not land at the R.A.E. airfield.[252]

But the 1964 Farnborough Air Show closed its gates on 13 September, 11 days before the first flight of the TSR2, so the TSR2 never flew over the crowds at Farnborough. If it had, perhaps this story would have had a different outcome.

The substantial 164-page official programme for the 1964 Farnborough SBAC[253] Air Show also gave much emphasis to the long-awaited TSR2. The public information available concerning the TSR2 project led a major feature article in the programme entitled 'Air Warfare at Tree-Top Height'.[254]

The cover of that Farnborough official programme is a fine example of British futurism. Inside, the publication is illustrated with numerous original artworks in colour and black & white. Design and production of the programme is credited to Scott-Turner and Associates Ltd of London, but individual artists are not identified.

Much of British industry took pride in its association with the TSR2 project.[255] But after the Farnborough Air Show had closed its gates that Sunday, the news of the following week was dominated by one thing – the announcement of a UK general election. On Tuesday 15th *The Sun* newspaper launched its first-ever front page, running with the story 'Election Race is On', although the main headline was, unsurprisingly, 'Good Morning! It's Time for a New Newspaper'.

Bill Gunston reports that during the election campaign Denis Healey asserted:

> TSR2 will only drop ordinary high explosive on tanks and bridges ... new anti-aircraft weapons will be able to shoot it down by the time it is in service, so at £16 million an aircraft it is going to make all Mr Amery's other blunders look like chickenfeed.[256]

The Times supplement, 'Survey of British Aviation 1964',
7 September 1964 [The Times / News Licensing]

In those words we see the full text of the remarks introduced more briefly in Chapter 5. Gunston goes on further to observe: Conservative ministers said £16 million was 'an exaggeration by a factor of 10' but they would not be precise about the actual figures. It seems likely that the best estimates were somewhere in between the numbers in the rhetoric from the left and the right. Internal documents at this time were quoting figures of around £5 million.[257]

Labour's election manifesto was carefully crafted on the issues of defence. The party rank-and-file contained influential pacifist elements, but the pragmatic realities of possible government were also clear. The manifesto declared:

> The Government bases its policy on the assumption that Britain must be prepared to go it alone without her allies in an all-out thermo-nuclear war with the Soviet Union, involving the obliteration of our people. By constantly reiterating this appalling assumption the Government is undermining the alliance on which our security now depends. …

> We are not prepared any longer to waste the country's resources on endless duplication of strategic nuclear weapons. We shall propose the re-negotiation of the Nassau Agreement. Our stress will be on the strengthening of our conventional regular forces so that we can contribute our share to Nato defence and also fulfil our peacekeeping commitments to the Commonwealth and the United Nations.

> We are against the development of national nuclear deterrents and oppose the current American proposal for a new mixed-manned nuclear surface fleet (MLF) [multi-lateral force]. We believe in the inter-dependence of the western alliance and will put forward constructive proposals for integrating all Nato's nuclear weapons under effective political control so that all the partners in the alliance have a proper share in their deployment and control.[258]

It is clear from these words that if Labour were to win the election, the TSR2 would be in trouble.

Right-wing Tory MP Stephen Hastings wrote of the choices facing Britain at this time:

> there lies before us a nation a clear choice, either to regain the main stream of history with all its risks, its dangers and its rewards or to turn into a backwater.

> Of course it is open to us to choose the backwater. Its aspect is already clear. Economically, we can rely upon the whisky distilleries and the manufacture of plastic buckets and perambulators. We can surrender to the no risk, welfare-first philosophy which has so insidiously pervaded our thinking since the war. In the backwater personal security comes first, the prowess of the nation second. Here is the stagnation of egalitarianism and of trade-union nihilism; where youth wanders gloomily and mischievously about the sea fronts looking for something to bash up; where nobody resigns on a principle, because of the pension; whence ex-imperial Britain gawps into the skies – at other people's achievements.[259]

Stephen Hastings' autobiography reveals an interesting life, shaped by 20th-century history. Joining the Scots Guards at the start of the Second World War, he moved to the SAS and then the SOE along the way, seeing extensive action in North Africa. After the war he continued his journey away from the life of an ordinary soldier. He recalls his life after 1948:

> Thus for the next twelve years, like many others, my efforts were dedicated to this hidden combat with Marxism/Leninism and its executive arm, the KGB.
>
> Secret service is necessarily something of a strain if only because of the necessity to lead a double life. The rewards are rare and can only be acknowledged among close colleagues but the hunt can certainly stimulate the adrenalin and an insight into the ruthless nature of international politics is a safe guarantee against many illusions. I am grateful for this.
>
> Years after I left the service, when I was already a Member of Parliament, Sandy Glen, then a director of what was still British European Airways, kindly invited me to join their inaugural flight to Leningrad. Visas duly arrived for all his guests – except for me. Enquiry at the Foreign Office disclosed that I had been declared persona non grata in the Soviet Union. I consoled myself with the thought that this was, after all, some sort of accolade.[260]

Going into the 1964 election the Labour party was led by Harold Wilson. Wilson was from Huddersfield, now in West Yorkshire, where today a statue stands in the main square in his honour. During the British election campaign *Life* magazine introduced its American readers to the possible next British prime minister with the words:

> Wilson represents a new image in the top echelons of British politics. As one political columnist described it recently, 'Harold Wilson is the first of a new classless generation of grammar school boys to reach the top.' Tory leaders have invariably been drawn from the aristocracy or upper middle class and have traveled by the Eton–Oxford route to the top. Labour leaders have either been intellectuals who took a similar Eton or Winchester–Oxford route and have sometimes seemed a little misplaced among the slums and factories that are the heartbeat of the labor movement, or they have been passionate working-class men who have fought their way to the top from humble beginnings and little education. Harold Wilson, a native of Yorkshire, is the first champion of a brash new route from working-class beginnings, via the grammar schools to which only the most promising students are admitted, and a scholarship to Oxford he won entirely on merit. His accent, although still slightly flavored by his north of England childhood, is the nearest that any Briton can achieve to a classless accent. It has neither the rough-hewn quality of a fighting trade unionist nor the smooth, sophisticated polish painstakingly honed on an old Etonian.[261]

Harold Wilson aged 8 in front of Number 10 [Getty Images / Hulton Archive]

Life magazine also reproduced a photograph of a young Harold, aged 8, taken in front of Number 10 Downing Street.

TEST FLYING

During the election campaign the test flying of the TSR2 finally got under way. The first flight was to be undertaken by BAC test pilot Roland Beamont. The role of the test pilot was key at this stage in the history of aviation, even arguably at its zenith. Roland Beamont observed:

> A test pilot is often asked about his job as if it was not quite respectable, no doubt because of the misleading image sometimes conjured up of the pilot by reporters on the occasions of prototype first flights or more dramatic events.

The test pilot's function is in practice a key point in an essentially team effort. The design, engineering and development of a successful aircraft is dependent on the sustained and dedicated effort of a team of specialists covering a wide field of activities. In these the test pilot's task is no more and no less important than many of the others, but it is perhaps inevitable that certain pressures occur in the course of his job which are unique and not experienced by other members of the team because, in the nature of things, one of the aspects occurs at the focal point in the process when all the other specialists have done their task, namely the flying programme. At that stage all the efforts and aspirations of the responsible members of the team and of the many hundreds of people down the line whose future livelihoods may depend on the success of the venture, are focused on one thing – successful flight testing; and this must depend on, among other factors, the capability of one man, the test pilot.[262]

In the lead-up to the flight-testing programme further tensions arose between the Vickers and English Electric engineers.[263] Vickers proposed that the programme should be undertaken somewhere in the south of England because the first aircraft would be built at Weybridge, in Surrey. English Electric, however, was adamant that the better location would be Warton, Lancashire, in the north of England. Warton provided superior test equipment and had a history of supersonic flight testing. The debate dragged on, putting the whole programme under unnecessary pressure. Beamont describes the difficult journey towards a solution:

Then one day, at one of the hundreds of specialist meetings, a Weybridge man was recorded as stating that it had been decided to fly from Wisley. Cross-checking failed to confirm this as agreed policy either at Warton or Weybridge, so I asked to see Sir George Edwards [GRE], BAC's managing director. As always GRE was quickly ready to see the pilot, but he did not seem enthusiastic about this subject saying that of course with the prototype building at Weybridge, the Vickers flight test department would be responsible for the flying programme, but that I would be in charge, as arranged at the time of the contract. The only problem he saw was that to tow the aircraft down the road to Wisley and do final preparation there would be too time-consuming, and so the Weybridge solution was to fly it out of Brooklands. This was a surprising proposal as I had come prepared to argue against Wisley with its usable 2,200yd runway on technical and professional grounds, and now we were apparently being asked to take from a runway half as long! The advice given to GRE by Vickers was apparently that Jock Bryce had recently (and very capably) flown the prototype VC10 airliner out of Brooklands, and so there should be no problem with TSR-2 which was smaller and STOL (short take-off and landing) anyway!

But the facts were somewhat different. The VC10 for first flight with a crew of five, no passengers and two hours' fuel, had a wing loading of about half that of the TSR-2 first flight case and a similar power-to-weight ratio (the initial TSR-2 Olympus 22Rs being severely de-rated). So that if Vickers had been prepared to accept an almost non-existent V-stop[264] case for their VC10 the decision was theirs, but for the TSR-2, the ministry demanded full safeguards for testing the tail parachute and wheel brakes to cover an acceptable V-stop case at wherever the first flight was to occur. It was at this point that we had come to put to GRE as the Warton calculations had indicated that the prototype would overrun at Wisley, across the Portsmouth road, if the tail parachute failed at V-stop and the brakes overheated subsequently.

GRE seemed unhappy with this proposition and said that it would otherwise mean taking the aeroplane to Boscombe Down, which would involve complications and delay; but when it was suggested that it would be better to go to Warton because of the excellent first flight facilities there and because we believed it was already becoming apparent that Warton would ultimately have to take over the flight testing fully, he replied to the effect that 'you can't have a debate with people who have made up their minds!' and the discussion was closed.

Beamont was soon vindicated in his aversion to the Wisley option. During a September 1964 taxi test to check parachute deployment at Boscombe Down the chute failed and the aircraft ran forward such a distance that if it had been at Wisley the aircraft would indeed have ended up on the Portsmouth road.[265]

Many years later Roland Beamont provided further comments on troubling question of the base for first flights. He said of the Boscombe location:[266]

Nobody really wanted us there, although they did their very best to help us, I must say. We didn't want to be there. We had the worst of both communication worlds – we were 150 miles from Warton and 60 miles from Weybridge where we ought to have been doing all that work on one base with all the experts just round the block.

Despite the inherent need to dismantle and reassemble the aircraft, George Edwards took the view that it was most important to undertake the first flights at a venue neutral with respect to the two main factions of BAC.[267] Edwards had led BAC since mid-1961; he was managing director with executive authority for all aspects of the company.[268] Neutrality between the former Vickers and English Electric sites implied that neither Weybridge nor Warton could be chosen, and as noted above Edwards selected the Aeroplane and Armament Experimental Establishment at Boscombe Down, near Salisbury.

The months leading up to the first flight had revealed one concern above all others for the flight test crews: the safety of the Olympus 22R engines. Roland Beamont recorded his misgivings at the disturbing test record of the engines.[269] The background to Beamont's concern was that the engine test programme had suffered a series of catastrophic failures including the December 1963 explosion of the first engine during a ground test. That problem had destroyed the Vulcan flying test bed (see figure captioned 'Vulcan XA894 flying test bed', Chapter 5). Through the early months of 1964 Bristol Siddeley engineers worked to establish the cause of the problem, known to be some form of resonant excitation. Meanwhile another engine failed catastrophically at the Filton test site, near Bristol.[270] Only in August 1964 was the engine problem finally pinned down, but there would not be time to modify the engines so as to remove the cause of the problematic excitation without badly delaying the first test flight. As the taxiing tests continued at Boscombe Down a meeting was held to decide what to do. The final decision rested with Roland Beamont, pilot of the first flight. He agreed to a plan that the initial flight would limit use of full engine power to two minutes at take-off. Beamont noted that 'the meeting ended without further discussion and on a slight note of relief – now we were committed'.[271] Beamont spent the Saturday before the first flight at home with his wife, Pat, before travelling south to Boscombe on Sunday 27 September 1964. It was a fine sunny day for the flight, taken in a Beechcraft Travelair hired by BAC for the trip. As they approached the airfield at Boscombe Down those aboard could clearly see TSR2 XR219 waiting for them with its flight test instrument vehicle, its servicing equipment and ground crew.[272] Later that afternoon the TSR2 would fly for the first time.

Prior to the flight, Roland Beamont and Don Bowen had a few brief words in the test team's offices with the flight test engineers, Dickie Dickinson, Derek Hargreaves and Dave Parry. Beamont and Bowen went over the latest weather and wind information before collecting their helmets and test equipment. They were ready to go out to the airfield.[273]

The team has a dedicated technical photographer John Whittaker, and he had gone ahead to join Jimmy Dell in a two-seater Lightning chase plane. A second chase plane was a Canberra flown by John Carrodus.[274]

Roland Beamont took TSR2 XR219 into the air for the first time at 15.28 on Sunday 27 September 1964. Roland Beamont's flight report is positive in tone, explicitly mentioning only one small unexpected problem. During the initial climb-out away from Boscombe Down the angle of the aircraft was such that Beamont found that he could no longer see ahead through the cockpit window. He raised his seat and he could see again. In his flight notes he reported: 'The seat raising switch was conveniently placed and easy to use in this situation'.[275] Two other, more serious, issues were alluded to: Beamont reported buffet vibration during the climb-out, and Don Bowen reported a concern that the starboard undercarriage bogie might not have been fully rotated into position at touchdown. During this first flight the landing gear was not retracted, as permission had not been obtained in time for the first flight; Bowen wondered if mis-positioned landing gear might have been the cause of the vibration encountered. The flight lasted 14 minutes.

With the aircraft brought to a safe stop, Beamont and Bowen opened their cockpit canopies and the clear, fresh Wiltshire air rushed in. 'It had been a splendid experience.'[276] Beamont looked down at the assembled ground crew with a smile on his face.[277] After some congratulatory handshakes from his ground crew and BAC staff, he found himself talking to a BAC press officer keen to note some upbeat messages to be spread around the world. As Jimmy Dell brought his Lightning chase plane in to land, Beamont said to the press officer: 'The aircraft handled perfectly. I expected to have to work much harder than I did during the

Don Bowen and Roland Beamont enjoy some tea after the first flight of TSR2 [BAE Systems Heritage Warton]

flight, but we had no trouble at all. I have just signed what we call the 'snag sheet' and there are no snags at all on it.'[278] The press officer was happy. Another positive message was coaxed from Beamont: 'The whole flight went according to plan. We completed everything we planned to complete, and I think we have a winner in this aeroplane. It has been long wait for this flight but we have got off to a good start. It was a thoroughly enjoyable flight.'[279]

The prime minister wrote to the TSR2 team:[280] 'Congratulations on the successful flight. It is a splendid achievement. Alec Douglas-Home.'

BAC also received supportive statements from Julien Amery, the Conservative minister for aviation. *Air Pictorial* magazine picked up on the BAC information and reported the words of Julian Amery:

> The TSR-2 is probably the most complex airborne weapon system ever to be developed. Yet less than four years have passed between the placing of the development order and the first flight. The TSR-2 will go into service with the R.A.F. in about three years' time. It will be a formidable addition to Britain's military power.

But with the election campaign moving into its final stages the sands of time were running out for Sir Alec Douglas-Home and his government. The general election of 15 October was a close-run thing: a small swing to Labour was sufficient to deliver victory for Harold Wilson's Labour party – but with just four seats Wilson had only a very narrow of majority. In the opening words of his government memoirs, Wilson recalls a television interviewer making a provocative point with the words: 'Lord Attlee once said that it was not possible in our parliamentary system to maintain a government with a majority of less than ten, What do you think of that?' His majority was tiny and indeed, proving Clement Attlee correct, the 1964 victory would need strengthening only 18 months later. However, the 1964 victory marked a major shift for the United Kingdom; under Harold Wilson's leadership much would change, especially for the TSR2 project.

That the TSR2 was in trouble was now obvious to all, so much so that it had become a figure of fun. The flagship BBC documentary programme *Panorama* aired a feature on how the outgoing and incoming prime ministers had fought the election campaign. The show featured a series of comedy sketches by the current affairs comedy troupe *That Was the Week*

That Was. The sketch, as featured in the Panorama programme of 19 October 1964, went like this:

Schoolgirl:	But Sir, what are you going to fight the next election on?
Man in cloth cap:	The British independent deterrent, the H-bomb and all that nonsense, you know …
Schoolgirl:	But surely we haven't got anything to carry it in?
Man:	Oh no, but we will have my dear, very soon, our wonderful new bomber the TSR2, you know, it costs two and a half million pounds – that's more than twice as expensive as the American one.
Girl:	Yes, but how will we pay for it?
Man:	Well by selling it to other countries like Australia.
Girl: *[laughs]*	but Australia hasn't got any H-bombs to put in the TSR2.
Man:	Oh really? [*with a worried tone*] … Well that explains a lot, doesn't it?

Clearly the BBC's comedy writers took the view that TSR2 was an overly expensive part of the strategic nuclear deterrent rather than the tactical strike and reconnaissance aircraft it was officially intended to be.

Meanwhile, the buffeting and vibrations encountered during the first flight, and worse vibration problems encountered in later ground tests, caused much concern to the testing team. Had the Olympus engine problems returned? Back in August it had been assumed that the engine problems had been resolved. In fact the problem turned out to have links to Don Bowen's concerns during the first flight: the second flight on the last day of 1964 showed that altering the position of the landing gear changed the vibration effect, which was still present although the engines were now supposed to be fixed. While the undercarriage had indeed affected things, the main source of the problem was finally pinned down to an out-of-tolerance fuel pump.[281] The engines were fine.

Even before the first flight in September, the engineers and flight crew had known very well that they had influential opponents. Roland Beamont recalls a visit from Sir Solly Zuckerman during the September taxiing tests. Zuckerman arrived at Boscombe in the early evening after most people had gone home for the day. Zuckerman's visit was very brief. He took just a cursory look at the aircraft, set against the colourful backdrop of the Wiltshire countryside and gleaming white in the autumnal evening sun. He then heard a short description of the trial from Beamont, and as Beamont recalls: 'with something like an expression of distaste he said it was a pity that people should be bothering themselves with such a scandalous waste of public money and then, saying he was late for an engagement anyway, departed'.[282]

It is important to remember the strength of feeling against TSR2 within the establishment even before the Labour victory. For example at this time, in October 1964, the chief of the air staff, Sir Charles Elsworthy, had urged the Conservative aviation minister, Hugh Fraser, to cancel the TSR2 and to acquire the F-111 in its place.[283] The strongest opponents of the TSR2, however, were to be found close to the Labour party, and arguably the most influential of them all was the aviation journalist Richard Worcester. Although Worcester had no formal role in Labour government defence policy, his influence is understood to have taken effect by way of Colonel George Wigg MP,[284] paymaster general in the new government – and most importantly, as mentioned earlier, a key adviser on matters of security to the new prime minister, Harold Wilson.[285]

George Wigg records his respect for, and the influence of, Richard Worcester with the words:

> I became increasingly concerned about the organization and efficiency of the aircraft industry and the way in which aircraft supply problems were being handled. I had the advantage of the friendship and advice of Richard Worcester, one of Britain's really disinterested experts in aviation matters.[286]

George Wigg is forthright and clear in his condemnation of the TSR2 and the wisdom of its cancellation. In his 1972 memoirs he recalls:

> We cancelled the T.S.R.2, not before time. The aircraft industry in 1964 absorbed twenty-five per cent of national expenditure on research and development while earning only two and a half percent of our foreign exchange. We continued, however, to support Concorde, another expensive project which I suggest may never earn its keep.[287]

In his autobiography Denis Healey recalls George Wigg as an opponent of the Polaris submarine-based nuclear weapons system, and nuclear weapons in general. Wigg favoured pre-Sandys ideas of a large army based on National Service.[288] Of Wigg's temperament and behaviour, Healey writes:

> his interest in security made him see and organise conspiracies everywhere. I cannot say my heart always rose when his long ant-eater's proboscis began to quiver, and his mouth began its gobbling splutter. In the end Wilson lost patience, and George was able to pursue his other life-long passion, as Chairman of the Horserace Betting Levy Board.[289]

In the months following the TSR2 cancellation, Richard Worcester published a book in which he outlined everything that was wrong with British aviation policy, and his sense of the future of defence. Worcester had hardly a good word to say about British efforts in aviation. He asserted that France and Russia did better, and that the representative of best practice, in his opinion, was the United States. British creative culture was inappropriate for advanced engineering, its legislative and constitutional structures were inappropriate for planning complex engineered systems and the industry had consistently failed to develop the right innovations. One sentence captures much of the message of Worcester's book: 'The Royal Aircraft Establishment at Farnborough has been at the root of numerous hurtful decisions and hidebound ideas such as the delay in getting started with swept wings and swing wings.'[290]

Worcester asserted that Britain made numerous errors in failing to see quickly enough the merit of swept wings for supersonic flight, arguing that the TSR2 ambitions had been more than five years too late.[291] As for swing wings, Worcester saw that approach as adopted by General Dynamics for the F-111 as far superior to the more conservative TSR2 approach. He wrote: 'in both the V-bomber phase, and in the Avro 730 and TSR-2 supersonic bomber phases that were to follow, these possibilities [swing wings] were systematically overlooked.'[292]

The notion that Britain was insufficiently aware of the merits of a variable-geometry swing wing or that it was not considered in the early days of what became the TSR2 both seem hard to reconcile with the facts. Arguably the whole concept of the swing wing had come from Barnes Wallis at the end of the Second World War, although it was clear by 1966 that Britain had encountered real problems with the idea.[293] What would not be so clear was that indeed the Americans would also encounter difficulty in trying to get the F-111 concept into an operational state. For Worcester in 1966 the F-111 looked highly capable:

> The F-111 can do more than the V-bombers on half the weight, two engines instead of four, and having some three times the speed. The F-111 can be configured as a strategic fighter or reconnaissance aircraft, as a high-level or low-level attacker, can be used as its own trainer and in effect the complete weapon.[294]

In a letter to *Flight International*, C.G. Milner captured the essence of such unrestrained advocacy for the F-111 over the TSR2 with the memorable epithet 'Worcester Sauce'.[295]

1965

The year opened for Denis Healey with his 15 January 1965 announcement to the government's Defence and Overseas Policy Committee, an announcement he himself called his 'aircraft purge' – an idea that went down well with Mountbatten and several others present.[296] The TSR2 survived that announcement, but that does not imply that Healey regarded the aircraft as desirable; rather it reflects awareness by government that the status of the TSR2 was different from the other aircraft in both industrial and public consciousness.

At Boscombe Down the test flights of XR219 continued, but all was not going smoothly. Flights three and four had failed to achieve proper undercarriage retraction, and in flight five the problem became positively dangerous. The fifth flight took place on 14 January 1965. Following a failure to retract the undercarriage, Roland Beamont could not reset the landing gear ready for landing, so he set the gear in an intermediate position, hoping that with care he could land the plane such that the first contact of the wheels with the runway would force the gear into the right position. He offered Don Bowen the chance to use his Martin-Baker

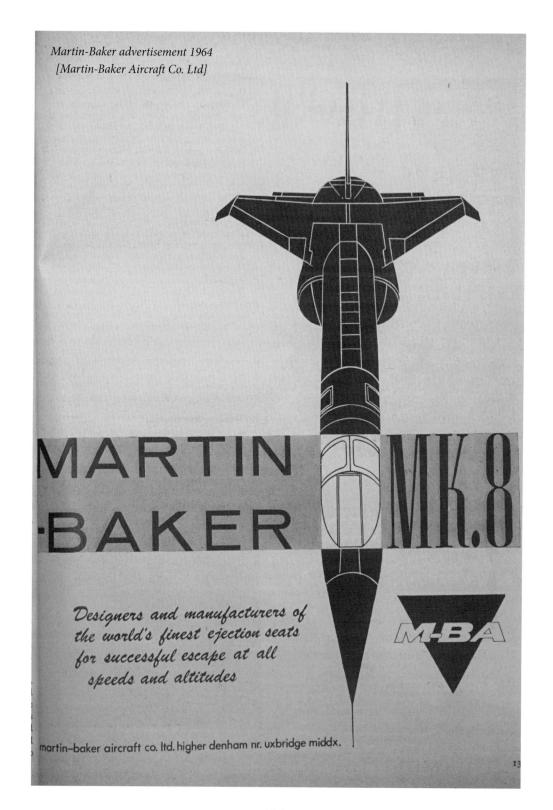

Martin-Baker advertisement 1964
[Martin-Baker Aircraft Co. Ltd]

104

ejector seat; Beamont recalled Bowen's response: ' "What are *you* going to do, Bee?" I said I thought I would try a landing, and Don came back with the classic: "You're not going to get rid of me that easily!" '[297] Beamont and Bowen knew that if they both ejected that would be the loss of XR219 and almost certainly the immediate death of the whole TSR2 programme. They landed successfully. With their brave decision the flight tests continued, and the hopes for TSR2 stayed alive.

In all, three pilots were to fly the aircraft: Roland Beamont, Jimmy Dell and Don Knight. Don Knight was the third pilot to fly the aircraft, and he had one extremely bumpy landing which broke part of a bogie assembly of the landing gear.[298] Beamont described that landing as being 'a lot of swerving and commotion'.[299] Peter Moneypenny was in the back seat, and he reported that after the initial hard touchdown he looked through the two small windows to the left and right of the second seat position. Through one he could see the Boscombe runway and through the other he could see blue sky.[300] Fortunately Knight kept control of the aircraft and they landed safely.

On 22 February 1965 Roland Beamont piloted XR219 on its 14th flight. This was the planned homecoming for Beamont and for English Electric, as he brought the aircraft to Warton – English Electric's well-equipped test base.

Warton was not as it had been when first used by Roland Beamont in 1947; he had flown Gloster Meteor 4 aircraft out of what was then a deserted former US aircraft maintenance unit site with, as Beamont recalled: 'broken windows, rusted hangars and tails of crashed Boeing Fortresses sticking up out of the mud of the nearby Ribble estuary.'[301]

Beamont recalled the 1965 flight up to Warton:

> We flight planned to the Wallasey TACAN beacon and from that point I intended to accelerate under the control of Warton radar up the approved supersonic test range over the Irish Sea starting from Liverpool Bay if all was well at that stage of the flight, before turning and descending to Warton.

> The flight went smoothly up to Wallasey (on the coast, near Liverpool); then at 28,000 feet, and after a brief check by radio with the flight test engineers concerning engine reheat, and taking care to ensure he was free of the coast, Beamont accelerated away from Dell [who was accompanying him in an English Electric Lightning chase plane], and crossed the sound barrier while still at 'dry power on the ASI'.[302]

The transition was smooth, and TSR2 went supersonic for the first and only time.

One former English Electric engineer described to me how TSR2 had made an impression on him as a young man. In the mid-1960s English Electric operated two sets of factories in Preston on opposite sides of Strand Road. He worked as an apprentice in the aircraft side of the business running down one side, while on the other side of the street were the traction works. He recalls the day that the TSR2 flew overhead. The apprentices were allowed out to see the beautiful plane fly past. It was a special day. Indeed it was only one of three days that the former apprentice could remember, from many years working with

English Electric and BAC, on which the workers had been allowed to leave their posts to witness an event. The other two had been a visit by the Queen and the rather formal funeral of a senior factory manager.

The former apprentice remembered the earlier 1964 election campaign and campaigning by Julian Amery for the Conservatives and from the local Labour MPs, all of them promising the workers that the TSR2 project would be safe. Events, as we know, turned out to be rather different.

He also recalled that after the cancellation there were terrible redundancies in English Electric, but somehow he survived the cull, and he continued to work for the company for many more years through all the subsequent mergers and amalgamations. As he put it:

> these days there is almost nothing left in Preston, many aircraft activities moved out to Warton and the non-aircraft business vanished entirely. Even more shocking than what happened to English Electric was what happened to Leylands in the town. It was enormous and made everything, but now it is gone.

February 1965 had opened with a sense of near-panic in the British aviation press; the editorial of the February 1965 issue of *Air Pictorial* was entitled 'Short Cut to Suicide'.[303] The magazine cover featured a cartoon of Labour Cabinet ministers as Snow White's seven dwarfs chopping up Britain's future aircraft. The editorial opened with the words:

> 'Cut Concord.' 'Scrap TSR-2.' 'Switch of defence policy – buy American' These are the cries that have been emanating from those with their ears to the keyhole of No. 10 Downing Street. In their first hundred days Mr. Wilson and his colleagues are well on the way to achieving what Hitler and seventy million Germans could not manage in five years: the destruction of British air power. By British air power we do not mean solely the Royal Air Force – the nation's *first* line of defence – but also the industry that supports it.

> By destroying that industry – buying American is a sure way of going about it – the Wilson government will not only put many thousands of people out of work (or at best the type of work at which they are most efficient) but will have thrown away the capacity for producing one of the most valuable forms of export on earth (a modern aeroplane packed with electronics is worth very nearly its weight in gold). We shall then be in a position of having to use aeroplanes which are not suited to our needs (being foreign they will naturally have been designed to foreign requirements which are often very different from our own), of having to pay for those aeroplanes with money which we have not got (certainly not dollars), and of having our defence policy decided for us by a foreign power (which could limit the choice of weapons available – e.g. no bombers for Britain).

> With the death of Britain's aircraft industry which, because of the exacting nature of the modern aeroplane, has to be in the forefront of technology, there would be

a drop in the benefits passed on to other industries ('technological fall-out'), which would suffer and would themselves be less able to export their wares. Since the dawn of industry Britain has had to live by importing low-cost raw materials and using its brains to convert those materials into high-value exports. We were told by a previous government 'export – or die.' Mr. Wilson has asked us to step up our exports and has promised expanding scope in the field of technology. Yet the government he guides seems bent on destroying the industry pre-eminent in exactly those two spheres.' (Emphasis original.)

With those words Air Pictorial's editor David Dorrell expressed his anger and fears concerning the storm clouds hanging over the UK aircraft industry. He was also, however, articulating a fear about Britain's future role in the world.

There was other bad news; in February 1965 the Vickers Valiant was retired after only nine years of operations. The previous year, in 1964, Valiant WZ394 had developed a crack in a rear wing spar while conducting a reconnaissance survey with two other Valiants over Southern Rhodesia (now Zimbabwe) and Bechuanaland (now Botswana). This stress cracking was found to be a weakness affecting all Vickers Valiants.

The V-bombers' strategic role had changed following the downing of Gary Powers (described in Chapter 5). They had been re-tasked from high-altitude attack to low-level penetration with concomitantly higher stresses on the airframe arising from thicker air and more weather. The planes had not been designed for such operations, and in essence the Vickers Valiant was not up to that particular job. A single prototype of a Valiant re-engineered for low-level operations was produced with designation Type 673 Valiant B. Mk. 2. The redesigned aircraft produced was WJ954 and it was fitted with reinforced wings and with a lengthened nose. This had further led to a complete redesign of the main undercarriage.[304] These developments, however, came too late: the stress cracking of the Valiants serving in Africa could have been remedied, but this was judged not to be an economic proposition.[305] The Valiant fleet was withdrawn from service in January 1965, and retired the following month. Only one Vickers Valiant, XD818, survives, and is located at the RAF Museum, Cosford. Interestingly it is the same aircraft that dropped Britain's first hydrogen bomb in the Grapple tests (described in Chapter 4).[306]

The unease in the press and the retirement of the Valiant was not, however, the full extent of the February 1965 turbulence.

On 9 February 1965 Defence Secretary Denis Healey presented to the Cabinet proofs of a book of 1965 defence estimates.[307] It is a thorough and detailed itemisation of UK defence capabilities and costs, and it outlines UK capabilities going forward. On reading its 59 pages one thing stands out starkly – the lack of emphasis given to TSR2. The only mention is on page 10 where it says 'Meanwhile work on the TSR.2 is being continued', a clue perhaps that in the mind of Denis Healey, at least, TSR2 was already dead.

Further insight is available from records of the Cabinet meeting held the week before. The official record of conclusions reports:

Cartoon depicting the new Labour government's impact on the British aviation industry by E.A. (Chris) Wren (1909–1982) as originally published on the cover of Air Pictorial *February 1965, and as republished subsequently.*[308]

The TSR-2 presented the most difficult problem. This aircraft had originally been estimated to cost a total of £325 million (including £90 million in respect of research and development), i.e. an average cost for 158 aircraft of £2.1 million. This estimate had now risen to a total of £750 million or approximately £5 million per aircraft, an increase which illustrated the uneconomic character of the manufacture of military aircraft in the United Kingdom. … Moreover, it was clearly necessary, on broader economic grounds, to reduce substantially the size of the United Kingdom aircraft industry.[309]

At this meeting the Cabinet decided to replace the Shackleton II with the Comet (later the Nimrod). It was decided to cancel the HS-681 transport aircraft and the P-1154 supersonic vertical and short take-off fighter being developed by Hawker Siddeley alongside the subsonic P-1127 Kestrel.[310] TSR2 was spared temporarily, in favour of a comparative assessment of costs and capabilities with the American TFX aircraft (later named F-111).

Following the concerns of January and early February, TSR2 next received Cabinet attention at the regular meeting held on 1 April 1965. Prime Minister Harold Wilson reported that in the preceding weeks it had not been possible to agree a fixed price for the TSR2 with BAC. BAC had offered a 'target price' and a willingness to absorb the first £9 million of any losses, but that after that further losses would fall to the government.

George Edwards' biographer, Robert Gardner, provides insight into the government's failed attempts to get TSR2 at a fixed price, a matter reported as being Harold Wilson's main concern. On 15 January 1965 George Edwards had met Wilson at the prime minister's country house, Chequers, at the foot of the Chiltern Hills in Buckinghamshire. Wilson asked Edwards if he could firmly agree to the figure of £750 million that was being quoted for TSR2. Edwards replied that he could not, because he was unaware of how it had been made up, as only about one third of that figure was attributable to BAC. The prime minister appeared surprised that this was the case.[311] He made it very clear that a truly fixed price was required if the project were to have a future. As the Cabinet noted on 1 April, the best that BAC had been able to offer was a deal in which they would be willing to forgo all profit, a figure that might have been as large as £46 million; they could in addition undertake to absorb up to £9 million of any losses. Arriving at this offer had taken several waves of effort within the company, and had caused much concern as to the risks that such an offer could bring.[312] BAC felt that its offer was unprecedented – but it would not be sufficient.

Denis Healey had cleverly arrived at the idea that he might be able to secure an insurance option for UK tactical strike and reconnaissance at a far lower price than continuation of TSR2 into production would require. The source of this option would be the American TFX/F-111.

The original TFX (F-111A) deal built into Healey's option appeared to be cheaper than the TSR2 alternative and to be at a fixed cost, but it required a dollar outlay of approximately £500 million at a time of fixed exchange rates, exchange controls and severe concerns relating to national balance of payments issues, especially with the US. These considerations led to the possibility of rendering the F-111A deal a 'false economy'.[313] In Cabinet on 1 April 1965, there was further discussion of the fact that TSR2 was simply too expensive. Also, the Cabinet took the view that if the full specification were to be met there were indeed only two serious aircraft to consider. The Cabinet noted: 'Other aircraft lacked both the range and the payload to fulfil either the strike or the reconnaissance roles for which the TSR-2 and the TFX [F-111A] were designed.' The F-111 option was an interesting idea, but the Cabinet wanted to be sure of the precise terms of the option. More information was needed, and quickly.

Cabinet met again at 10 p.m. There were only two items on the agenda: the TSR2 / F-111 decision and 'Space Policy'. Priority was to be given to the first item. At this meeting the Cabinet considered Denis Healey's F-111A option paper and the draft of a possible public announcement. The chancellor, Jim Callaghan, had also been busy, and the news he reported all pushed in favour of cancellation of the TSR2 and the benefits of the F-111 option. The official record of Cabinet conclusions reports:

> The Secretary of State for Defence [Healey] said that, in order to secure an option to acquire the TFX [F-111A] at the fixed price offered by the United States authorities, we should previously have had to undertake to buy a minimum of 10 TFX Mark I. He had been in touch with the United States authorities since the Cabinet's previous discussion and this condition had now been withdrawn. The United States Government would now accept an option agreement which would not commit us to the purchase of any aircraft.[314]

The Cabinet was also conscious of the wider messages that a robust cancellation of the TSR2 might convey; indeed 'a courageous decision to cut expenditure in the context of the Budget would be an important factor in the reaction to it of opinion overseas'. It appears that the Cabinet was hoping that in cancelling the TSR2 it might be able to send a signal to the global financial community that the new Labour government was serious in tackling the financial difficulties facing the country. Those who tend to the conspiracy theories circulating around TSR2 (see Chapter 9) might see in such ideas coded reference to a possible quid pro quo deal with the International Monetary Fund. I do not subscribe to such an interpretation.

In a paper prepared for the 1 April meeting, Denis Healey would advise the Cabinet regarding his F-111 option negotiated with the Americans:

> This arrangement will enable us to complete our defence review before deciding whether to place any orders at all, and it gives us two years from now before we need take a final decision on the total numbers we require.[315]

In the meeting itself the Cabinet also observed – perhaps bizarrely, given later hindsight regarding the national journey ahead from manufacturing to financial services – that 'skilled resources must be redeployed from the aircraft industry if we were to secure the necessary increase in productive investment and the consequent strengthening of our economy'. This was a much restated idea at the time.

In the Ministry of Defence statement released following the Budget speech announcement to cancel the TSR2, the following somewhat unpersuasive argument regarding skills and human resources was put forward:

> The Chancellor in his speech today estimated that the cancellation of the TSR.2 would release resources in this country totalling about £350m over the next five years. As regards manpower, many highly skilled designers, engineers and skilled workers of various kinds will become available. These abilities and skills are of a kind which we must apply in the civil sector of our economy if we are to achieve the increases in our exports which are essential to put our balance of payments right. We need to increase the output of goods which can be sold abroad or substituted for imports. But we cannot do this unless we can improve the relative competitive position of our

own industries. In an advanced economy the growth of productivity and competitive strength is increasingly reflected by the rate at which new products and processes are developed and marketed. Thus the release of highly qualified people from the aircraft industry must be expected to lead to an increase in productivity and speeding up of technological progress in other industries and thus a widely spread benefit to the economy and the balance of payments.[316]

In such wishful rhetoric we gain a clear insight into the Wilsonian notion of a Britain that would prosper by making things. This was the world of the White Heat of Technology. It was a vision in which the only path to British prosperity lay in making things – physical, tangible things – that the world would want to buy.

One letter writer in the 22 April 1965 issue of *Flight International* concurred with such an opinion in terms verging on sarcasm.

> Sir, – May I, as an ex-member of the aircraft industry, say how glad I am that our Government has at last relieved me of the task of helping to build these expensive monsters, and enabled me to take up work of more direct economic benefit to the country? I must say that, given time to get things in perspective, I shall find automatic vending machines just as challenging as the TSR.2 and with better export prospects. Our economy, and the lives and nerves of our workers, have been burdened far too long by the strain of making our own aeroplanes; let the Americans accept this responsibility, and let us hope that their economy and workers prove better able to withstand the strain!
>
> St Annes-on-Sea, Lancs   J.R. Daniels

Evan Davies has explored the weakness of the notion that British prosperity in the late 20th century would require a White Heat of Technology in his BBC book *Made in Britain*.[317] Davies explains that conversely 21st-century Britain has achieved prosperity on the back of an international service economy while acknowledging the concerns of some that the British economy has become too reliant on services and has failed sufficiently to support manufacturing.

The notion that those made redundant by the TSR2 cancellation might somehow pioneer a new Britain, one manufacturing better television sets and motorcycles for export, was ably rebutted by a TSR2 flight test engineer, G.J. Corner, in a letter published in the 22 April 1965 edition of *Flight International*. He wrote:

> While it is true that a fitter, turner or borer, or even a systems or aero-mechanical engineer, might relatively easily find alternative employment, the aerodynamicists, wind tunnel and performance engineers, flight control experts, specialist ground crews and, very likely, aircraft stressmen, will have the greatest difficulty in transferring to other industries with retention of their status and earning capacity; and they will, in the main, have no desire to do so (unless they seek the comparative security of an academic life, teaching aeronautical science – but to whom?).

From the perspective of the 21st century, Corner's question appears to have been remarkably prescient. Today, higher education is a major UK export industry, which includes the training of post-graduate engineering skills to classrooms dominated by international students. To an extent which would undoubtedly have surprised Mr Corner, today in the UK we teach what we don't do.

At its late-night meeting on 1 April 1965 the Cabinet formally resolved to cancel the TSR2 and to establish the F-111 option negotiated by Denis Healey. It was further agreed that the announcement would be made in the Budget speech on 6 April, and it would be followed by a press conference led by the defence secretary in consultation with the minister for aviation, Roy Jenkins.

In his paper *The Need for an Option on the F-111A* presented to that late-night Cabinet meeting, the defence secretary, Denis Healey, had summarised his paper with the words:

> I believe that there are grave political and military dangers in cancelling the TSR.2 unless, at the same time, we secure an option on the F-111A. Without such an option, once we have cancelled the TSR.2 we shall be entirely in the hands of the Americans as to the terms, price and politico-military conditions under which we might subsequently buy the F-111A, if this proves necessary.[318]

Healey's paper further argues:

> The United States has made a far more attractive price offer for the F-111A. This would make the first ten aircraft available at £2.125 million and later Mark II aircraft at £2.32 million. These figures *include* about £335,000 per aircraft for a research and development charge which the United States Government has said it will waive in full if necessary to maintain the basic aircraft price (including any effect of wage awards) at the level quoted. This is as firm and as good an offer as we could hope to secure. There can be no doubt that the existence of the TSR.2 has produced it. Once the TSR.2 were cancelled, we could not rely on getting such an offer again. For comparison, the TSR.2 cost estimate is £2.9 million *excluding* the research and development cost of up to £300 million. (Emphasis original.)

Attached to Healey's paper were some proposed revisions to the text of announcement of the cancellation: 'On certain hypotheses about long-term commitments it might even be possible to dispense with this type of aircraft altogether.'

Jeff Daniels, author of the original contractor's edition of the pilots' notes of the TSR2, has commented that 'American F111s were ordered "instead", though my view remains that the intention was always to cancel those too (as eventually happened) as soon as was politically convenient'.[319] While such ideas deserve some consideration, it would appear that the reality at the time was rather messier than Daniels suggests. I take the view that while there may have been early thoughts in Healey's mind that such aircraft might not be needed, such thoughts did not go so far as to become a plan to avoid the need for such aircraft;

indeed, Healey would later fight hard for his F-111 option. In the event, the UK initiated the production of a UK variant of the F-111A known as F-111K. Construction of the first two aircraft commenced in July 1967, only to be finally cancelled one year later.

At the time of the TSR2 cancellation in the spring of 1965, Healey and others may have had some early thoughts about a possible retreat from East of Suez, with possible implications for RAF capability. By 1967, however, nuclear weapons policy would increasingly start to collide with East of Suez ambitions. Denis Healey increasingly saw competing pressures between the long-standing commitments East of Suez and the new challenges of Polaris deployment. In the Ministerial Committee on Nuclear Policy meeting of 18 May 1967, he linked Polaris and East of Suez considerations directly:

> '[It is the] independence of our deterrent which gives it credibility and assures Europe that it is not wholly dependent on [the] US. That is what [the] US resents: and that is why they want us to give up [our] nuclear role and devote savings to maintaining [the] East of Suez position.'[320]

We shall return to some of these ideas of national options in Chapter 8. First, however, we must address the matter of the cancellation of the TSR2.

CHAPTER SEVEN – CANCELLATION: 1965

There is more technology in the little finger of one Professor from the
Massachusetts Institute of Technology than in the whole of British industry.

Comment attributed to Sir Solly Zuckermann when looking at the TSR2.
Zuckermann was chief scientific adviser to the Ministry of Defence 1960–1966[321]

6 APRIL 1965

The story told in this book pivots around a single date – 6 April 1965. This was the date
on which Britain's leading aircraft project and arguably the nation's sense of technological
confidence appeared to be terminated by the second Budget of Harold Wilson's Labour
government announced less than six months after taking office.

The events of 6 April 1965 have been described by Frank Barnett-Jones in his books *TSR-
2: Phoenix or Folly?* and *Tarnish 6*. Other sources have referred to the same basic realities,
but place the key events in Andover or in a pub. Whatever the precise details, the story
starts on a fairly typical late spring Tuesday morning in the small Wiltshire market town of
Amesbury. The early fog was lifting and the weather was looking pretty good, with just the
prospect of some typically English scattered showers in the afternoon.[322]

On this particular day the second TSR2 aircraft, XR-220, was being readied for its first
test flight. The allocated test crew, Jimmy Dell (TSR2 chief test pilot) and Pete Moneypenny
(observer) drove into the town from the base at nearby Boscombe Down.

Jimmy Dell was chief test pilot of the TSR2 programme. reporting to Roland Beamont
who by that point was director of flight operations at Warton. Dell and Beamont had great
respect for each other, but they were very different people, as Jimmy's son Kevin explained
to me:

> I think my father always felt naturally in the shadow of Beamont, for one reason:
> Beamont was well known for being an ace Battle of Britain pilot in World War II. My
> father was frustrated that he wasn't actively involved as a front-line pilot during the

War. He was about five years younger than Beamont, born in August 1924, so that would have made him just 16 in August 1940 just prior to the Battle of Britain the following month. So, I believe he joined the RAF in early 1941 whilst still only 16, below the joining-up age I believe – as he mentioned that he 'adjusted' his age to get into the Air Force. Immediately upon joining up, he and several hundred colleagues were put on a ship that stayed at anchor in the River Mersey for three days before joining a convoy, that criss-crossed the Atlantic three times, and none of the troops know where they were going. They eventually arrived in South Africa, and then taken by train to Rhodesia. He was taught to fly and then he was retained there as a flying instructor on Tiger Moths for the remaining duration of the War. Then, upon return to the UK, he was only three out of about 300 people in that particular cohort who decided that they wanted to stay in the Air Force, instead of being demobbed. He actually wanted to go out to Korea, the War was still not over in the Far East, but in fact, for various reasons, that didn't happen. So his wartime service was a rather cushioned existence, away from imminent danger as a flying instructor down in Rhodesia, where he had not been directly involved in the thick of air-to-air combat action such as the Battle of Britain.[323]

As Dell and Moneypenny drove into Amesbury perhaps they used one of the small vans that the test establishment held ready for use in and around the base. The story goes that the two men walked into a social club, perhaps the Dunkirk Social Club on Church Street. As the two men ordered a light lunch, the bar manager turned on the television set. It was Budget Day, and the new Labour government chancellor, Jim Callaghan, was expected to be raising a few taxes, given the parlous state of the national finances.

Back in 1965 two military types in town would not attract much attention or interest. Military personnel were common in Amesbury and these were the days, long before the troubles in Northern Ireland, when men in uniform were frequently seen in towns across England.

As winter turned to summer, sleepy Amesbury was waking up to the Swinging Sixties, as was the whole country. Earlier in the year the Beatles had stayed at the Antrobus Hotel on the outskirts of town while filming their movie *Help!* on nearby Salisbury Plain. That had caused a commotion that was still much talked about in the town. But Dell and Moneypenny's thoughts would surely have been elsewhere: as they waited to be served,

Two of the six TSR2 test crew: Pete Moneypenny and Jimmy Dell [BAE Systems Heritage Warton]

they knew that they should be at 6,500 feet taking the second TSR2 aircraft XR220 through her paces at 220 knots in a short, 15-minute, first test flight.[324] But last-minute delays had shifted their plans from the morning to the afternoon, hence their morning off in Amesbury.

XR220 had completed a series of taxi-run tests and this was to be the day that the second aircraft would follow XR219 into flight testing. XR220 had not just suffered from last-minute delays – in fact the whole programme had been a catalogue of problems. Indeed, XR220 should have finished its flight and shakedown programme by 6 April, and Dell and Moneypenny should already have followed Bee Beamont and Don Bowen up to Warton. The worst delay had been caused by unfortunate events seven months earlier.[325] On 9 September 1964 a remarkable convoy had passed through the heart of the nearby market town of Andover. Shoppers and townspeople had turned and stared as the enormous fuselage of a supersonic bomber passed down the main street. This was the second of the TSR2 aircraft XR220 squeezing through the town. It was like Gulliver among the Lilliputians – strapped down and oddly out of scale with its surroundings. XR220 was tied to a long, flat trailer connected to a tractor unit by a long towing bar. The pair of huge outlet ducts of the plane's Olympus-22R engines extended far beyond the back of the trailer. The overall length of the combined road vehicle was nearly 40 metres, leading to it being known as the Queen Mary, after the great ocean liner. Somehow, however, and despite the difficulties, the convoy, heavily escorted by police, had already made its way from the British Aircraft Corporation factory at Weybridge in Surrey, 60 miles to the north-east. Everything had gone like clockwork. The journey had been sedate and careful. Andover was successfully navigated and, as the convoy approached Boscombe Down, the ground crew could see it coming for miles – in 1964 the airfield was still surrounded by beautiful open country.[326] Later in the day, however, on arrival at the Aircraft and Armaments Experimental Establishment's base things went horribly wrong. The driver of the tractor unit attempted to reverse the plane into B Hangar for the night, but the improvised trailer unit could not match the tight right turn he made in preparation for reversing.[327] Rather than turning the aircraft into a better orientation, the tractor unit dragged the trailer sideways and toppled it over. XR220 and the trailer crashed to the ground, leaving the great plane stuck on its side like a wounded animal. The taileron spigot gouged a deep groove into the concrete of the apron.[328] It took two long weeks just to get XR220 upright and separated from its trailer. Despite only superficial damage, XR220's test flying was delayed by a month, from early March to early April. That delay would prove significant and give rise to sad events that capture, in one small drama, much of the TSR2 story.

It is said that at some point Dell and Moneypenny started a game of ten pin bowls, although it has to be said that today there is today no sign of such a facility at the Dunkirk Social Club. If there was such a game then it would have had an air of Sir Walter Raleigh awaiting the Spanish Armada; fitting for the drama that was about to unfold for the two men. Customers in the bar now started to pay attention to the Budget which was, as the story goes, being reported on the television. At this point it must have been mid-afternoon, because the Hansard Parliamentary Record tells us that the Budget speech started at 3.34 p.m.[329]

XR220 being lifted following its September 1964 accident [Brooklands Museum]

The BBC announcer was commenting on the creation of a new type of investment account that investors could open at their local post office.[330] The next item concerned public expenditure announcements, and at this point Dell and Moneypenny started to pay attention The announcer relayed the chancellor's comments on government spending and in particular the defence budget … and then he said:

> Government have had to consider the future of the TSR2 project. The Defence Secretary plans to make a fuller statement on the matter this evening. The government has decided to cancel the project.

The two airmen looked at each other in shocked disbelief. They both knew that Defence Secretary Denis Healey might cancel the project, but they never expected to hear the devastating news on TV. Without saying anything more the two aviators rushed back to Boscombe. The military policeman on the gate asked if they had heard the news. They both nodded grimly.

As they came up to the apron, where that morning XR220 had been fuelled and ready to fly, they now saw the aircraft being wheeled backwards into its hangar. Several people were milling about around the flight operations director. I imagine Dell strode up and said 'Can we take her through her paces, boss?' But the reply came back 'Sorry, no, Jimmy, we've just got orders from on high – she's not going anywhere today.'

And so it was that the gleaming white bird was wheeled out of the fading late afternoon sunlight and back into her hangar. On that day she had been ready to fly, but she never would. At the time of writing, more than 40 years later, she can be found at the RAF Museum at Cosford in Shropshire.

In the days following the Budget announcement there was much anger and disbelief. TSR2 was an iconic prestige project for Britain, and it was one that had greatly captured the public's imagination. Members of the opposition Conservative party, which had supported TSR2 when in government, insisted on a Censure Debate in Parliament. That debate was held on 13 April, but the government was unwavering in its determination to kill the TSR2 programme. The plane's manufacturer, BAC, would propose a limited, relatively low-cost, test flight programme using the two flight-ready aircraft, XR219 and XR220.[331] It was argued that such testing could be very helpful to the nascent Concorde programme, but even this modest request was rejected by the government. In the weeks, months and years that followed, the cancellation of TSR2 has lost none of its contentiousness. Never has a single public expenditure item in a British Budget caused such long-lasting controversy. The issues are very much with us today, and arguably in the early 21st century they are growing, not diminishing. In times of economic uncertainty prestige national projects are back on the agenda, and globalisation and liberalised market approaches to technology appear to be in retreat. As for Jimmy Dell, whatever his politics had been before April 1965, he never voted Labour again.[332]

He commented directly on the day's events to Frank Barnett-Jones:

> I heard of the cancellation in a rather bizarre fashion from a TV programme reporting on the Budget Speech. It came over in the form of 'twopence on beer, sixpence on cigarettes, oh and by the way, TSR2 has been cancelled'. You can imagine the general feeling of all concerned on receiving this information. Hearing this way it took some time to sink in. This was a project at the forefront of technology and I, personally was looking forward to many years leading the flight test team. Once I had become reconciled that this was not to be, my thoughts turned to all the designers, flight testers and all those engineers that had lived that project for five years. The rug had been yanked from under their feet.[333]

In fact the cancellation in the Budget came before discussion of taxes on cigarettes and beer. The actual tax rise on beer amounted to a rise of 1d per pint.[334]

For the thousands of people connected to TSR2 through its construction, military planning, or simply as a popular news story, the announcement of its cancellation came as a shock, which is perhaps rather odd given the months of public speculation that the project was too expensive and unsustainable. Despite the sense of unsustainable ambition around the TSR2 project, Roland Beamont noted that at the time of cancellation no major problems remained:

> Trouble areas at cancellation still included engine development which was behind airframe progress and also the undercarriage vibration and associated fuselage modes. But these problems were well on the way to solution and the aircraft was close

to evaluation by Service pilots as a first stage towards acceptance by the RAF when it was cancelled on 5 (*sic*) April 1965.[335]

While Beamont had rather enjoyed his Second World War exploits being written up by the British newspapers, Jimmy Dell had been less pleased when in August 1952, while serving with the USAF as an exchange officer, he was forced to eject from an American F-86 over Connecticut. The local newspaper, the *Hertford Herald*, exaggerated and mangled the story in every way, putting the news on the front page under the headline 'RAF Flight Officer Dell – battles his way out of flaming jet'. Actually, the jet had run out of fuel when he battled his way out of it, and he was definitely not an RAF flight officer (a female rank equivalent to a flight lieutenant).[336]

As I asked Kevin Dell to recall his father's interactions with Roland Beamont, it was actually the reaction of his mother, Marjorie, that came to mind first:

> 'She used to get quite frustrated [*laughing*]. My father would naturally shy away from publicity, unlike Roland [Beamont] who often seemed to be in the news, so that used to annoy her – I remember that.'

> To which I replied: 'But it didn't annoy your Dad?'

> 'No, he was quite humble and publicity-shy really. He was quite happy to get on with the job and do what he was paid to do and not seek glory.'

Dell and his family had moved to Lancashire in December 1959 to join the English Electric team under Beamont. Dell and Beamont were to work together for more than 20 years thereafter. Two years earlier Dell had been associated with the Warton team as a serving RAF wing commander; Roland Beamont remembered the idea of a serving RAF man joining his team:

> Jimmy came to Warton in 1957 after a number of telephone conversations between me and the Air Ministry, during which many names were suggested. It was necessary to make sure whoever they sent up to Warton was not someone we, at English Electric, would have any reason for not wanting to have with us. It had to be a mutually satisfactory activity, because here they were putting into a civilian establishment a RAF representative who was going to take part in everything we were doing and be party to it all; therefore it was quite essential the new chap was not seen as a hostile representative of the customer!

> However, I knew of Jimmy Dell by reputation, which I understood to be excellent, and which suggested he would be very suitable for the position. Eventually he joined us as 'Fighter-Command Liaison Officer'. ... We got him flying Lightnings as soon as we could and, of course, he took to it extremely well. Jimmy was an exceptional pilot with a flair for test flying and he soon showed the right qualities.[337]

The other character at the heart of our tale of the shock of the TSR2 cancellation is Londoner Pete Moneypenny. The bond between Dell and Moneypenny extended beyond the cockpit, as Kevin Dell recalls: 'Both my parents and Pete and Daphne Moneypenny were very good friends. We used to see a lot of them socially and went on driving holidays to Spain together.'[338]

Jimmy Dell had first met Pete Moneypenny when Moneypenny was working for a commercial outfit known as Silver City Airways. That company had the contract to ferry English Electric aircraft, including the Canberra, to distant overseas markets such as Latin America. Later Dell thought this work could usefully be carried out in house; and with Moneypenny now employed by English Electric, he pioneered such an approach. On his second such run in May 1966 he was accompanied by Moneypenny as they delivered a Canberra to the Peruvian Air Force. The trip was plagued by technical faults with the aircraft and other bad luck, but they did the job successfully.[339]

Roland Beamont's main experience of the base near Boscombe dated from his earlier days testing Lightnings in the summer of 1954. When down south he would stay at the Pheasant Inn on the Stockbridge–Salisbury road. He remarked: 'it was pleasant to walk across the Wiltshire Downs glistening with dew in the early mornings of June and July.'[340] At the time of the Budget announcement and the events at Boscombe Down surrounding the second TSR2 aircraft, XR220, Roland Beamont was not there; he was in the north of the country at Warton, where the testing of XR219 had been proceeding well.

Beamont wrote about those days and what had been lost:

> None of the three pilots who flew the TSR2 in the fateful months of early 1965 will ever doubt the quality of the aircraft. Those of us who experienced skimming through the Pennines down to treetop height on low-level high-speed tests in rock-steady security while the Lightning 'chase' pilot had often to pull away up to higher, smoother air, saying that he couldn't stay down with us owing to the extreme turbulence, knew that in TSR2 we had in our grasp one of the most remarkable designs in aviation history. But our grip on it was forced and the consequent loss in potential power and flexibility of the RAF became a significant factor in our national affairs in the latter half of the century.[341]

In the weeks that followed he would help a BAC attempt to keep some test flying going, but it was not to be – TSR2 was finished.

There was much anger, especially in the aviation press.

> The Commons was not at its best on Tuesday, April 6. It was not only the Chancellor's sixpence extra on cigarettes and four shillings on whisky, it was the incidental cancellation of an aeroplane called the TSR.2. This, the Government decided, should be a part of the Budget speech. This, the Leader of the Opposition declared, was a scurvy trick.[342]

The following week the letters page of the same magazine featured the following remarks in defence of the TSR2 decision:

'Sir – The decision to cancel the TSR.2 reflects great credit on the Government. However much one wishes to buy British aircraft, it's not possible to run a Rolls-Royce car on a Morris Minor income. Finishing off the TSR.2 has been no vote-catching move. It's a refreshing change to have a Government that puts Country before Party.

Bristol.

F. J. Devrell.

As noted earlier, the Tory opposition responded to the cancellation announcement with demands for a Censure Debate in Parliament. The Cabinet, when it met at 10 a.m. on Thursday 8 April 1965, considered its position for the upcoming debate.[343] It was agreed that no amendment would be proposed to the Tory motion and that the government would simply invite the House to reject the motion, which is exactly what happened.

One of the most famous aspects of the whole TSR2 story is that following its cancellation the order went out to destroy everything associated with the project, including the only aircraft to fly, XR219. Denis Healey has denied that the order came from him.[344] It appears, however, that in fact two aspects of the story of TSR2's destruction are not as profound as is sometimes presented. First the destruction was far from total. One complete aircraft (XR 220) and one completed airframe (XR222) survived. Substantial pieces of TSR2 aircraft survived in various locations. There was even in 2010 a 'BAC TSR2 RAF Aircraft Olympus 320 Jet Engine TSR 2' available on eBay.[345] The second aspect that appears exaggerated is the notion that somehow the order for the destruction of the TSR2 following cancellation was special or even unique. Although George Edwards could not recall the source of the order to break up the TSR2 production jigs, he did recall that he himself had issued a very similar order following the cancellation of the Vickers V1000 cargo aircraft 'so as not to leave dead corpses lying around'.[346]

CHAPTER EIGHT – FALLOUT: 1966

It is really hard to explain to the public that the waste of £40 million is a small sum of money. But in fact it is tiny compared with the amount wasted on Blue Streak, the TSR2, Trident, Concorde, Nimrod, high-rise council flats, British Rail, British Leyland, Upper Clyde shipbuilders, the atomic power station programme, comprehensive schools or the University of Essex.

Yes Minister script, Anthony Jay and Jonathan Lynn[347]

The early solstice dark hanging over London on Tuesday 21 December 1965 was being pushed back by the bright lights of a confident swinging city intent on Christmas shopping. In Leicester Square film fans gathered to see Sean Connery and other stars arrive for the premiere of the new James Bond *Thunderball*, a film which had a long gestation, spanning much of the TSR2 period. The novel, based on the movie screenplay, had first appeared in 1961. The London audiences were destined for a treat evoking the old, pre-TSR2 cancellation, Britain, replete with gung-ho aerospace excellence. Prominent in the movie is the capture, by the evil agents of SPECTRE,[348] of a nuclear-armed RAF Vulcan bomber cleverly crash-landed in the sea near the Bahamas. Needless to say, the all-British hero James Bond would save the day with a little help from his love interest, Domino Vitali. The film was a critical and commercial hit despite, or perhaps because of, the fact that the Cold War Britain which it celebrated was now in apparent decline.

As noted earlier, following the cancellation, factions within BAC pushed to maintain a flying programme focused on Concorde and future military aircraft. Derek Wood points to an internal memorandum from the BAC publicity department, noting that such a programme would involve embarrassment for the government and observing that such a test programme would therefore require the company to put the government under political pressure if the idea was to be successful.[349] Wood further observes:

> BAC, however, were due to receive a large sum of money in compensation for losing TSR2 and this was earmarked for the company's civil projects. The Ministry of Aviation made it clear that if research flying was continued, then the cost would

come out of the compensation payments. That settled it; BAC withdrew their proposals.

The aviation press were struggling to come to terms with what had been done by Healey and the Labour government. One week after the announcement the editorial in *Flight International* said, under the title 'How did it happen?':

> Months will pass before Britain's aircraft industry can adjust itself to the blows of the last few months, culminating in the cancellation of the TSR.2. The loss of three major military aircraft programmes, each at the very forefront of technological endeavour, is serious enough, and will impoverish the entire technical ability of the nation. What we must be concerned with now is the total failure of the national system of aviation policymaking and decision. While British aircraft factories close, £1,000 millions' worth of orders are being placed with American factories. How did it happen?[350]

The editorial suggests that the fault lay with the British constitution. Too much power rested with the government and not enough with Parliament, which in the 1960s was poorly informed on technical policy issues and unable to hold government to account properly. To a 21st-century eye his criticisms of the UK constitutional position in the mid-1960s appear fair. Select Committees were relatively recent and had arguably not yet found their feet, and the Parliamentary Office of Science and Technology had not yet been conceived. Whether, however, a more technically literate Parliament would, or should, have saved the TSR2 seems far from clear.

Roland Beamont was also angry with what he perceived to be the destruction of the British aircraft industry by meddling Whitehall bureaucrats. His concern prompted him to write *Phoenix into Ashes,* a memoir dedicated to the topic.[351] In it he wrote:

> in the middle '60s when Government spokesmen would publicly insult and smear the efforts of industry without perceptible attempt being made by industry to refute them, the craven attitude that 'We must not argue with the Government customer lest he may not be nice to us in the future', did much harm to the aviation industry and was a root cause of many critical examples of lack of resolution and decision on the industry's side in this period.[352]

The April 1965 TSR2 cancellation announcement had been noticed in the United States, where some small media manipulation of the message was apparently under way for domestic reasons relating to the F-111. On 12 April, David Hoffman reported from Washington:

> On April 6 the influential *Washington Star* front-paged the response of its military correspondent, Richard Fryklund. "Great Britain will buy the American TFX fighter bomber instead of its own TSR.2", said Mr Fryklund, putting the words in the mouth of Mr McNamara, who did not disclaim them. "The British purchase will amount to about $1 billion", he said, avoiding that "option" word as if it would corrupt his copy.

As a result Mr Fryklund continued, the Defense Secretary can "say that the General Dynamics design is a recognized success and that his decision to save $1 billion by developing only one aircraft for both services has proved as logical for the United States as it is for other countries". This remarkable sentence was written three weeks after Rear Admiral William Martin, assistant chief of Naval Operations (Air), told a Senate sub-committee "it is too early to say" whether the Navy F-111B can shed enough weight adequately to defend the fleet at sea.[353]

The description of the F-111 'option' was much more carefully laid out by the British government. The MoD statement released on the day of the announcement said:

> The nature of the option on the F-111A is such that Her Majesty's Government has until the end of the year to decide whether to take it up. Any initial order would be a very small number for training purposes. It would not be necessary for her Majesty's Government to place a follow-up order until April 1967. This arrangement will enable us to complete our defence review before deciding whether to place any orders at all, and it gives us two years from now before we need take a final decision on the total numbers we require.[354]

Given the importance placed in the UK on public-sector spending cuts and on the extreme sensitivity concerning the spending of precious US dollars in an era before freely floating currencies, the British rather bristled at the notion that the Americans were celebrating a $1 billion order from the UK when all the British had done was take a relatively small option. At a press conference held immediately after making the MoD statement on 6 April 1965, it was observed:

> [When] told that Mr McNamara, US Defense Secretary, had said that Britain had ordered £357m ($1,000m) worth of F-111s, Mr Healey said: 'I can't believe he said it in that way.'[355]

In January 1966 *Air Pictorial* magazine reported on a visit made by British aviation journalists to the General Dynamics plant at the Fort Worth, Texas, production site of the F111 aircraft.[356] Perhaps unsurprisingly, the journalists were presented with an upbeat assessment of progress on both the US Air Force F-111A and the US Navy F-111B (later cancelled). *Air Pictorial* was concerned for the prospects for the UK aircraft industry following the cancellation of the TSR2. One possibility for new British activity would be if the British were to use Rolls-Royce Spey engines in the F-111 aircraft on which an option had been secured. It was pointed out, however, that any such step would come at the price of a six-month delay. *Air Pictorial* also noted that although the British government had regarded only the F-111A as a possible alternative to the TSR2, BAC was in 1966 pointing to the idea of a collaboration with France to produce a Spey-engined version of the Mirage IV. *Air Pictorial* reported:

This aircraft, they claim, meets virtually all the requirements of the original TSR-2 specification (OR.339) and would cost only about £2.2 million per aircraft, compared with perhaps £3.5 million for each F-111. Even more important than cost is the fact that adoption of the Spey-Mirage would give the British aircraft industry at least a share of a major military aircraft – and thus save it from extinction.

The Spey-Mirage was not to be. But neither was the future of the British aircraft industry immediate extinction, as it found success later in European collaborative projects such as the Sepecat Jaguar and the Panavia Tornado.

There was much British interest in utilising the Rolls-Royce Spey engine in new military aircraft. While the F-111 and Mirage IV ideas would come to nothing, the Spey engine did feature in another UK aircraft, the US McDonnell-Douglas Phantom F-4 modified by BAC, yielding the F-4M for the Royal Air Force and the F4-K for the Royal Navy.[357] The UK variants of the F-4 filled a gap created by the cancellation of the Navy's P.1154 supersonic vertical take-off aircraft and the winding down of the Lightning with the RAF. Despite the F-4 fighter being fundamentally a US aircraft, its British variants helped keep the UK aircraft industry going following the cancellation of the TSR2.

In January 1966 *Air Pictorial* vainly hoped that TSR2 might be resurrected when it said: 'Perhaps the Labour Government, … who have now had a year or so to learn the facts of military aircraft life, should do their sums again and see whether it might not be better to reinstate TSR-2.'[358]

However on 17 August 1966 the 12-ton fuselage and tailplane of XR219 arrived at Shoeburyness, Essex, from Warton. The wings had arrived the previous week. Other TSR2 fuselages (such as those from XR223 and XR226) and other bits would arrive in following months.[359]

In September 1966 the Royal Aircraft Establishment (RAE) Farnborough asked for XR219 to be rebuilt, and following distraction and delays this task was completed by May 1968.[360] Then in April 1973 the physics department at RAE Farnborough issued a programme of trials works for TSR2. XR219 was pounded in gunnery tests up until May 1975. The fuselage was designated as scrap in January 1977, and the remains of XR219 were disposed of by 1982.

In February 1966, the Cabinet returned to the issues of the F-111A option; Denis Healey presented a paper entitled *Defence Review: The F.111A option.*[361] The paper sought to challenge the emerging notion that the Buccaneer might be able to serve the RAF in place of the F-111A. Various maps were submitted, showing the far more limited range of the Buccaneer compared to the F-111A. Suggestions were also put forward for various possible aircraft for the 1970s, including a proposed Anglo-French variable-geometry (or 'swing-wing') aircraft and the Jaguar, a planned light-strike aircraft and trainer. Rather than go with the Anglo-French variable-geometry plan, the RAF would in fact acquire an Anglo–German–Italian swing wing aircraft, the Panavia Tornado, which had its first flight in 1974. This would be joined by the Jaguar and – despite the irony – the Blackburn Buccaneer.

Between them, and together with the ageing English Electric Canberra, these aircraft would seek to fill the spaces left by the TSR2. The Tornado would make use of much of the avionics technology originally intended for the TSR2.

As regards the supersonic strike and reconnaissance capabilities envisaged for the TSR2, the 6 April 1965 MoD statement had advised: 'On certain hypotheses about long term commitments it might even be possible to re-shape our defences in such a way as to dispense with this type of aircraft altogether.'[362]

Which 'certain hypotheses' might the MoD have been referring to? In seeking to understand the concerns of Denis Healey at this time it is important to observe a small set of overarching considerations and observations. In his later years, Lord Healey decided that he did not wish to elaborate further on this period of his life: for detailed insights he pointed interested parties to his memoirs, *The Time of My Life*.[363]

On 5 December 2009 he did, however, offer me a summary insight: 'I now believe we should have bought the Buccaneer for the Air Force – that they were unwilling to accept an aircraft created by the Navy – typical inter-service jealousy!'[364]

This chimes with his published observation:

> The real tragedy is that the TSR2 should ever have been begun; it would have been possible to develop the naval Buccaneer strike aircraft to meet the RAF's needs much faster and at far less cost. But under the conditions of internecine warfare which then ruled between the services, the RAF would never accept an aircraft originally designed for the navy – a syndrome described in the Ministry as NIH, or 'Not Invented Here'.[365]

The second observation is that the cash-strapped nature of Britain's public finances in the mid-1960s were indeed fundamental to the decision to cancel the TSR2.

Denis Healey said on 13 April 1965 in his Policy Statement made in the Parliamentary Censure Debate:

> The first detailed estimates of cost were made in October 1960, when the contract was placed with BAC. By that time the R and D cost for the aircraft had more than doubled – it was estimated at £90m – and the production cost was estimated at at least £1.5m each. On the basis of these figures, and assuming an order for rather more than 150 aircraft (which was the previous Government's programme), the total capital cost for research, development and production would have been about £330m. At this stage the target date for the aircraft's entry into service was the end of 1965 – the present year.

> I readily admit that if these targets for cost and delivery which were set and accepted in 1960 had been maintained, the aircraft would have been worth the money. Indeed we might have sold a substantial number to other countries too. But by October 1963, only three years later, the time when the Australian Government decided in favour of the American aircraft as against the TSR.2, the forecast of total costs had doubled again. The writing was on the wall.[366]

However, arguably the most important part of Healey's thinking had been revealed by remarks he made at a press conference held on 6 April 1965. *Flight International* reported him as saying:[367]

> During the next nine months we must see if TSR.2's strike role can be carried out by other aircraft – possibly by sea-based Buccaneers, or land-based Buccaneers or Phantoms. On certain extreme hypotheses about long term commitments it might even be possible to dispense with this type of aircraft altogether.

Healey goes on to echo the Ministry of Defence statement referred to earlier. When asked to elaborate on the 'extreme hypothesis', Mr Healey said: 'No. I do not find it easy to envisage a situation in which we could do without these types of aircraft.' His feeling 'at the moment' was that they would be needed if Britain was to retain her ability to fight limited wars. It seems possible that he is considering a more European future in which the Buccaneer or a similar aircraft would have been more than sufficient, and the advanced capabilities of the TSR2 or the F-111 would not be essential. Interestingly he only says that it would not be easy – he does not say 'impossible' – to imagine a new British set of circumstances, for example a future freed from the challenges and costs of maintaining effective force projection East of Suez.

In the defence policy announcement of 13 April 1965, Healey gave a small further insight into his thinking about the future and what he had described as an 'extreme hypothesis'. It seems possible that he was indeed already starting to conceive of a British defence strategy focused closer to home.

> I do not wish to be specific here, for reasons which we will all understand, but if Hon. Members think for a moment about our present problems outside Europe they will realize that it is the knowledge that we could, if necessary, strike successfully at the enemy's main bases which is the best guarantee against the dangerous escalation of a local conflict into a major war. I am talking here, of course, exclusively in terms of conventional weapons.[368]

For those seeking insight into Healey's thinking, his paper of 11 February 1966 is interesting, as it includes an intriguing line concerning opportunities in defence that might avoid the need to exercise the F-111A option. In it, he states: 'I still hope to secure one or two further gains on which discussions are still proceeding.'[369]

Denis Healey was the central figure in the decision to cancel the TSR2. It is easy with hindsight to forget the complexity and uncertainty surrounding the job of British defence secretary at this crucial point in an unavoidable transition away from imperial power. Certain aspects of Healey's thinking appear clear, while others retain a measure of uncertainty. It seems clear that fundamentally Denis Healey saw the TSR2 in purely tactical terms using conventional munitions, and that he did not envisage a major role for it as a delivery system for nuclear weapons, at least in Europe. It seems also that he may already have been focusing attention on the European theatre in which the advanced capabilities of TSR2 would be less essential.

Fundamentally Healey trusted that the long-term strategic defence of the United Kingdom in Europe would be assured by the expected delivery of the Polaris submarine system in 1967. He recalls, however, that in his first week in office he received a top secret briefing on Polaris concerning the need to revise NATO strategy.[370] The content of that briefing remains secret. Whether in October 1964 it contained any hint of possible future problems with Polaris, as discussed in Chapter 10, is not known, but seems probable. In any case Healey would have been aware of the numerous difficulties faced by other advanced weapons systems and especially of the US actions surrounding Skybolt, which had so disrupted British strategy only a couple of years earlier. He may have drawn some comfort that his no-cost F-111 option covered the crucial period up until the point when Polaris would be deployed.

It is important to note that Healey denies that in 1966 he held Britain's East of Suez commitments to be anything other than of the highest importance. He writes: 'At that time I myself believed that our contribution to stability in the Middle and Far East was more useful to world peace than our contribution to NATO in Europe.'[371] The Ministry of Defence understood very clearly the importance of an aircraft such as TSR2 to the delivering of British commitments in Southeast Asia, where support infrastructure was weaker and distances greater than in Europe. Later, Healey would lead the UK towards the closure of practically all military bases East of Suez except Hong Kong. Lord Healey has always maintained, however, that such considerations were not on his mind in early 1965 when he was making his decisions concerning the TSR2 and his negotiated option with the Americans on the F-111.

He recalls his first trip to Australia in February 1966 with the words:

> On this first visit to Canberra I still believed it was right and possible for us to stay East of Suez. I told the National Press Club: 'we intend to remain, and shall remain, fully capable of carrying out all the commitments we have at the present time, including those in the Far East, the Middle East, and in Africa and other parts of the world. We do intend to remain in the military sense a world power.' But even then I did not think we should plan on keeping our base in Singapore indefinitely. However, when I explored with the Australians the possibility of replacing it with a new base in their own country, they were unenthusiastic.[372]

Denis Healey later observed that the prevailing sense in Britain was that the government had been too slow in recognising that the reality that the presence East of Suez was unsustainable. But he countered any suggestion that Britain should have pulled back sooner by observing that in the mid-1960s British troops were fighting in both south Arabia and Borneo.[373]

The notion that the key to understanding TSR2 and its cancellation lies not in Europe but in East of Suez policy has been developed by Guy Finch. Finch has further observed that the aircraft developed as the Panavia Tornado had first been specified by the British in 1961 with OR355; the idea had gone quiet for eight or nine years but was resurrected by Healey after the TSR2 cancellation.[374] He adds that, with hindsight, the Tornado could have been seen as a good bet from as early as 1959.

Finch further observes:

> Both the Minister of Defence Denis Healey and James Callaghan at the Treasury were supporters of Britain's East of Suez commitment and were concerned that the cancellation of TSR2 would be seen as a message indicating imminent withdrawal. It was a double irony, therefore, that Healey found the solution to this dilemma in Elsworthy's suggestion that TSR2 be cancelled in favour of the F111. This ensured not only the demise of TSR2 but also, paradoxically, the survival of the role that had been specifically tailored to fit it. …
>
> Almost inevitably, the F111 order was later cancelled but not until after the last British troops had left Aden. [375]

Meanwhile the UK was attempting to redirect its vast military aviation industry towards more civilian challenges: on 12 September 1968 the world's second Concorde, and the first 'British' one, 002 G-BSST, was rolled out of the main assembly hall at Filton.[376] It was the first chance for the factory workers and journalists to see the aircraft out in the open air, albeit in an incomplete state.

In several respects Concorde would be the successor to the TSR2; much of its technology (especially the supersonic engines) went into the new aircraft. The trajectory away from defence technology development towards civil industrial growth were well suited to the Labour government's hopes for a new balance to British industry. As events later showed, supersonic civil air transport turned out to be – in the 20th century at least – just as unsustainable a 1960s idea as supersonic bombers in advanced air forces.

LABOUR PARTY MODERNISATION

The TSR2 occupies a particular place in the history of British science and technology policy. The cancellation decision falls within a context set by the Labour government even before the October 1964 election victory. Norman J. Vig, an American Fulbright Scholar at Manchester University in the early 1960s and subsequently an active researcher in the UK, captured the technology policy issues of the time well in his 1968 book: *Science and Technology in British Politics*.[377]

Vig explains Wilson's perspective on the future of British industry through a contrast with his predecessor as Labour party leader, Hugh Gaitskell, who died in 1963. Concerning Labour party strategy for the 1964 election Vig writes:

> The Labour Party felt a similar compulsion to revamp its "cloth cap" image after its crushing defeat of 1959. At the post-mortem party conference of that year, Gaitskell

sought to repeal Clause IV (the party's constitutional commitment to nationalization), but also warned more broadly of the changing nature of the labor force resulting from technological advance. And the need to develop a "modern mid-twentieth century party, looking to the future".[378]

These ambitions would only be achieved nearly three decades later. Under Tony Blair's leadership the party would connect with business and leave behind its working-class origins, becoming 'New Labour'. For the party itself, Clause IV remained the litmus test of modernisation; under pressure from Blair it was finally reformed in 1995.

In the lead-up to the 1964 election a major focus of Labour party attention was devoted to military technological development. Vig notes:

> from 1960 a recurrent theme of Wilson and others was the "waste" in "prestige" military projects, and the need to concentrate scarce scientific and technical resources on "productive" civilian developments.[379]

Gaitskell's bid to reform Clause IV had failed, but for the right of the party it was clear that in 1959 nationalisation had been a major vote loser. As Vig notes:

> The Party's left wing, on the other hand, argued that the ideological commitment to nationalization was too basic to discard: rather its relevance to contemporary circumstances must be emphasized.[380]

Vig quotes Wilson as apparently having said:

> What was needed … was not to drop Clause IV but to redefine our socialism in terms of the scientific age. Instead of nationalizing old, ailing sectors of the economy, we should apply public ownership at the growing points of industry – in the manufacture, for example, of products created by Government-sponsored research and development.[381]

This would have particular importance in the military technology area, as according to *The Times* of 2 April 1963:

> That is why the central thread of Labour policy, the key to our plan to redynamize Britain's economy is our plan to mobilize the talents of our scientists and technicians, redeployed from missile and warhead, on research and development contracts, civil research and development to produce the new instruments and tools of economic advance both for Britain and for the war on poverty in underdeveloped areas of the Commonwealth and elsewhere.[382]

The Attlee Labour government of the late 1940s had started British support for technology with the creation in 1949 of the National Research Development Corporation, dedicated to the task of establishing worldwide patent protection for ideas emerging from British government laboratories.[383]

Clearly the TSR2 project was going to have few friends in the 1964 Labour government: key to its plans for reorganised technological development was to be the new Ministry of Technology, which began by amalgamating the Atomic Energy Authority, the National Research Development Corporation and the industrial functions of the Department of Scientific and Industrial Research.[384] One key issue facing the early days of MinTech, as it became known, was when and how it might take over functions from the Ministry of Aviation, which many in the upper reaches of the Labour party wanted to see phased out.[385] A key step in such a process was to be the Plowden Report, published in December 1965, after the cancellation of the TSR2. The report concluded that the aircraft industry should in future receive 'no more support or protection than that given to comparable industries in Britain.' And it further amplified a strong theme of the Labour government when it said that some of the 8,600 qualified scientists and technologists could beneficially be redeployed to 'problems concerning the whole range of British industry'.[386]

These Labour government actions, and others such as the Selective Employment Payments Act (SEPA) 1966, were an attempt by the Wilson Administration to construct a new future for the UK based upon what would today be termed High Value Manufacturing.[387] The SEPA created a rather unusual and short-lived tax, the Selective Employment Tax (SET), which was repealed at the first opportunity by the Conservative party when it returned to power, at the point that Value Added Tax was first introduced. SET charged a levy on workers in the growing service economy, while exempting employment in the manufacturing sector. But Labour's 1960s experiment to build a high-tech manufacturing Britain largely failed. The decline of former high-technology centres of excellence was more apparent than the emergence, in industrial estates across the land, of a new, more commercial, manufacturing base.

In combination with Barbara Castle's attempts to curtail trades union power, Wilson's government had sought to build a new Britain. In almost all key respects Wilson's policies failed, but one can argue that: in many of them lay the seeds of reform that Margaret Thatcher would build upon in the 1980s. As such, the Wilson era industrial restructuring, which in many ways had shaped the attitude of the Labour party to the TSR2, would echo far beyond the mid-1960s. Today, in the 21st century, we live with the legacy of many of those developments.

RUSSIAN VERSION

In the 1990s while Labour sought to reinvent itself, an entirely separate echo of the TSR2 story could be heard in the Soviet Union. In May 1967 the Sukhoi T-61 had flown for the first time. The story of this aircraft and its direct successor, the Sukhoi Su-24, provides a fascinating insight into how the USSR saw the TSR2 story. Originally the T-61 reflected the TSR2 approach of small swept wings ducting some of the engine output over their top surface, but when modified into the SU-24, the design reflected the swing wing approach of the American F-111.

In the years after 1965 TSR2 was not forgotten. In September 1973 Bill Gunston asked in the pages of *Aeroplane Monthly*: 'TSR-2: What went wrong?' He added two important observations to the understanding of the story:

> upon TSR.2 fell the cost burden of an entire generation of advances in structures, propulsion, systems, materials and a thousand and one other items that in the United States were available off the shelf after being funded by a score of programmes developed in parallel. The second was that, as TSR.2 was the only project of its kind, there was no obvious yardstick against which to judge its costs and timing. Taken together, these two factors were to prove not merely important but lethal to the entire programme.[388]

Gunston was not in fact persuaded that TSR2 was such a great idea. In particular he closes the same 1973 article with the important observation that if the TSR2 had proceeded as originally planned and gone into full production it would have undermined the prospects for the Tornado fighter-bomber of the 1970s, which he regarded as a 'much better thing for Western Europe to have developed'. Bob Fairclough concurred with that assessment when he wrote in 2007 with the full benefit of hindsight. He observed:

> This joint venture [Panavia Tornado] with Germany and Italy was perhaps the most significant aspect of the TSR2's cancellation. The consortium built some 1,000 Tornados and it is unlikely that Britain would have entered the project had production of TSR2 continued. As only about 120 to 150 TSR2s were envisaged for the RAF, there is little doubt that Tornado was a greater industrial and commercial success than TSR2 could ever have been.[389]

Back in the late 1960s, though, the rival aircraft to TSR2 was not the Panavia Tornado, then still on the drawing board, but rather the American F-111. It is interesting to pause to consider how it actually progressed into production and service.

C.G. Milner had, as early as 8 April 1965, warned the readers of *Flight International*: 'It will be surprising if Australia gets the F-111 at the original specified price – unless the USA is prepared to sell at a loss.'[390]

Bill Gunston observed eight years later:

> BAC's final target price for the production run of 158 [TSR2s] was £575 million, or £3.64 million a copy … On cost grounds alone there seemed a good case for buying the F-111, and ministers had a field day for four years afterwards thinking up ever more astronomic totals for the amount of money this would save. They even went on doing this long after the real F-111 prices had more than doubled, which was not allowed for in any of their calculations.

Elsewhere in the article Gunston notes that the F-111 ended up costing roughly three times the nominally fixed price that the Australians had agreed on 24 October 1963, and that the first aircraft finally arrived at the RAAF base at Amberley several years late – in 1973, the year in which he was writing. Coming so late, F-111 would not have been a good choice for Britain.

Roland Beamont did not share the sense either that Britain had learned lessons quicker than the Americans with F-111, or that the Panavia Tornado had been the shining success to emerge from the failure of the TSR2; rather he reflected in 1996 on the decline of a once-great British aircraft industry and saw little merit in falling back on international collaboration:

> The cancellation of the TSR.2 was the pivotal point. Before that date the British aircraft industry was a world leader in supersonic technology with the capacity to design, build and deliver the supersonic aircraft needed for UK defence and export customers. After the cancellation this capacity was allowed to fade away. No new all-British supersonic design has been produced for the RAF in the 30 years since 1965. The capacity is no longer there and will not return in the continued absence of a national will to meet our own defence requirements from our own industrial resources.

> The argument that single nations can no longer have such capacity 'to go it alone' is clearly refuted by the technical successes of the Swedish SAAB supersonic fighter programmes, and the Rafale of France. But with the hindsight of 30 years it can now be seen clearly that while the cancellation of TSR.2 was the pivotal point in the run-down of the British aircraft industry, that run-down began inevitably with the crass government decision five years earlier to force amalgamation in the industry.[391]

Roland Beamont is very clear that the 1960s represent the key point in British industrial policy, and he is adamant that the decisions made were wrong. In 1996 he wrote:

> In a 40-year association with the aircraft industry, mostly at management and later board level, I witnessed many examples of strange, inexplicable and often downright incompetent decision-making at procurement level, and of course some also by the contractors. Often no single centre of influence seemed to be to blame, but in the 1960s we all shot ourselves in the foot![392]

In the years after the TSR2 cancellation the RAF would slowly lose its role in nuclear weapons delivery – a role it gave up completely in 1998, as an early act of the incoming Labour government led by Tony Blair; the 1998 decision ended the nuclear WE.177 capacity on Tornado GR-1 aircraft.[393] The TSR2 decision had arguably been a visible sign of the journey to the UK nuclear deterrent being a matter for the Royal Navy alone, a process that had started with Macmillan's 1962 Polaris agreement won from John F. Kennedy in Nassau, Bahamas.

Robert Gardner reports an important insight from Freddie Page, in that while in those early TSR2 years BAC had acted as if it was Vickers, with a recalcitrant subcontractor in English Electric at Preston, the early 1963 transfer of responsibility for TSR2 away from

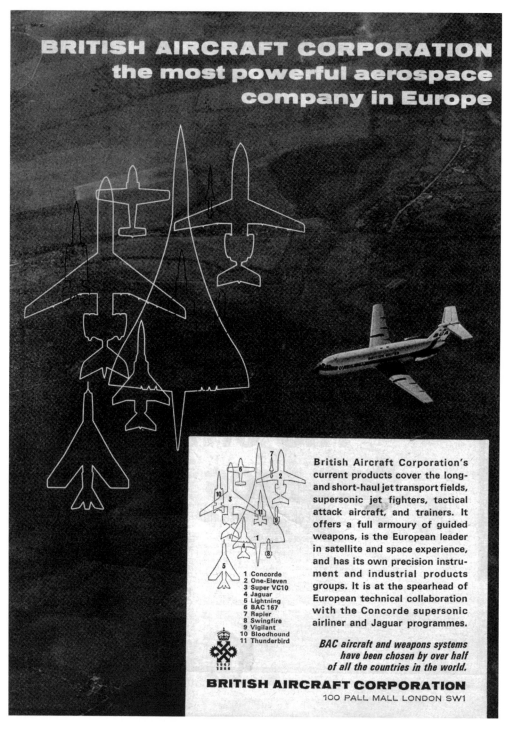

'The convergence of BAC completes following the cancellation of TSR2 [Author's collection – as published widely in aviation magazines in 1968, e.g. Air Pictorial, November 1968]

Arthur Sheffield's empire at the main English Electric Preston works to English Electric Aviation was 'a key TSR2 achievement and the foundation of the successful military aircraft division of BAe at Warton and Samlesbury'.[394] (Samlesbury Aerodrome was located in Lancashire, midway between Preston and Blackburn.)

CHAPTER NINE – CONSPIRACY!

Technology is … a queer thing. It brings you gifts with one hand,
and stabs you in the back with the other.'

C.P. Snow

The story of the TSR2 and its times provides parallels between the past and the present. A central motivation for this book is that these stories of British industrial and military transition reveal lessons for the present in terms of national identity, foreign policy and defence ambitions. These lessons do not rely on conspiratorial notions of dishonesty or hidden truths. The TSR2 story is interesting and relevant in the absence of conspiracy. That reality, however, does not alter the fact that since its cancellation the TSR2 has been the heart of numerous provocative theories and allegations of hidden truths.

Soon after the cancellation, Stephen Hastings published his polemic *The Murder of the TSR2*.[395] Years later he commented on the destruction of the TSR2 airframes after cancellation, in many cases by the very workers who had built them:

> I think it is the most shameful aspect of this sad story. There is no sort of reason whatsoever, except a … what you could really describe as a selfish determination to ensure that that aeroplane would never be built under any other circumstances or in the future. I never heard of anybody connected with this project who was other than shocked by this decision. I can't tell you who took it, but the figure must point at the government in … one department or other … I called my book *The Murder of TSR2*, and that I believe is exactly what happened, though to put your finger precisely on the murderer is less easy. There were a good many.[396]

One persistent allegation is that the United States put pressure on the British to cancel the TSR2, so as to favour prospects for US defense secretary McNamara's beloved F-111 project. It is alleged that the spring 1965 IMF loan to the UK was contingent upon a British promise of cancellation of the TSR2. Roy Jenkins, minister for aviation at the time of the TSR2 cancellation, denies there was such a deal. He recalled:

I don't think international diplomacy operates quite so crudely as that. We wanted good relations with the Americans, but there was never any suggestion in my mind that ... um ... a condition for having IMF support ... the Americans wanted a variety of things. They wanted to sustain sterling as a sort of auxiliary currency to the dollar. ... They wanted us to maintain an East of Suez role, as it were to share a world-role with us; and they were quite keen, to, ... um ... not specifically that we should cancel the TSR2, but they would like us to buy the F-111 for exactly the same reasons that we would have liked the Australians to buy the TSR2.[397]

Denis Healey is more emphatic in rebutting the allegation of a linkage between the IMF loan and the TSR2 cancellation: 'The IMF had already decided a week earlier to give us the loan we needed and we got the necessary loan from other governments as well, so that didn't enter into discussions in any way.'[398]

Less prominent theories include the sense that TSR2 was already obsolete before it was born, with anticipated improvements in over-the-horizon radar technology and phased array radar. Similar perceived improvements in radar technology had arguably undermined the low-level case for the USAF B58 Hustler. This is reminiscent of the warnings made by Denis Healey when in the lead-up to the 1964 election campaign he suggested, regarding TSR2: 'new anti-aircraft weapons will be able to shoot it down by the time it is in service' (see Chapter 6).

Another idea is that perhaps the TSR2 had a major undeclared technical problem. Problems with the Olympus engines during development and the problems with the undercarriage during early test flying are well documented, but perhaps there was another deeper problem known to government. There is little evidence for such a view. In considering the possibility I am drawn to mention three ideas. First, a possible problem with the onboard computer technology; the breakthroughs of miniaturisation that were to occur with the advent of integrated circuits could not be fully appreciated in the mid-1960s. It is known that the flight computers were a major source of difficulty for the TSR2 project at the time of its cancellation. It is noteworthy, however, that TSR2-based terrain-following radar and flight control systems were later perfected for the Panavia Tornado. A second possible source of technical difficulty concerned the metals used in the TSR2 structures – types of metal which once worked become very brittle. The third idea is perhaps the most seductive. The rumour goes that a major issue lesson affecting TSR2 was learned from the US Navy. The Americans had been developing for Navy use a plane with a very similar design, presumably the North American A-5 Vigilante. Like the TSR2 it had a large rigid tailplane for supersonic operations. The American aircraft's tailplane was a sizeable fraction of the size of the wings (as on TSR2), hence it rather unusually contributed lift, not downward force, on the aircraft. If the pilot wanted to climb he would alter the angle of attack of the tailplane to exert a moment with respect to the plane's centre of gravity so that the nose would rise and the thrust of the engines would cause the plane to climb. On the US plane (and, if the rumour is correct, on TSR2 as well) this process was also accompanied by a loss of lift at the tailplane.

Crucially this loss of lift affected the whole aircraft, so that when the pilot needed to climb the aircraft started by descending. This is a major problem in an aircraft designed for terrain following. The US had spotted it in connection with their aircraft, and the story goes that the information was passed to the British team. Importantly the Blackburn Buccaneer with its different design did not suffer this problem. Likewise the F-111 did not suffer from this weakness with its swing wing concept, which had much better lift properties at low altitude, with the wings swept forward.

Whatever the merits of rumoured technical failings and problems, in my opinion the cancellation of the TSR2 made good defence policy sense, and certainly there is no evidence of devious decision making. As noted previously, one overarching conspiracy theory more than any other dominates lingering British impressions of the TSR2 saga. The story goes that in some devious way the Americans had something to do with the killing of a great British project for their own self-serving reasons. I see no evidence to point to such a cynical conclusion.

Perhaps Roy Jenkins captured the actual issues well when he said:

> I think what was the case was that I, and maybe some other people too: the Chancellor (Jim Callaghan), George Brown who was first Secretary of State, thought – I think, thought with some justification – that the aircraft industry was consuming too large a proportion of our research and development resources and also that it was too keen, for understandable reasons, – not unworthy reasons; it was too keen on breaching the frontiers of knowledge on aircraft design rather than making and selling planes that it could make and sell.[399]

For those attracted to more conspiratorial thinking, the TSR2 is arguably not the best example to start from. An earlier and even sadder story dates back 20 years before the TSR2: the story of the Miles M.52. It is the story of how the British lost their lead in the race to supersonic flight to the Americans.

Before the war Miles Aircraft had been a successful, albeit rather low-technology, aircraft manufacturer. Coincidentally it was in this period that a young Douglas Lowe first became interested in flying. He recalls his own interactions with the pre-war Miles Aircraft:

> I didn't enjoy my school terribly much, and I left I suppose at 16, and looked around to find a job, and tried to get into Lloyds Bank because that seemed the thing to do. … But, they didn't want me, and my father, at that stage, was working at Woodley Air Field … Phillips and Powis had this air field there, and, in about 1938, F.G. Miles and his brother, George, and his wife, Blossom Miles, who had been at Shoreham Air Field designing mono-plane light aircraft for sport flying … moved to Woodley, where [they] designed, and started building, the Miles Hawk, which was a single-wing light aircraft. … By the end of 1938, just as they were getting this under way, the whole business of potential war came on the horizon, and the RAF suddenly panicked and decided they needed to expand, very rapidly indeed, and, although they

were reasonably content with the Tiger Moth as a training aircraft, they didn't think that it looked quite modern enough for the new Spitfires and Hurricanes which were obviously in the pipeline … So, suddenly, Miles, and Phillips and Powis, received an order for 500 Miles Hawks, which were to be brought up to the military standard, if you like, … and that became the Magister. So, here was [Miles Aircraft], with this order for 500 aeroplanes, which required an enormous expansion at the Woodley Air Field, and it demanded an enormous great new production hangar to be built, a test facility set up and so on and so forth.

My father was … what I call a general odds-body. He could turn his hand to anything. And he became the sort of maintenance engineer for this vast expansion that was going on … My father happened to mention, on one occasion, that I was looking for a job and was having trouble, you know, just having left school, so I ended up getting a job at Miles Aircraft. They stuffed me in the drawing office, and I was most unhappy. I was the dogsbody, you know, 'Go and get this drawing,' 'Go and get some more tea,' and so on and so forth, and … got desperately unhappy with the whole thing. And, fortuitously, they got this order for these Magisters. It required the aircraft to comply with RAF and Government regulations, which meant they had to have all the materials tested. They needed a test house. And I managed to worm my way out of the drawing office and into this test house, so … and I was absolutely in my element, going round, picking up samples of the glue, picking up samples of Medapalin and so on, and taking them back to a laboratory and testing them.

They imported a chap called Dr Steer, who was a great man, in what was then the extremely new [technology] of castings. These were magnesium alloy castings … I introduced the idea that we should X-ray these things, so, in our test laboratory, I got involved in installing a Philips X-raying machine. I was 16 and a half or 17, right in the middle of [the research and development community].

We were attacked on one Saturday morning. I was working in the laboratory, and this wretched Heinkel came over, I dived under the desk and the bomb went [off] … He'd flown right down the line of the hangars, released the bomb, and had miscalculated on the wind, and it just blew it sideways, and the bomb, instead of coming straight down on the hangar, went in about 100 yards to the left, into an allotment area. So, that's as close as I got to *not* being in the War [*laughing*]! So, that and the Battle of Britain and Churchill and all the rest of it, I'd suddenly got this urge that I'd better get out and do something, and I'd always, you know, looked at aeroplanes and loved them, so I joined the RAF in November 1940.

Douglas Lowe's experiences with Miles Aircraft predated by two years the start of the M.52 project, but his early efforts in bringing Miles Aircraft towards the high-technology end of the business may indirectly have had a role in the later story.

Between 1942 and 1946, Miles Aircraft designed and developed a remarkable turbojet-powered aircraft, the M.52, which if taken to completion could easily have been the first aircraft to break the sound barrier. It included several world-leading developments, and most especially the all-moving or 'flying' tailplane. Fast subsonic aircraft used control surfaces on the trailing edges of fixed wings and tailplanes, but Miles realised that these control surfaces were insufficient for the transition to supersonic flight and that much more aggressive control would be required. An all-moving tailplane gave such strength of control, and was a key innovation in supersonic design. Another innovation was a pilot escape pod not entirely dissimilar to the one later deployed on TSR2's rival, the F-111. The Miles M.52 also employed a shock cone designed to slow the air entering the engine to a subsonic speed despite the aircraft itself flying supersonically. A jet-propelled piloted aircraft was never built, that aspect of the project having been cancelled in February 1946 with the first of three prototype aircraft almost finished and with trials and testing just around the corner; rather considerable amounts of money were spent on rocket-powered models, one of which flew successfully on the last test flight, lasting 50 seconds, on 10 October 1948. As with so many great British technology projects, such as the later TSR2 aircraft and the Black Arrow satellite launcher, cancellation swiftly followed success; the Miles M.52 project was cancelled almost immediately after the successful flight.[400] The project was cancelled by the Labour government, conscious of the need to cut costs in times of great national austerity. The use of rockets for the model programme was controversial, as a key element of the aircraft project was the Frank Whittle-designed high-speed jet engine, the W.2/700, to be produced by his small, high-technology company, Power Jets.[401]

Eric Brown, who had been directly involved with the project, wrote a first-hand account of the project with assistance from another participant, Dennis Bancroft. In their book, *Miles M.5:2 Gateway to supersonic flight*, they dismiss various theories concerning the cancellation of the M.52, but they give some oxygen to three possible stories:

- The first idea is that the project fell victim to personal dynamics and industrial rivalries. It is argued that the major aircraft engine companies resented the role being played by Power Jets. Power Jets had been nationalised on 28 April 1944 at the suggestion of Sir Frank Whittle, but he soon started to feel constrained. Rival and larger private companies started to complain about unfair state-subsidised competition, and managed to restrict the role of Power Jets to R&D, much to Sir Frank's dismay. His response was, in late January 1946, to resign from the company, taking several key staff with

61 per cent steel scale model of the Miles M.52 as used in wind tunnel tests at RAE Farnborough [Blacker Limited]

him. It is argued that Sir Frank's decision more than any other could have fatally wounded the project, which limped along for a couple more years.[402]

- A second idea is that the project suffered unfairly because of a prevailing sense that a treasure trove of aeronautical innovations had been found in Germany following the defeat of the Third Reich. These innovations included the swept-back wings characteristic of the German attempts to break the sound barrier. In fact the innovations in the Miles M.52 were arguably superior, but Brown and Bancroft point to the possibility that confusion and miscommunication may have played an unhelpful part in British decision making.[403]

- The third idea is suggested by Eric Brown alone in a postscript to his book, and again refers to the power of a single individual and his ambition.[404] In this case the individual is General H.H. 'Hap' Arnold of the US Army Air Force. Brown points to the idea that Hap Arnold's driving ambition was to transition the USAAF into a truly independent US Air Force (USAF), and that coincident with that achievement he wanted a headline-grabbing US achievement in military aviation. The best possible goal was to break the sound barrier. The problem was, as Brown says: 'in 1945/46 the M.52 loomed as a threat to his plans'. Indeed, Arnold achieved his ambition, in that the US Bell X-1 with Chuck Yeager at the controls broke the sound barrier on 14 October 1947; the same day that the USAF came into existence. Brown and Bancroft describe in their book how the X-1, and even more so its successor the X-2, benefited from innovations developed for the Miles M.52. As for evidence that there was a reciprocal pay-off from the USA in return for the cancellation of the M.52 in this regard, they report a total lack of evidence. No paperwork exists at all – as befits a true conspiracy theory, and as Eric Brown readily concedes.

Despite these provocative thoughts and ideas, few would disagree with the notion that the death of the Miles M.52 was simply a consequence of a manifest truth – that a cash-strapped Britain needed to make deep cuts in aviation development and that in so doing some world-beating projects had to be let go, even if it did mean leadership later passing to the Americans. It is in this regard that I suggest that the parallels between the Miles M.52 and the TSR2 really lie.

As with the TSR2 innovations adopted later in the Panavia Tornado, the Miles M.52 and its model rocket test programme also left a positive legacy for the British aircraft industry. While Britain was not the first to break the sound barrier, the Miles M.52 left a legacy in two remarkable aircraft. One was the Fairey Delta 2 test aircraft which on 18 November 1955 broke the world speed record by 30 *per cent*, a record held for more than 18 months;[405] the other was the Lightning, English Electric's magnificent cousin of the TSR2.

CHAPTER TEN - DEFENCE OF THE REALM

> I think the real tragedy is that the Tories should have had the sense to develop the Buccaneer into a strike/reconnaissance aircraft for the air force, but the air force wouldn't agree to that, and Varyl Begg later told me that he thought that the decision to go for the TSR2 was, in a sense, compensation to the air force for the government's decision to give the nuclear deterrent to the Navy, and Varyl Begg was head of the navy.
>
> *Denis Healey*[406]

Thus far we have considered the issues shaping British defence concerns in the 1950s and 1960s. We have focused on the TSR2 aircraft cancelled in the spring of 1965: that decision is still remembered with regret by a large number of aviation commentators. We have sought to explain the context of that decision and to reveal the concerns of senior policymakers at that time. From the perspective of the early 21st century it can appear that the cancellation of the TSR2 represented a high water mark of British engineering excellence and that from that point on the nation went into a slow decline, including a concomitant loss of ambition. In this chapter we seek to challenge that perception. What follows is a story of ambition and challenge at least equivalent to that associated with the TSR2. In order to tell this story, a story of the 1960s and 1970s, we will need to step back somewhat and go back over some ground already covered. The price we will pay is some slight repetition of our narrative, but our destination will be different. In order to start this new journey, let us step back to the fulcrum of this book: 6 April 1965 and the cancellation of the TSR2.

The engineers and flight crew involved in developing the TSR2 were dismayed by the cancellation of their flagship project. Despite months of media speculation concerning the fate of the TSR2, many were nevertheless unable to comprehend the decision coming down to them from the politicians. It is important for understanding to consider the TSR2 decisions in the wider context of British Cold War defence policy. In order to do this, we must step back further to the early days of our story and repeat our chronological journey, but this time from the perspective of the defence policymakers.

TSR2 - A STRATEGIC ROLE?

In the late 1950s TSR2 was intended to be, as suggested by its name – Tactical Strike and Reconnaissance 2 – a tactical aircraft. One theme, however, will recur. Might TSR2 usefully have evolved into a more strategic weapons system able to deliver megaton-scale nuclear weapons deep inside the Soviet Union?

The minister of supply in Harold Macmillan's government of 1957–1959 was Aubrey Jones.[407] Born into a South Wales mining community and educated at the London School of Economics, he was an unlikely Conservative. He was responsible for the TSR2 contract, and he explained its planned role clearly: 'not a deterrent weapon. It is not a bomber in the conventional sense of the word but an aircraft intended to give strike support to ground forces.'[408] Despite such official statements there was, however, from the beginning a sense that TSR2 might indeed be able to assume a strategic role in the RAF's defence of Britain and her overseas dominions and interests. In fulfilling such a function, it would have the secondary consequence of defending the RAF's power and position within the British military.

In Chapter 4 we noted that the Royal Air Force never felt comfortable with the notion of a separation of 'strategic' and 'tactical' capabilities. For them the issue was the simply the ability to strike, and some of its targets would be deep in enemy territory. Despite the aversion to such terminology, the RAF knew very well what others meant. In particular the perspective of US Strategic Air Command (SAC) was known well in the UK. In the United States the Strategic Air Command had a role central to Cold War planning, and from 1946 it had grown in power and importance. For the SAC there was a clear distinction between the realms of the tactical (to be fought in central Europe with short-range weapons and with targeting determined by the course of battle) as against the strategic (fought mostly in, on and above the Arctic Ocean, with engagements in space and with pre-determined targets deep inside the Soviet Union, each to be hit with megaton weapons). As regards the UK, however, the distinctions were less clear-cut: for the US, British core interests, such as to preserve an inhabitable homeland, while undoubtedly strategic for the UK, were mere steps in tactical war planning. For the UK, the strategy and tactics of any nuclear war would inevitably be intermingled.

The ideas of a nuclear tripwire in Europe, as described in Chapter 5, further blurred the boundary for the UK between the tactical and the strategic when considering the use of nuclear weapons in a European war.

While TSR2 was consistently presented as a 'tactical' weapon, there were voices at various times that stressed its potential benefits in essentially strategic terms. The voices stressing strategic credentials for the TSR2 were heard most forcefully in the early years (1958–1960) and towards the end of the project (1963–1965). The evidentiary base for the first wave of interest is strong, while that for the second is arguably little more than inference. We shall explore both phases of the strategic capability argument.

Richard Moore reports that in 1958/59: 'The Air Ministry also wanted a (secondary) strategic role for TSR2, which was especially controversial and *never* formally agreed.' (Emphasis original.)[409] He further notes that:

from November 1959 there were requirements for between 9–600kt yield depending on target and assumed accuracy. [There were] various discussions in the year following this around similar yields. By March 1961 [there were] more solid plans. Fixed yields between 10 and 300kt in the requirement, and (unrequited) Air Ministry longing for a Mt yield for strategic use on TSR2 – but this was probably never formally proposed outside the Air Ministry.[410]

One constraint on TSR2 as a strategic weapon would have been its range. Even a 1,000-nautical-mile sortie would have been insufficient for a return mission from British bases to targets around Moscow, 1,600 miles distant. Any strategic mission would require:

- mid-air refuelling, with which the RAF was becoming ever more experienced
- forward operations from West Germany (although a host of NATO and related considerations would then come into play)
- one-way missions
- lesser, nearer, targets within the Warsaw Pact.

The NATO Supreme Allied Commander Europe (SACEUR) had his administrative headquarters at NATO Supreme Headquarters Allied Powers Europe near Mons in Belgium. In the late 1960s NATO enforced a separation which itself defined the 'tactical' and the 'strategic'. Richard Moore offers insight when considering UK interest in 1963 for a 450kt warhead. He asks:

Was 450kt too much for Eastern European (or Middle or Far Eastern) targets? Later, in the 1960s, it was certainly the case that weapons with a 450kt yield could only be used, under SACEUR rules, against targets in the USSR, which was towards the outer limit of the TSR2's practical combat radius.[411]

To my understanding, during the Cold War RAF aircraft based in Cyprus would tend to have targets in the Southern Soviet Union,[412] perhaps around Kiev, while aircraft based in the UK might have the Leningrad (St Petersburg) area as a target.[413] One thing was clear: nobody wanted to try to fly to Moscow.

By 1962 plans were well under way to replace Red Beard with a weapon which was to become the mainstay of RAF nuclear weapons capability in the last quarter of the 20th century – the WE.177. Richard Moore notes of the WE.177 that in 1962: 'the 24.5 inch maximum diameter over the fin became the real governing requirement for size, and was determined by the TSR2 bomb bay – to which no modifications could possibly be contemplated by the Air Ministry'.[414]

Paul Lucas, in his book *Lost Tomorrows of an Eagle*, has paid close attention to the early wave of interest in TSR2 as a possible strategic nuclear deterrent weapon delivery system.[415] He refers to an internal Air Ministry memo of 16 October 1957 which suggested that TSR2 with its range extended by in-flight refuelling might carry a megaton bomb using an Orange

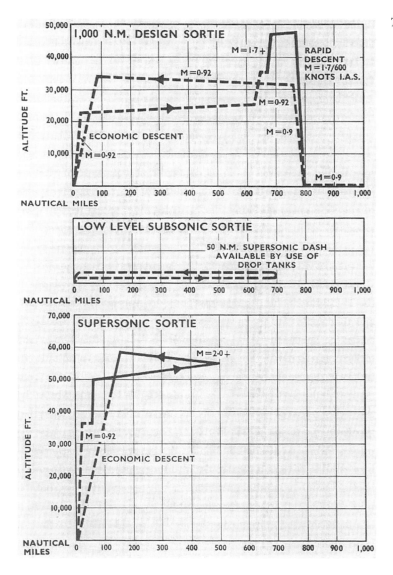

TSR2 operational sorties
[Brooklands Museum]

Herald warhead with a diameter about 6 inches greater and a length 2 feet longer than Red Beard while still matching the bomb load weight specified in the TSR2 requirement, GOR 339. Lucas reports that the memo went on to say that TSR2 might complement a British ballistic missile (presumably Blue Streak) to form the strategic deterrent going forward.

Lucas devotes the first chapter of his book to the early question of a strategic role for TSR2, equipped with higher-yield warheads. Referring to the possibility of such a capability, he says:

> This was due to the low altitude flight of which it was capable, giving it a chance of penetrating the defences around major Soviet cities, whilst its take-off performance

when operating from major airfields made it possible to overload the aircraft with fuel to extend its already long range to that which might be necessary for strategic operations. It was realised however that an attempt to give TSR2 a more effective strategic capability for the future must involve equipping it with a propelled weapon fitted with a megaton warhead.[416]

However, propelled or 'stand-off' weapons of the time, such as the Skybolt under development in the US and the British Blue Steel, were too large for use with TSR2. Lucas does refer to some interest in Skybolt being matched to TSR2 – but the large relative size of the Skybolt weapon would have made such a pairing very challenging.

STAND-OFF

As early as 1956 intelligence reports had indicated that the Soviet Union was developing surface-to-air guided weapons capable of intercepting the V-bomber force at the Blue Steel launch radius.[417] This would force the V-bombers into the zone of vulnerability. Two solutions were clear: either a very long-range stand-off weapon such as Skybolt, or – as became ever clearer after the Skybolt cancellation and the Gary Powers incident – an aircraft capable of coming in low and fast, such as the TSR2.

The desire to extend the range of the TSR2 to allow it to attack heavily defended targets inside the Soviet Union more easily was not the only possible motivation for a stand-off capability. If TSR2 were ever to be used in a strategic manner, then each aircraft might have been expected to fly in anger only once (in notable contrast to the recurrent nightly raids of the heavy bombers in the Second World War). In such a scenario the strategic calculus would not have required the aircraft or the crew to return safely: it would be sufficient to hope that they might be able to find a friendly airfield somewhere, perhaps even in a neutral country. It would however be required that if gravity-drop bombs were to be used then the aircraft, its crew and most importantly the nuclear weapon, must be able to access the target zone. Coming in low, the pilot would find that the target zone could be a dangerous place. The reality of such concerns was to be clearly revealed in the first Gulf War of 1991: even sophisticated low-flying strike aircraft, such as the RAF's Tornados of the 1990s, were vulnerable to defences based simply on a blizzard of upward small-arms fire close to the target. The potential vulnerability to such primitive defence motivates in part a stand-off capability, albeit without the long range achieved by Blue Steel (nominally 100 nm, but less with low-release), and certainly much less than that envisaged for Skybolt (more than 1,000 nm). The capabilities of the TSR2 could be greatly enhanced if it could be given short-range stand-off weapons. In 1963 when some were hoping that TSR2 could be a strategic gap-filler, the possibility of stand-off capability received much close attention.

Chris Gibson and Tony Buttler have observed:

> over the years the RAE [Royal Aircraft Establishment] and the Air Staff had reached the startling conclusion that a stand-off weapon with a range between 60 and 400nm

(111 and 740 km) was a waste of time. They wanted a small 25 nm (46.3 km)-range missile that could be launched from TSR.2 or Buccaneer as well as the V-bombers, or a larger, long-range weapon for the V-bombers. The RAE declared that a Blue Steel capable of low-level launch was not what was required.[418]

Although, in fact, it is what was developed.

Perhaps the most elegant of the stand-off concepts proposed for TSR2 was the Tychon proposal from Bristol Guided Weapons. It dates from the first wave of interest in TSR2 stand-off capability in the late 1950s. It was to have been a powered version of a concept known as the 'momentum bomb' first developed by the renowned aeronautical engineer Barnes Wallis of Vickers.[419] The concept allowed a low-flying TSR2, below the radar screen, to skirt the zone of anti-aircraft protection around a target and then to turn directly away from the target while still at low altitude (see p.148). In this way the pilot needed neither to climb nor to enter the heavily defended target area and once he was flying directly away from the target he could release the momentum bomb. Shortly after separation, elevators on the bomb would put it into a steep climb behind the faster-moving aircraft. The bomb would then travel up beyond the vertical to perform a large loop as it travelled towards the target as the aircraft continued to fly away from the target. The path of the weapon, if projected onto the ground, would show that it had reversed its direction following release and that relative to the plane's course it flew backwards into the target as the plane escaped. However, as with so many advanced concepts of the time, the Bristol Tychon was never put into production.

Following the December 1962 cancellation of Skybolt, and in the closing months of the Conservative government, there came a second wave of interest in stand-off capability for the TSR2. In particular, BAC sought to remind the air staff of the wider nuclear strike capabilities of the TSR2. A series of brochures were submitted to Whitehall in January 1963 by BAC, illustrating a wider variety of nuclear delivery roles than had previously been considered.[420] The BAC submissions formed part of a process in 1963 through which the British government realised that it faced a looming gap in its nuclear strike capability. The Skybolt decision, and the awareness that the lifetime of the V-bombers as a credible force was limited, had precipitated the sense of concern in defence policy circles. Although the British had won the Nassau Agreement (the precursor to the US–UK Polaris Sales Agreement), it was not until April 1963 that the crucial Polaris Sales Agreement was to be secured. Inter-service rivalries of the time were always going to ensure that the Royal Air Force would be reluctant to take any comfort from the Polaris possibilities, and in these first months of 1963 there was a clear sense that something needed to be done to ensure the continuation of the RAF as a nuclear strike force. Even among those that recognised that the strategic nuclear deterrent would pass from the RAF to the Royal Navy, there was hope that the TSR2 might be able to fill the gap between the departure of the V-bombers and the arrival of Polaris. As it turned out the delays with TSR2 were to erode that possibility, and arguably the only lasting consequence of those days for the RAF was the development of the free-fall WE.177 series of weapons;[421] weapons designed originally to fit the bomb bay of the TSR2.[422]

Momentum Bomb In Action

Toss/Loft Bombing Attack Profile

Strike aircraft performs a toss bombing attack, but enters Air Defence Zone and is vulnerable.

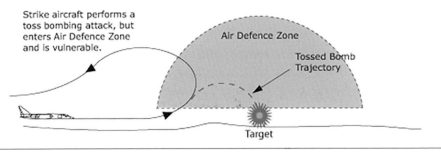

Air Defence Zone

Tossed Bomb Trajectory

Target

Momentum Bomb Attack Profile

Strike aircraft maintains low-level attack altitude under the Air Defence Zone. Momentum Bomb is launched after aircraft has passed target.

Elevators Reversed At Top Of Loop

Momentum Bomb Trajectory

Air Defence Zone

Target

Momentum Bomb climbs at an ever increasing angle after release. On reaching the top of the loop, the elevators are reversed and the weapon flies onto the target.

By flying an offset path and releasing the bomb in a turn, off-track targets can be attacked with impunity.

Air Defence Zone

Target

Momentum Bomb Trajectory

Strike aircraft flight path avoiding Air Defence Zone

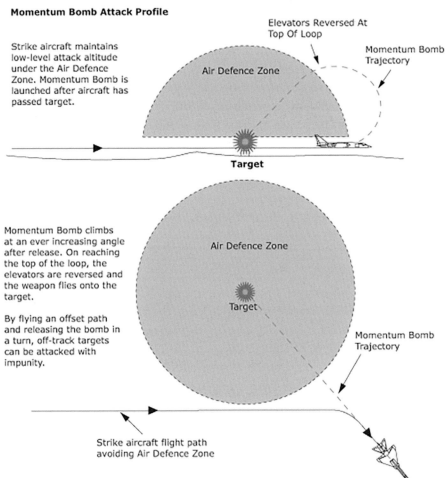

Conventional loft bombing and the safer momentum bomb attack profile considered for the Bristol Tychon concept [Courtesy of Chris Gibson, British Secret Projects – Hypersonics, Ramjets and Missiles, www.crecy.co.uk]

148

As Derek Wood discusses in his book *Project Cancelled,* the TSR2 weapons delivery thinking at the time had already evolved from a 'forward loft manoeuvre'. In this manoeuvre the bomb is released as the aircraft climbs from 200 feet at an attitude of around 30 degrees, throwing the bomb forward approximately 4 miles. The release would occur at 1,840 feet, and the aircraft would reach a maximum altitude of 10,600 feet in a 'chandelle' escape manoeuvre. The new plan recognised improvements in target air defence, and suggested a laydown deployment from 200 feet (in laydown, the low-flying aircraft releases the bomb, a drogue parachute slows its forward speed until impact with the ground, and the delayed firing allows the delivery aircraft to escape). This is despite the risk of close-in small-arms fire discussed earlier. The laydown option is that for which the Red Beard replacement weapon (OR.1177) was being developed, but in the event that role would be filled by the WE.177 weapon. Wood notes that with two such weapons at the forward end of the bomb bay and additional fuel, a strike radius of 1,860 nm was considered for TSR2. As such, with take-off from the UK or Cyprus, difficult Soviet targets could be attacked with mainstay British nuclear weapons such as WE.177, whose yield had been increasing in the early 1960s.[423]

It is also important to note that in the mid-1960s the accuracy of aircraft-delivered weapons was significantly greater than that of ballistic missile systems. As such the on-target damage expected from an airborne strike could be expected to be significantly more effective than that achievable from ballistic systems of similar nominal yield. Although such arguments favoured RAF options over Polaris, they would not be sufficient to win the argument.

The second wave of interest in stand-off capability for the TSR2 can be seen in the early 1963 lobbying by BAC for a range of options including stand-off options. Derek Wood refers to these activities including the proposal for an airborne version of the Blue Water missile that was under consideration as a TSR2-launched weapons system.[424] Blue Water was 7.6 metres long and weighed 1,400 kg. In comparison Skybolt was 11.66 metres long and it weighed 5,000 kg. The history of the Blue Water weapon is discussed in Chapter 5.

The multiple stand-off options for the TSR2 have been described in detail by Paul Lucas in his book *TSR2: Lost Tomorrows of an Eagle.* He refers to the BAC proposals concerning 'strategic weapon system' options for TSR2, including the Blue Water option also considered by Derek Wood. Lucas refers to the suggestion of a megaton-upgraded Blue Water extended from the original army version for greater range. Such a weapon might be carried under one wing of a TSR2. The aircraft itself could have its range enhanced with a non-jettisonable fuel tank taking up most of the weapons bay; such a fuel tank is known as a ventral tank. In addition there would have been a drop tank under the second wing. Such a configuration would clearly be a strategic system in every sense.

In his book Wood also refers to the weapon system known as 'Grand Slam' that was under consideration for the TSR2. This is not to be confused with the British Second World War bunker-busting bomb of the same name. Wood describes the TSR2 Grand Slam weapon as weighing 3,402 kg and with a length of 6.10 metres. The warhead was to be the same as that planned for Skybolt.

Chris Gibson and Tony Buttler consider the BAC Grand Slam proposal in some detail. BAC proposed two variants of the concept.[425] The first was a 100 nm (185 km) range rocket-propelled toss bomb to be launched from TSR2, while the much larger Grand Slam II could be carried only by the V-bombers, and was intended, not unlike Skybolt, to be a long-range (in excess of 1,000 nm) stand-off weapon. One key attraction of the Grand Slam idea was that it was British. As such it fitted with the pervasive post-war narrative of British engineering excellence and national self-reliance. In particular it would be free of the vicissitudes of dealing with the Americans, and lastly it would not require the use of precious American dollars, a major government concern in these years of the Bretton Woods agreement.[426] Any technical preference for TSR2-compatible solutions would also favour the Grand Slam idea, coming as it did from the same BAC stable as the TSR2. However, as thinking went forward, the BAC Stevenage concept of an air-launched Blue Water was the one that survived longest. It is interesting to note that following the withdrawal of Blue Steel in 1970, the RAF lacked a stand-off weapon until the introduction of the MBDA Storm Shadow in 2003.[427] A variant of that weapon was later developed into a cruise missile,[428] for the French navy.

Gibson and Buttler have referred to a paper from the British National Archives at Kew, dated 2 January 1963, which lists various (non-naval) options for the UK following the Skybolt cancellation.[429] These included: enhanced electronic countermeasures for the V-force; a stretched Blue Steel weapon; a silo-launched two-stage Black Knight ballistic missile; a nuclear-tipped TV guided Martel missile (AJ.168); and an extended-range TSR2. This last option has provocatively been dubbed as a possible 'SSR2' by Gibson and Buttler – Strategic Strike and Reconnaissance.

In its 10 December 1964 issue, *Flight International* magazine ran an editorial that nicely captured some of the key military issues relating to the TSR2. The arguments presented appear from a current perspective to undermine somewhat the case for TSR2, but the writer was not intending to make a case against it; rather, his aim was to weave a strong case in defence of the aircraft by invoking the notion of a strategic role. The editorial said:

> The TSR.2 is in many ways the ultimate aeroplane designed from the outset to penetrate the defences of a fully developed nuclear power, surviving long enough to deliver its weapon or to return its reconnaissance information. What may prove to be a trump card in the penetration business is that the TSR.2 is designed to fly lower than any of its equivalents, and immunity lies in flying low much more than in flying fast.

> Would a defending general dare to assure his government that a sufficiently high percentage of attacking TSR.2s can be destroyed? The answer seems to be that a sufficiently dense network of defensive weapons would be economically feasible only on a target defence basis. This the TSR.2 could overcome with stand-off weapons. Vast belts of defensive weapons, however effective, would probably be economically unjustifiable.

In the same way any less well equipped defender, even though he had been given missiles and supersonic interceptors, would not lightly flout the threat of TSR.2s. And the threat is accompanied by capabilities so varied in terms of extremely accurate strike and reconnaissance by day and night that the TSR.2 is a deterrent to conventional as well as to nuclear war threats.

The original operational requirement has remained surprisingly unchanged since 1959 and, on military as well as on industrial grounds, we can no more afford to cancel the TSR.2 than at any time during those past five years. We repeat the key question: would a defending general dare to assure his government that a sufficiently high proportion of attacking TSR.2s can be destroyed?[430]

Despite such propositions, TSR2 was never officially adopted as a deterrent weapon concept. The Foreign Office declared in a telegram of 10 April 1963 that TSR2 was not, and had never been intended to be, the basis of a British deterrent.[431] Yet despite the official position, there were diverse opinions in circulation. Bill Gunston notes:

In 1959 Supply Minister Jones has announced, 'TSR2 is not a deterrent weapon. It is not a bomber in the conventional sense of the word, but an aircraft intended to give strike support to ground forces. The reason for delay in deciding on it was the redesign of the aircraft to make it suitable for limited war-contingencies overseas.' One marvelled at how it could need to be redesigned in order to meet such an obvious requirement, and how it could give strike support carrying no weapons except bombs and yet not be a bomber. As for not being a deterrent weapon, the central requirement from day 1 had been the ability to deliver a nuclear weapon. In February 1963 new Air Minister Hugh Fraser stated: 'TSR2 will operate in the strategic role, both before and after the introduction of Polaris submarines.[432]

Despite the official statements, the idea that TSR2 might be capable of a strategic role recurred repeatedly in the course of the project. In November 1964, for instance, *Air Pictorial* magazine, in an article entitled 'TSR-2: The Most Important Weapon in Britain's Armoury', revealed the progress with the TSR2 and reported its ability to undertake its tasks 'in any weather and at low-level supersonic speeds that present known defensive systems with an almost impossible problem.'[433] This strong statement as to low-level capability was nuanced later in the same article with the statement: 'No details of its performance may be released, but it can be said that it is capable of a speed in excess of Mach 2 at altitude, and of flight at about the speed of sound at very low level.' Echoing the words of Air Minister Forster, the article further noted: 'In the strategic role TSR-2 will be fully capable of forming part of the nuclear deterrent, not only before the introduction of the Polaris submarines but also, later to supplement the Polaris force.' The UK was to deploy its first Polaris submarine in 1968.

Adding another voice to the notion of a strategic role for the TSR2, the *Air Pictorial* writer further noted: 'Although it was designed as a tactical strike-reconnaissance aircraft,

TSR-2 possesses a payload/range performance which gives Britain's defence planners a very useful strategic bonus'.

As 1965 began, Charles Keil, editor of *Aircraft Engineering*, caught the nervous mood of the British aircraft industry well when he penned an article entitled: 'Scrap TSR-2 and Concord at Britain's Peril!'[434] He further reinforced the potential strategic attributes of the aircraft:

> To consider TSR-2 first, this integrated weapons system was designed as a tactical strike/reconnaissance vehicle capable of pursuing a variety of mission profiles … But has the requirement for TSR-2 changed? Plainly, the answer must be in the negative. Britain still has important defence commitments throughout the world. She still requires an aircraft such as TSR-2 with the inherent versatility to operate in: (i) the strategic nuclear role, whether alongside a purely national Polaris fleet or as part of a Western nuclear force; (ii) the tactical strike role …; and (iii) the reconnaissance role.

One important point of distinction regarding whether TSR2 would be strategic or not relates to the weapons carried. The aircraft was clearly technically capable of carrying the high-yield WE.177B. Weapons of this yield were reserved for targets within the Soviet Union. As an officially tactical system, TSR2 would have been subject to a 10kT weapon yield limit. In a technical sense, however, the only major obstacle to its strategic capability would be the much-discussed matter of range.

STRATEGIC AIR COMMAND LEAVES EUROPE

As the Cold War developed, the US Strategic Air Command increasingly turned away from strategies based upon the European deployment of heavy bombers. For example, the B47 Stratojet heavy bomber programme was cut back as the SAC increasingly devoted its attention to intercontinental ballistic missiles: the last operational B47 was retired from bomber operations in 1966.[435] Through the 1960s it became increasingly clear that each European air base capable of supporting heavy bombers would be targeted not just by one high-yield nuclear weapon from the USSR, but most probably by two. In any 'bolt from the blue' surprise attack, nuclear devastation could arrive with less than five minutes' warning. Such short warning periods greatly eroded the planned retaliatory capability from medium and heavy bombers based at British airfields.

The US had first deployed the B52 Stratofortress in 1955. (This aircraft was to become the mainstay US heavy bomber of the late 20th century, and with its service life planned until 2040 its combat history is clearly going to include much of the 21st century.) As the US Strategic Air Command pulled back from European bomber operations in the late 1960s, the SAC B52 force was deployed directly from the north-eastern United States, where warning times were sufficient to get the force airborne in the event of an attack. In this new position the greatest threat to the B52 force came from Soviet submarines in the North Atlantic, but these threats were closely monitored by US forces.

The prospect that all British air bases might be doubly obliterated in the first ten minutes of a nuclear war also rendered the British V-force distinctly vulnerable to a first strike, and reduced its capability as both a strategic retaliatory weapon and a deterrent. In an attempt to minimise such risks, the RAF had contingency plans to disperse the V-force to 27 separate airfields in the event of a major crisis, in the hope that some might survive a Soviet first strike. Such a hope contained within it elements of optimism, however, as all the 27 dispersal bases would have been easily predictable; a greater level of protection could have been provided if the aircraft to loiter in an airborne state, but this was not a posture that could be maintained for very long. The TSR2 specification held within it a key relevant capability: the ability to disperse not just to well-established and well-equipped airfields, but to a multitude of locations including grass strips and improvised runways. It is as a consequence of such issues of vulnerability and dispersal that UK access to the Polaris submarine system, with its potential for near-invisibility, became of key importance to British defence planners in the early 1960s.

As we have seen, during the Cuban Missile Crisis the V-force was taken to high alert, fuelled, crewed and ready to launch at a moment's notice. It is interesting – and telling – however, that in this gravest hour the V-force was never dispersed as the strategy had envisioned. Was this Prime Minister Macmillan signalling his preference to avoid any escalation of the crisis, or perhaps a desire to reduce the scale of an attack should it occur? I tend to the former view: the proposition that strike bomber dispersion is itself escalatory, while highly plausible in the European context, would appear to be of less importance in far-flung potential conflict areas such as those found East of Suez. We shall return to such ideas when we confront the credibility of the plans for the extreme dispersion of TSR2 aircraft in a crisis to small ill-prepared airstrips.

The issues of military posture and risks of escalation are not restricted to the status of aircraft, although they are perhaps greatest in such cases. As described in Chapter 5, the Cuba crisis saw the Thor IRBM force taken to a high state of readiness,

A VERY BRITISH BOMB

If we are properly to understand the defence thinking of the mid-1960s we need to take a step back to times with which we are by now familiar.

As discussed in Chapter 5, in the early 1960s Britain faced some difficult strategic choices. First it had been forced to abandon its plans for a medium-range ballistic missile in the form of Blue Streak, cancelled in 1960 when it was recognised that a system reliant upon slow-to-fuel liquid propellants in hardened silos might invite a massive Soviet first strike rather than deter it. In the early 1960s the V-force was armed with very large gravity bombs such as the 10,000-lb Blue Danube fission weapon, described as a 'monster' by those that worked on it. But Blue Danube had a modest yield, equivalent to 16,000 tons of TNT (kilotons). As such, its destructive power was only slightly greater than that of the weapons dropped on Japan at the end of the Second World War.

Blue Danube, Blue Streak, Blue Steel and Blue Water are all British codenames from a series known as the 'rainbow names' and as used up to 1959.[436] Each rainbow name comprised a colour and a noun, but similar-sounding names were applied to very different technologies: for instance, Blue Yeoman was a radar system, not a nuclear weapon.[437] The codename system was deliberately confusing and opaque, but in describing Britain's Cold War options we must, sadly, continue to work with it.

Blue Danube saw fully approved RAF service from 1957 to 1961[438] and was followed by the Violet Club weapon, which placed a Green Grass warhead inside a Blue Danube casing. It was a huge, megaton-scale, fission weapon, and as such it required vast amounts of hugely expensive plutonium. If the UK were to retain its status as a top-tier nuclear weapon state, megaton weapons based upon nuclear fusion would be needed. The British were keen to follow the Americans into full two-stage thermonuclear weaponry in which megaton yields could be achieved based largely on fusion yield. This capability would be demonstrated via the test of a series of devices denoted by the codename Granite. (For a more detailed insight into the relationship between the Americans and the British on such matters, one can consult the work of John Baylis.[439])

The Violet Club weapon was only briefly deployed from 1958. In 1959 it was followed by the improved Yellow Sun designs of the early 1960s.[440] The later versions of Yellow Sun were indeed true 'hydrogen bombs'. It had been intended that the warhead for these British weapons would be provided by technology based on the entirely British Granite thermonuclear devices, which had, after some difficulty, been robustly demonstrated in the Grapple series of tests undertaken at Malden Island and, more importantly, at Christmas Island in the South Pacific in 1957–1958 – but, as we shall see, events were to take a different turn.

AWE Grapple Y test 28 April 1958; at 2.8 Megaton yield this was Britain's biggest ever explosion, and it provided clear evidence of its status as the third member of the hydrogen bomb club, after the USA and the USSR. [AWE Aldermaston – Open Government Licence]

THE AMERICAN WAY

The thermonuclear hydrogen bombs deployed for the V-force in the form of the later Yellow Sun weapons were actually based directly on an American design shared with the British under the terms of the Mutual Defence Agreement signed between Britain and the United States on 3 July 1958 for the express purpose of sharing nuclear weapons know-how, nuclear materials and nuclear submarine propulsion technology.[441] When discussing the use of American design know-how in the later Yellow Sun weapons, it is usually said that the technology was 'anglicised'. The major boost to US–UK nuclear cooperation involved in the Yellow Sun story occurred, however, only after it had become clear, via the successful Grapple X, Y and Z testing series, that the British could if need be achieve a megaton thermonuclear weapon independently. The journey to such a demonstration of capability had, however, been far from straightforward.

Britain had originally intended to demonstrate its capabilities, including the crucial Granite technology, via the Grapple series of tests. The tests had started with the detonation of air-dropped devices over Malden Island in the South Pacific in May and June of 1957. The results, however, were to prove disappointing. While the second test did indeed yield close to a megaton yield it was not based upon the Granite concept. The Granite devices had failed to meet expectations, and it was hastily decided that new tests would need to be conducted. These were the Grapple X, Y and Z series, and they would be undertaken at Christmas Island, today known as Kiritimati (both Malden Island and Kiritimati are today part of the Republic of Kiribati). The experiences of those involved have been recorded by Kenneth Hubbard and Michael Simmons.[442]

The Grapple X, Y and Z series of November 1957 to September 1958 would successfully deliver what Britain felt it needed,[443] but it was all done in a huge rush because of growing global pressure for a testing moratorium – so much so that only two international observers, both American, made it to the Grapple X test.[444] The Grapple X, Y and Z series tests demonstrated genuine two-stage thermonuclear devices fully in the megaton range, but importantly these devices were still far from being deployable weapons. British progress in weaponisation (i.e. arming, fusing, and assembling firing devices into a deliverable 'dropping kit') had been delayed by the testing moratorium that had followed President Eisenhower's statement of 22 August 1958 to the effect that the USA would halt nuclear weapons testing if the USSR and the UK would do the same.[445] Britain felt the pressure and fell into line, but nevertheless all three countries rushed to do as many key tests as possible during 1958, as the moratorium approached and negotiations for the Partial Test Ban Treaty got under way. Even with uninterrupted access to nuclear testing, the process of weaponisation would have taken several years.[446] The US warhead revealed to the British was the US Mk 28, which, once anglicised, became known as Red Snow. It is the Red Snow warhead that saw service in the later versions of the Yellow Sun bombs. The nuclear fundamentals of Red Snow were equivalent to the technology developed by the British independently. The process of the US Mk 28 being anglicised involved significant re-engineering and was not a trivial business. It involved much tricky work at Aldermaston, but it was done quickly. Aldermaston experts from this period are also at pains to point out that this has been the only occasion in the entire history of British nuclear weapons than a British warhead was produced directly from an American design.

Red Snow had a relatively short but unproblematic life in service. It was finally withdrawn in 1972 following difficulties with internal corrosion.[447] It was replaced by the WE.177 series of British nuclear weapons, which from 1969 were to be a mainstay of the RAF for almost 30 years. The WE.177 also saw service with Royal Navy aircraft. If TSR2 had been deployed, it is certain that some of its core armaments would have been the WE.177A boosted tactical fission weapon. The WE.177 weapons were designed to be extremely robust in order to meet a requirement for low-level laydown deployment, a role for which the TSR2 would have been extremely well suited. At the trans-sonic and supersonic speeds of the TSR2, the stresses induced in the weapon in a laydown release when its drogue parachute opened were expected to be extremely severe. Richard Moore has observed that 'the tail was [made] of a very strong light alloy to withstand [the] forces experienced on deployment of the parachute and/or on impact. Parachutes were designed to retard the 1000lb weapon dropped from 50ft from aircraft at Mach 1.15 (875 mph) to impact at 165 ft/sec (112 mph); i.e. with a deceleration load of 240g.'[448] Additionally, the intended tail-first slap-down of the weapon and the risk of multiple impacts if it bounced back from the ground also presented a major challenge for the bomb designers.

Successful laydown delivery can have the military benefit of sending a severe shockwave into the ground, destroying underground bunkers and facilities – but this benefit comes at the price of far greater fallout when compared with an air-burst detonation.

Following the Skybolt cancellation in December 1962, attention turned to the possibility of deploying the thermonuclear, and hence arguably 'strategic', WE.177B on TSR2. A paper on that topic had been prepared by the RAE in January 1961, and it is believed to have inspired official plans in January 1963:[449] the longer length of the thermonuclear WE.177B would have required the bombs to be mounted side by side in the TSR2 weapons bay as opposed to the tandem plans for the WE.177A.[450] Such thinking once again hints at the strategic potential of the TSR2.

WE.177 warheads were configured into a range of weapons, including free-fall bombs, parachute-retarded bombs and anti-submarine weapons. The UK Polaris warhead developed by Aldermaston had many similarities: the weapon-primary design for UK Polaris was based on the WE.177 concept as originally developed for the TSR2, miniaturised to fit the Polaris A3 re-entry vehicle.[451] The Polaris warhead was tested in Nevada from 1964 to 1965.[452]

The V-force from 1958 onwards had the ability to drop individual nuclear weapons with yields measured in hundreds of kilotons, but as we have seen the vulnerability of the V-force was becoming ever clearer. In contrast to the V-force, TSR2 had from the outset been specified to be operable from poorly prepared airfields for up to three weeks, and furthermore it was to be able to operate without any external support for 48 hours. This ambitious capability would have given the TSR2 a key advantage at a time when the V-force was looking increasingly vulnerable. As was alluded to earlier, the TSR2 was not restricted to a few dozen possible dispersal sites; it could operate from almost anywhere. The ideas underpinning the ability of TSR2 to operate away from conventional airfields had already been successfully implemented in Sweden in the late 1950s. Sweden has a long history of preparing its highways as potential improvised airfields. The Swedish Air Force's Saab JAS 39 Gripen fighter force continues, at the time of writing, to plan for such tactics, and the Swedish Air Force trains its pilots accordingly.

Unlike the V-force, a full squadron of very widely dispersed and hidden TSR2 aircraft equipped for nuclear retaliation might realistically have been expected to survive a massive bolt-from-the-blue attack, especially if it were to follow a period of escalating international tension. The TSR2 aircraft might even have been deployed to flying club airfields equipped only with short grass runways. With its far greater potential for effective dispersal, the TSR2 concept had within in it elements required for a potential deterrent role, although the practicalities of such a strategy are debatable, and the problem of an escalatory signal arising from dispersal at times of crisis remained.

FAST AND LOW

When Gary Powers was shot down, apparently by a Soviet S-75 Dvina surface-to-air missile over Sverdlovsk, Russia, it was not only to prompt an international incident, but it also forced a major reassessment of western military planning which would in the early 1960s favour the TSR2 concept over other aircraft-based nuclear weapon delivery options.

The downing of Francis Gary Powers' U2 spy plane from approximately 65,000 feet shocked the west. Military analysts soon accepted the official Soviet line that he had been shot down by a surface-to-air missile (see Chapter 6). If lightweight high-altitude spy planes could not safely gather intelligence over potential Soviet targets, then there could be little confidence in the ability of the west to get a lower-flying heavy bomber with free-fall bombs over a well-defended target deep inside the USSR.

US thinking in the late 1950s had planned for the B70 which was to be a supersonic high-altitude bomber for the Strategic Air Command. Two prototypes, the XB-70 Valkyrie, were built by North American Aviation using engines from General Electric. But the ambitious plans for the B70 were cancelled following the Gary Powers incident; it was clear that such high-altitude missions were no longer feasible.

At the time of the Gary Powers incident, the US had one aircraft that suited the new conditions better than any other – the B58 Hustler, built by Convair. Originally designed for high-altitude supersonic penetration, the B58 was quickly repurposed for low-altitude penetration, albeit with a significant penalty on speed and range.

Perhaps more than any other American aircraft, the Convair B58 Hustler is an aircraft whose history was shaped by the forces in play in the early 1960s.[453] Originally designed as a high-altitude supersonic bomber for the US Strategic Air Command, it was forced into a low-level penetration mode by the Gary Powers incident. However, at low level the aircraft was forced to operate subsonically; furthermore, operating at low level was fuel-inefficient, and the airframe suffered excessive fatigue. The B58 was operated in such a mode for a short while – but, importantly, its lack of terrain-following radar restricted its capabilities. The necessary radar and control systems upgrade was deemed to be too expensive, and the plane was phased out; the last one left service only eight years after the production line closed. US Defense Secretary Robert McNamara, previously president of the Ford Motor Company, sought to bring systems thinking to public policy challenges. He looked beyond the B58 and pointed to the arrival of the F-111A as a more capable aircraft. On 8 December 1965 McNamara announced the phase-out of the B58. This was to occur within five years.[454]

It might initially appear rather odd that the growing challenges faced by the B58 and the forthcoming TSR2 and F-111 were not as problematic for the older, and massive, B52. The key strengths of the B52 were its great weight and its ability to carry very heavy payloads, which made it relatively simple to fit ever more sophisticated electronic countermeasures to jam and confuse the target acquisition radars of Soviet air defence.[455] As the B52 was capable of carrying the largest stand-off weaponry, it avoided the need to come close to target.

THE BUCCANEER – GOOD ENOUGH?

The official British requirement to be met by the TSR2 was for a merely tactical strike and reconnaissance aircraft. In such terms it seems apparent that from the outset the Blackburn Buccaneer would have been more than sufficient for such a role, in Europe at least. Tactical battlefield capabilities, with no thought for strategic deterrence capability, would largely avoid the need for crisis dispersal and operations from grass runways, which, given the Cuba crisis experience discussed earlier, was arguably never going to be a practical proposition for TSR2, in Europe anyway.

Derek Wood has referred to plans for a supersonic version of the Buccaneer.[456] But even as such ideas were under consideration it was becoming clear that 'supersonic' was already yesterday's attribute. Supersonic capability had been key to the 1950s aspirations for high-altitude deep penetration of enemy air-space. At those high altitudes the air is thin, and air resistance low. Planning for fast and low attack, however, raised a host of new technical challenges including the need for sophisticated terrain-following technology and the need to cope with much greater mechanical stresses arising from thicker air and greater turbulence. The TSR2 and the Buccaneer were both highly capable in the face of such difficulties, but the thicker air at low altitude also gave rise to difficulties with range and rendered sustained supersonic flight effectively impossible, owing to very high fuel consumption at such speeds. This reality made the supersonic capability of the TSR2 largely meaningless.

The tension between the Royal Air Force with its desire for TSR2 and the Royal Navy with its preference for the Buccaneer is revealed by the following probably apocryphal tale:

> There was a wedding in the mid 1960s between an Admiral and a lady that had worked for the RAF on Blue Streak. The cake decorators had arranged for a plane to be put on top of the white wedding cake and they chose a model of a Blackburn Buccaneer. White, like the cake, it looked like a Buccaneer prepared for an RAF nuclear strike role and as such it was perceived by the RAF top brass present as a strongly anti-TSR2 statement. Apparently several senior people got up and left the wedding.

BACK IN THE USSR

Meeting the challenge of detecting low-flying NATO strike aircraft was the task of the Protivovozdushnaya Oborona Strany.[457] The PVO Strany, one of the five official branches of the USSR armed forces, was one of their key components. So esteemed was the PVO Strany within the USSR that the date 10 April was designated as a Union-wide day of celebration dedicated to it.

During the early 1960s developments were under way in Soviet air defence of which the PVO Strany were very proud. These developments gave the Soviet leadership, and more importantly the UK and US leadership, the impression that the USSR would indeed soon have the power to bring down a sufficiently high proportion of incoming low-flying fast bombers. As we have seen from the downing of Gary Power's U2 spy plane, Soviet air defence, or rather perceived Soviet air defence, had already successfully ended earlier western ambitions for a high-altitude bomber force.

By the mid-1960s the PVO Strany was starting to threaten even fast and low attack. Any such Soviet defence would be a major threat to the TSR2 programme.

At that time, air defence systems still needed a few seconds to acquire and process information to lock onto a target and launch anti-aircraft missiles, and a low and fast attack removed those vital seconds from the defence. However by the early 1960s it became clear that in-depth improvements in Soviet defence might soon circumvent this difficulty, at least for key targets such as Moscow. The idea in essence was that targets could be acquired with forward-deployed radars positioned to observe likely paths of attack, and that this information might be passed rapidly and electronically back to air defence weapons systems so that they might anticipate the time and place of arrival of an incoming attacker. Such capabilities would increase Soviet defensive capability – but, importantly, could not achieve the very highest levels of protection: the range of attack options were too numerous and too broad for that. If the Soviet Union were to secure a fuller defensive capability against fast and low attack, then it would need its target acquisition radars to be looking down from above. But this was not achieved until March 1977, by the US Airborne Warning and Control System (AWCS), by which time it had been under test for roughly ten years.[458] Soviet efforts to achieve such capacity lagged far behind Boeing-led activity in the west, and arguably by

TSR2 is capable of modern reconnaissance or of the pin point delivery of any kind of weapon. It is designed
operate at very high speed under the radar screen in all weathers, and has a high degree of invulnerabili
against any known defence. Its STOL capability frees it from large prepared bases and its long range gives it
flexibility hitherto unattained by any other aircraft. TSR2, which is now on the production line, will augme
the operational power of the Royal Air Force in a wide range of roles.

UNDER
THE RADAR SCREEN

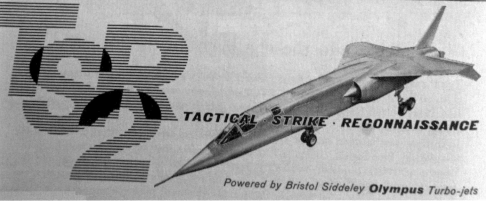

TACTICAL · STRIKE · RECONNAISSANCE

Powered by Bristol Siddeley **Olympus** *Turbo-jets*

*BAC TSR2 publicity [British Aircraft Corporation: as originally
published in Air Pictorial, December 1963 (Author's collection)]*

the time of the fall of the Iron Curtain in 1991 the USSR still had not achieved a reliable and workable system.

Even back in the early 1960s, future Labour defence secretary Denis Healey had clearly believed that the TSR2 would be vulnerable to Soviet air defence. As we recall from Chapter 6, Healey said: 'New anti aircraft weapons will be able to shoot it down by the time it is in service, so at £16 million an aircraft it is going to make all Mr Amery's other blunders look like chickenfeed.'[459]

TSR2 – IT'S NOT ABOUT EUROPE

The British, as Europeans, had very real anxieties about the consequences of any battlefield use of nuclear weapons in a European war. While tactical nuclear war-games were played, it all felt like a rather American construct. For the UK there was the nuclear tripwire mentioned in Chapter 5: once nuclear weapons were used in Europe, frankly Britain's policy of deterrence would have failed – all too quickly it would be 'game over'. In the Far East, however, it could have been different; the British might have been able to engage in a nuclear war that did not immediately escalate to Armageddon. Hence, there was no tripwire East of Suez.

MOSCOW CRITERION

Although the British were never as exuberant as the Americans in the use of the notion of 'strategic' defence; there was one Cold War consideration in UK defence policy that helps make a useful distinction between the strategic and the merely tactical, and that was known as the 'Moscow Criterion'. The Moscow Criterion required that the United Kingdom should possess the ability independently to destroy the heart of the USSR – Moscow. Not simply because Moscow represented the USSR's most important asset, but also because it represented the USSR's most heavily defended redoubt. Moscow had been defended unsuccessfully and successfully against the armies of Napoleon Bonaparte and Adolf Hitler. In the Cold War, the Soviet Union resolved to defend Moscow above all else.

The importance of the Moscow defensive system became clearer during the 1969–1972 discussions towards the Anti-Ballistic Missile Treaty (1972). That treaty specifically exempted one ABM site for each of the United States and the USSR, and for the USSR the clear choice was Moscow. Discussion of the 'Moscow' ABM system can, however, give the wrong impression. Peter Jones has summarised this point nicely:

> For those who may think of this loosely termed 'Moscow' ABM system as a ring of interceptors on the outskirts of Moscow let me transpose it to a 'London' ABM system. The nearest early warning radar would be somewhere near Berlin; the battle control Doghouse radar near Newbury; the 128 Galosh interceptors in batteries near Ipswich, Margate, Hastings, Brighton, Portsmouth, Swindon, Northampton and

Cambridge, protecting any target within an arc from Penzance to Edinburgh and on into the Netherlands and northern France.[460]

The Moscow ABM system, based on long-range Galosh nuclear-tipped surface to space missiles, was a system designed to intercept incoming warheads in the vacuum of outer space, and before the re-entry vehicles (RVs) could enter the atmosphere. The megaton-range warhead on the Galosh missile, if detonated in space, would produce a very high radiation flux capable of disabling incoming warheads at a distance of many nautical miles.[461]

Meanwhile the Soviets were also putting in place ever more sophisticated measures to protect against incoming low-altitude bombers, although realistically such a system would not be able to offer comprehensive protection to all possible targets in and around Moscow.

THE F-111 OPTION

The option negotiated by Denis Healey in early 1965 for Britain to purchase F-111A strike aircraft from 1967 is central to the story of the cancellation of the TSR2. Obtained at no cost to the UK tax payer, the F-111A option allowed for the prompt ending of the massive development costs of the TSR2. The criteria under which the option might, or might not, be exercised have never been made clear. It seems likely however that Healey could foresee that the UK might have little long-term need for advanced next-generation aircraft such as the TSR2 or F-111K. He might have imagined such a future even before the cancellation of the TSR2. In Europe such an aircraft would face a purely tactical strike role, a task readily handled by other aircraft such as the Buccaneer; and East of Suez, where TSR2/F-111K capabilities might have been more necessary, British commitments would soon diminish.

It is important to recall that, as noted earlier, Denis Healey had reported to the Cabinet on the night of the TSR2 cancellation decision that: 'On certain hypotheses about long-term commitments it might even be possible to dispense with this type of aircraft altogether.'[462]

In February 1965 *Air Pictorial* attempted to flag what its staff believed to be a government misconception that the TSR2 and the F-111 were essentially equivalent. Indeed, in key discussions in Cabinet later that same month, an equivalence between the two aircraft and their capabilities appears to have been generally assumed. *Air Pictorial* had reminded its readers that TSR2 was to be a very low-level tactical strike *and* reconnaissance aircraft (emphasis original).[463] The F-111, it was pointed out, was intended by the Americans as a successor to tactical *fighters* such as the F-105 in the USAF, and fleet defence *fighters* such as the Phantom II in the Navy. *Air Pictorial* stressed that while F-111 could fly low for limited periods, 'it has not been designed for all-out long-range low-level penetration'. It seems that *Air Pictorial* was warning its readers that F-111 would not be the strategic weapons system that TSR-2 arguably had the potential to be. The Cabinet, however, had no such strategic ambitions for the TSR2, and hence for them the assumption of equivalence may have been justified.

Shaping the decision as whether or not to exercise the F-111 option were not just the various considerations of military aviation but also much wider issues of UK defence policy, strategy and capability.

As we have seen, at various points throughout the 1957–1964 story of the TSR2 the notion that the aircraft might represent a British strategic follow-on to the V-bombers had been of recurring interest to politicians, defence planners and the military. For the military it was at the heart of a rivalry between the RAF and the Navy as to whether the RAF, with its larger budgets in the Second World War and its role in UK strategic defence in the 1950s, had the potential to become the cornerstone of British strategic defence in the late 20th century. The Royal Navy held the claim to be the Senior Service of the British military by virtue of being the first branch of the military to have been formally and properly established. The term 'Senior Service', however, evokes a sense of far more than mere longevity; it implies a supremacy of status that had come under increasing threat from the RAF. Would the Royal Navy, which had defeated the combined navies of France and Spain at Trafalgar in 1805, and which had allowed Britain to 'rule the waves' throughout the 19th century, be relegated to second place in the British defence pantheon? At the time of the TSR2 that possibility appeared to be very real, and, as we have seen earlier, Lord Mountbatten fought any such diminution of naval status tooth and nail.

ROYAL NAVY ASCENDENT

In the early 1960s one issue determined whether the Royal Navy would re-establish its leading role in the defence of Britain, and that issue was Polaris. Prime Minister Harold Macmillan had secured a quite remarkable offer from John F. Kennedy at Nassau, Bahamas, in 1962. The offer of Polaris to Britain was made in the context of the unilateral US cancellation of the airborne Skybolt programme. Despite having achieved a remarkable compensation in Polaris, the British must have remained concerned that this too would not be delivered, as promised, within five years. The 21 December 1962 joint statement by Kennedy and Macmillan stated: 'The first of a dozen Polaris submarines are due to go into service in the UK within five years. Each submarine will cost around £35m each (*sic*) and each missile costs £350,000. The total cost of the nuclear naval deterrent is estimated at about £300m.'[464]

While in the event Polaris was not in UK service within five years of the political announcement, the project did run to schedule from its formal initiation in 1963, and as such it is widely regarded as having been one of the best managed UK military projects. The first Royal Navy submarine equipped with Polaris nuclear missiles, HMS *Resolution*, left on her first patrol in June 1968. As the UK adoption of the Polaris system and the development of the new Resolution class submarines made good progress during 1966 and 1967, the UK held onto Denis Healey's option to deploy the F-111 if need be. (The reference to 'a dozen Polaris submarines' in the Kennedy and Macmillan statement is rather odd. It seems unlikely that there was ever any intention of so many submarines. The British plan focused initially on five vessels, although this was later cut back to four.)

As Christmas came in 1962 it seems likely that in Whitehall there was a sense that in Polaris Britain had found itself a powerful nuclear deterrent that, unlike the V-force, was not vulnerable to a first strike. However, as we shall see, there would still be an ongoing, and at that juncture highly secret, concern; could the UK get past Soviet defences?

As we shall see, the mid-1960s would present a series of worries to defence planners concerned with the future of UK nuclear weapons. For much of this period Healey would hold on to his F-111 option, and for as long as he could he defended it aggressively. The end would come in early 1968 just a few months before the first Polaris-armed patrol by HMS Resolution. In his memoirs Healey looked back on the TSR2 cancellation and the ending of the F-111 option:

> there was a powerful lobby in Cabinet for me to cancel the F111 purchase as well. I was finally compelled to do so three years later, in January 1968, as part of a further cut in defence spending – partly to save money, partly to avoid buying a third American plane [after the Hercules and the Phantom]. When the decision went against me, I was on the point of resignation, because I felt my honour was at stake: I had been able to persuade the air force to cancel the TSR2 only by guaranteeing them the F111 in its place.[465]

Healey has denied that East of Suez withdrawal was on his mind at the time of the TSR2 cancellation in the spring of 1965. On whether such matters were relevant to the decision not to proceed with the F-111 option, he further comments:

> I would have found it impossible to justify, either to the Party or the public, resigning over the cancellation of the F111. PEG (Programme Evaluation Group) had just concluded that, in the light of our pending withdrawal from the Middle and Far East, we had no operational requirement for such an aircraft, though I was not then aware of their conclusion.[466]

He does not mention whether he had already reached the same conclusion independently.

The F-111K as a British capability was a dead plan, but Healey still continued to believe that there was a need for an RAF strike aircraft with nuclear capability. In a European context, such a role could be played well by the Blackburn Buccaneer; and as we know, he would in later years, and with much hindsight, express the view that the Buccaneer would have been the best choice from the start.[467]

In 1968 the decision was made to equip the RAF with the Buccaneer, and the first aircraft arrived at 12 Squadron RAF Honington the following year. Despite the successful arrival of Polaris and the dropping of the F-111K requirement, the RAF would retain a fast and low nuclear strike capability in the form of the Buccaneer. In the period leading up to these decisions (1965–1968) it had become increasingly clear to high-level defence planners that there could be a serious problem ahead for Polaris.

POLARIS HAS A PROBLEM

It might have been expected in the late 1960s that the shifting of Britain's nuclear deterrent to a submarine-launched ballistic missile system (Polaris) would ensure the ability of the UK to achieve its goals for strategic capability far into the future. It must have seemed that all of the difficulties associated with airborne delivery had finally been circumvented. Such confidence, however, was very short lived. If one is properly to understand the strategic options facing the UK from the mid-1960s onwards, it is important to consider the difficulties that lay ahead for Polaris.

AWE Aldermaston refers to the emerging risks to Polaris when it says under the title 'UK starts Chevaline Programme':

> By the mid-1960s, the Government had concluded that the Polaris system was at risk from Soviet improvements in anti-ballistic missile defences.
>
> The Americans responded with a new system – Poseidon – but in Britain a decision was taken in 1972 to improve the ability of Polaris to penetrate these defences. In this way was born the uniquely British system known as Chevaline.
>
> AWRE's scientists and engineers, together with those at RAE Farnborough, Hunting Engineering and many other British companies, redesigned the original Polaris 'front end' to greatly improve its ability to penetrate enemy defences.
>
> The new design included a warhead which was 'hardened' against nuclear attack; two warheads were mounted on an 'Improved Front End' capable of manoeuvring in space to deploy its payload. This was fitted to existing Polaris missiles and was in service from 1982 to 1996.
>
> It was a tribute to the skill and ingenuity of the many hundreds of specialist staff involved.[468]

The risk to the planned UK Polaris system posed by Soviet ABM systems was apparent very early on, and far in advance of the actual Polaris deployment in 1968. Indeed, the whole history of UK Polaris from its earliest days is bound up with concerns regarding Soviet ABM capabilities. Matthew Jones, author of the official history of the British deterrent, summarises the situation well when he observes:

> As technical preparations for the introduction of Polaris missiles into Royal Navy service gathered pace during early 1963 it was apparent that the ability of Polaris to overcome the Soviet ABM environment that could be expected to appear in the 1970s was already an issue that would require attention.[469]

A study group was soon established in May 1964, bringing together officials from the Ministry of Aviation and the RAE, and tasked with considering penetration aids for Polaris.

Working under designation 'HR 169', its task was to examine the risks posed by possible Soviet ABM systems especially as the warheads descended through the atmosphere to their targets.[470] The study group worked quickly, and it completed its primary task by producing a rather troubling report in November 1964. That same month things took another difficult turn as the Galosh ABM weapons system was seen in a Moscow military parade.[471] The upshot of these developments was that by the start of 1965 it was becoming very clear that the Polaris system faced a serious problem.

According to British Cold War mythology, at the 1964 Red Square parade the British air attaché had managed to snap a photo illegally. Later, back in Britain, analysts used the known size of the masonry stones in the background to calibrate the size of the new missile. In this way the British managed to satisfy themselves that this must be a new, slow, long-range missile. It was the nuclear-tipped anti-ballistic missile system that had been feared for several years. The sentiment in the Ministry of Defence was, 'We're in trouble, boys.'

By July 1966 Aldermaston director Ted Newley had set up a Vulnerabilities Committee, or 'V-Committee', to work on the scraps of intelligence that came in concerning Soviet radars and defensive systems insofar as they posed a challenge to Britain's planned Polaris deterrent.[472] The V-Committee was supported by a Physics Working Party, under hydrodynamicist Arthur Bryant, to assess shock and heat effects.[473] The V-Committee had started to become aware of a serious problem for Polaris in the form of the Soviet Moscow ABM system based around the nuclear-armed Galosh space interceptor missiles. It soon became clear that the UK Polaris system was uniquely vulnerable to these Soviet developments because the UK Polaris deterrent was based on a small number of submarines.[474]

The Moscow ABM system relied upon phased array radars that looked in all directions, including east towards China. It was a sophisticated battle management radar, sending target acquisition information to, in full deployment, about 100 Galosh missiles. The system was built up through the late 1960s and early 1970s, but the threat it would pose to British strategy was apparent well before it was fully deployed.[475]

By January 1967 even the British public was becoming aware of the looming difficulties, partly as a consequence of a report in the *Sunday Telegraph* stating that Polaris was 'no longer regarded as a 'credible' deterrent and looked as though it would be obsolete before we have finished deploying it, or still less paying for it'.[476] The sister newspaper, the *Daily Telegraph*, went further later the same year, revealing that much of the risk was associated with exoatmospheric X-ray-based defence. On 19 May an article appeared entitled 'Fears for Future of British Polaris', in which it was specifically suggested that the Russians might, like the Americans, be interested in using X-rays to damage incoming nuclear warheads in flight outside the atmosphere. While some of the technical details may not have been correct, the overall premise of the article was powerful.[477] Pressures were growing that these problems must be fixed if the British deterrent was indeed going to be credible.

In order to understand the vulnerabilities of the Royal Navy Polaris system it is important to understand its technical fundamentals.

The system comprised three warheads deployed from each missile. The warheads would re-enter subsonically with heat shields, and the falling weapons would form a triangular damage pattern. Each detonation would yield roughly 100kT exploding at a selected altitude. Taken together, the three blasts all directed to a single target would yield damage equivalent to a megaton blast.

The concerns about the ability of Polaris to get past the Moscow ABM system were a uniquely British problem. The difficulties arose because of the small size of the British Polaris fleet: only four vessels, of which only one, or perhaps two, would have been at sea at any one time. The Americans took the view that they faced no serious threat from the Moscow ABM system. The US had so many warheads available that it could first attack the perimeter acquisition radars and then slowly, in an increasing programme of nuclear attacks, roll the defensive radars right back until metropolitan Russia became vulnerable. Furthermore, the United States had a clear numerical ability to overcome a defensive system based upon only roughly 100 interceptor missiles. The British, however, had only 16 Polaris missiles on one boat, and maybe 32 missiles available if two boats were at sea. In the mid-1960s it started to become clear that by the early 1970s the Russians would have more than enough interceptor missiles to have a chance of completely blocking any British attack by the Polaris submarines. This was because each Galosh interceptor missile would have the capability of taking out all three warheads from one Polaris missile, since these would still be close-clustered and drifting apart relatively slowly in space into their final re-entry footprint. The Royal Navy Polaris fleet was rightly intended as a retaliatory weapon to deter Soviet aggression. If Britain were to lose its ability to retaliate credibly by causing unacceptable damage, then Britain would become more vulnerable to Soviet threats and aggression. In strategic terms this was a major problem.[478]

The solution developed was to become known as Chevaline. It had its origins in a series of Polaris improvement studies in the period 1967–1970.[479]

Chevaline was an utterly British technology in two respects. First, it was a unique British invention – yes, assisted by the Americans, but completely British nonetheless. The second aspect was that it was only necessary for scenarios in which the UK might alone and independently seek to retaliate against an attack from the Soviet Union. While NATO more generally, and the Americans in particular, would always have been able to overwhelm Moscow's Galosh-based defences, for Britain acting alone the Moscow Criterion was a particularly difficult challenge to overcome.

This book is entitled *Britain and the Bomb*, but it is important to stress the emphasis placed publicly, especially by Labour governments, on the British deterrent having a wider role, indeed its dominant role, as part of NATO capabilities. While notions of independent British action were staunchly protected by all British governments, only Conservative governments felt comfortable in giving such positions public prominence. For Labour the notion of independent action was a sensitive matter in the 1960s. Matthew Jones devotes much discussion to these dual roles for the British capability.[480] The Chevaline system deserves particular mention in this context, as its special capabilities would only ever be needed if the British were to act alone.

The Labour party had come to power in 1964, winning the election with a manifesto which included a pledge to renegotiate Polaris.[481] The manifesto said:

> The Nassau Agreement to buy Polaris know-how and Polaris missiles from the U.S.A. will add nothing to the deterrent strength of the western alliance, and it will mean utter dependence on the U.S. for their supply. Nor is it true that all this costly defence expenditure will produce an 'independent British deterrent'. It will not be independent and it will not be British and it will not deter. Its possession will impress neither friend nor potential foe.

> Moreover, Britain's insistence on this nuclear pretence carries with it grave dangers of encouraging the spread of nuclear weapons to countries not possessing them, including Germany.

> The Government bases its policy on the assumption that Britain must be prepared to go it alone without her allies in an all-out thermo-nuclear war with the Soviet Union, involving the obliteration of our people. By constantly reiterating this appalling assumption the Government is undermining the alliance on which our security now depends.[482]

The sensitivities around nuclear weapons within the Labour party at this time are clear. In 1966 Labour won a second term, and by 1967 'renegotiation' was finally under way.[483] This led to the reduction in the size of the Polaris force from five submarines to four at a cost saving of £60 million.[484] The direct consequence of this decision was that the Royal Navy would no longer be able to promise to keep more than one boat at sea at all times. As will become clear, this decision to save £60 million and to reduce from two submarines on patrol to one may have amplified the later challenge of beating the emerging Moscow anti-ballistic missile defences. As things turned out the UK would spend almost 20 times as much as had been saved, approximately £1 billion, on the Chevaline upgrade designed to maintain the core strategic capabilities originally planned for the Polaris system.

It is important to appreciate that the key steps of initially understanding the threat posed by the Soviet Galosh ABM system, and the subsequent planning of a response, were taken during the Labour governments led by Harold Wilson in the period 1964–1970. They were making private decisions aimed at preserving stand-alone British capabilities while publicly giving emphasis to multilateral, NATO-based ideas for which these capabilities would have little relevance.

While Chevaline would ensure the credibility of an independent British deterrent, such independence brought with it both opportunities and responsibilities. For the UK, it removed a need to rely on a US (or NATO) nuclear security guarantee, and removed any need to worry about whether the United States would really risk its major cities to guarantee

London's survival. A key responsibility came with the reality that the UK would represent a second centre of decision to be assessed by an aggressive Soviet Union. If the USSR were to consider aggression against western Europe, it would face the possibility of having to make two (or perhaps three, if one considers France) separate decisions concerning a possible western response. In this way the Soviets faced a greater risk that one of the three western powers would choose retaliation using nuclear weapons. Contemplating such risks would surely increase the power of the western deterrent in Soviet minds.[485] Of course if Britain were to retaliate with the use of Polaris missiles, one could not assume that the Soviets would know that a British, rather than an American, missile was on its way.[486] In that context the risk of escalation would be very high. These risks relate to fears that would in turn further boost the power of the British deterrent to Soviet eyes.

FORCED TO CHOOSE

The two central narratives of our story – the Royal Air Force's ambitions for TSR2 (and subsequently for the F-111) and the Royal Navy's plans for a submarine-based nuclear deterrent – finally collided in government on 5 January 1968 in the Ministerial Committee on Nuclear Policy. There, and also in Cabinet, chancellor of the exchequer Roy Jenkins argued that 'we could not afford to continue with both the F-111 and Polaris programme'.[487] In response Denis Healey tried valiantly to defend both projects, but the economic realities were overwhelming and with the withdrawal from East of Suez having already been announced the previous November,[488] it was clear that Polaris, and the Chevaline upgrade, must prevail.

This single decision exemplifies a profound shift for Britain in the late 20th century. Fading away were notions of distant dominions and the power of Bomber Command. In its place was a new reality of European security, friendly with the Americans but wary to ensure independence of British action in defence of the home islands. The Empire was gone, and arguably the Commonwealth would soon start to fade. In its place would be decades of emphasis on NATO and what would later become the European Union.

As noted earlier, concerns for the viability of Polaris as a British deterrent had existed from the very beginnings of the UK programme. As early as 1961 and into 1962, the Soviet Union broke the 1958 nuclear testing moratorium, including tests of high-altitude rockets.[489] It would be surprising if these had not given rise to fears among defence strategists about nuclear-armed ABM systems (as would later be deployed in the form of the USSR Galosh missiles).

It is interesting to pause and note that fundamentally the Americans had a different philosophy about ABM capability. They did not set out to protect their capital as a bastion: they set out to protect their deterrent. The missile silos of North Dakota would emerge over time as the chosen focus of American defensive efforts.

In 1967, as Aldermaston researchers began considering the issues of weapons hardening for a Polaris improvement, it became clear that the RAE Farnborough and the Royal Radar Establishment, Malvern, had already been working for some years in the strictest secrecy on improved penetration aids or 'penaids'.[490] Much of their work had related to the abandoned Blue Streak programme. It is known that the Ministry of Defence had been learning from the Americans (and Canadians) about improved Soviet ABM technology for some time via the non-atomic Tripartite Technical Cooperation Panel (TTCP). The researchers at Aldermaston had apparently been unaware of those high-level exchanges before 1967.[491]

A colourful character on the margins of our story worthy of mention is Lord (Victor) Rothschild. Heir to the prominent banking family, he enjoyed his time at Cambridge University in the 1930s before joining MI5 for the Second World War. Despite some vague and apparently misplaced concerns that he might have come too close to his contemporaries, the Cambridge spies, during the pre-war years, he went on to become an influential figure in UK technology policy during the 1960s and 1970s.

He has a special role in the story of the independent British nuclear deterrent. In particular, he was a member of a very small group led by Lord Kings Norton (Harold Cox) tasked by the Ministry of Technology with assessing the work of the Atomic Weapons Research Establishment with the hope in mind of securing economies through rationalisation. The group started work in April 1968.[492] As it turned out, the dominant opinion was that only modest saving would be achievable, and AWRE continued undiminished. Rothschild, however, did not support the dominant opinion: he pushed at the boundaries of the group's terms of reference, seeking consideration of the wider challenges faced by the AWRE. His dissent went so far that he produced a minority report challenging the pro-AWRE consensus. Rothschild, like Sir Solly Zuckerman, persistently questioned and challenged the dominant narratives and decision making that shaped British nuclear weapons policy in this period. While the various policies largely survived Rothschild's attacks, and while some of his critiques were perhaps misplaced, the fact that British decision making admitted such dissonance is impressive. The inclusion of someone of Rothschild's strength of character, challenging as he did sensitive and important decision making, points to the robustness, and open-mindedness, of British policy making at this time. The roles played by Lord Rothschild and the Kings Norton Group feature prominently in Matthew Jones' official history.[493]

The Polaris improvement studies were a 'black programme' known only to a few people, and initially only Aldermaston was working on it. In an official sense it was not a project at all, and this reflected political sensitivities at the top of the Labour government's decision-making system. The studies were funded on a six-monthly basis. Normally nuclear weapon projects had a heavy reliance on outside contractors, for instance those with rocketry experience, but in this case that was not possible:[494] no contractor would agree to tool up for a body of work that might be cancelled in less than six months. An inevitable consequence of the early stages of Chevaline not being a 'project' was that it had no project management. Peter Jones, the director at Aldermaston, had to cope as best he could, having to steer technical challenges with very long-term implications with only the most short-term tools. By the time that Chevaline finally became a project it was already running fast, and the project management took some time to catch up with it. For these reasons Chevaline has a bad reputation to this day, in certain policy circles, as a project that was mismanaged and went horribly over budget. In recent years this standard opinion has begun to be challenged.

Chevaline only officially became a project in 1975 when Labour defence secretary Roy Mason secretly gave his formal agreement.[495]

CHEVALINE – A TECHNOLOGY DEPLOYED, NOT CANCELLED

Earlier in this book we examined the story of the TSR2 in part to understand where Britain might be today if other decisions had been taken. In order to be able to gain a perspective on what might have been, it is important to have an understanding of the story as it actually happened. The years in which several TSR2 squadrons might have been deployed, some of which could in effect have had a strategic nuclear capability, were the same years as those during which the UK in reality struggled in complete secrecy to beat a major threat to British strategic deterrence; a threat posed by the Moscow ABM system. Britain of the 1970s and 1980s was not developing and deploying TSR2 – rather, it was developing and deploying Chevaline. Britain chose one path: Polaris to Chevaline. It simply could not have afforded the TSR2, or F-111, as well.

To understand the story of Chevaline it is important to understand that a strategic nuclear retaliation by Britain against the USSR would have started with a nuclear battle in space. If it were to take place at night then the night sky above northern Norway would have been lit by a large number of bright flashes, each as bright as the sun. These flashes would be the in-space detonation of the megaton nuclear warheads lifted by Soviet Galosh missiles and which had been launched with the intention of destroying the British Polaris missile warheads in flight.

There is a legend in the western nuclear missile community that the fundamental idea behind the Galosh system was inadvertently leaked by a Soviet scientist attending an American physics conference on X-ray deposition effects, when he declared in passing that X-ray physics effects provided the 'kill mechanism' for the Soviet ABM system. X-ray concerns had previously been considered and dismissed in the west, but following that crucial observation the Americans and others rapidly revisited the issues and soon realised that the claim could be true.[496]

If the story is true it is not necessarily the case that it was an accidental slip by an individual Russian academic. It could have been a deliberate step by the Russians to share an insight that needed to be shared if deterrence were to function. In some ways such thinking is reminiscent of the lines from Stanley Kubrick's 1964 polemical comedy *Dr Strangelove* concerning the Soviet 'doomsday machine':[497]

| Dr Strangelove: | Yes, but the … whole point of the doomsday machine … is lost … if you keep it a secret! Why didn't you tell the world, eh? |
| Soviet Ambassador DeSadeski: | It was to be announced at the Party Congress on Monday. As you know, the Premier loves surprises. |

We shall probably never know what really motivated the public disclosures of the 1960s, but I like to think that Kubrick's satire reminded the real Dr Strangeloves of the importance of telling the world of their discoveries and ideas.

In the spring of 1968 two high priests of American nuclear weapons physics, Hans Bethe and Dick Garwin, published a remarkably candid and wide-ranging assessment of the issues around nuclear-tipped anti-ballistic-missile technology, and revealed to the world the fundamental physics principles involved.[498] The ideas made public in 1968 were the same as those that had worried Aldermaston a few years earlier.[499] Garwin and Bethe had restricted their discussion to a consideration of US plans. Core to US thinking were two types of nuclear-tipped weapon – a larger missile intended to intercept in space (equivalent to the Soviet Galosh) known as 'Sentinel', and a smaller and shorter-range missile, 'Sprint', intended for terminal defence with interception in the atmosphere.

When a Galosh warhead, or any nuclear weapon, detonates in space there is no blast such as we would expect – that is, there is no sound, but there is a pulse of neutrons and even more importantly an extremely short-lived pulse of X-rays. In space this pulse is intense over a very significant distance. The key to the damage that the X-ray pulse can do to a nuclear weapon lies in the very short duration of the pulse.[500] Even at many nautical miles' range, the intensity of the X-ray pulse can be sufficient to produce, almost instantaneously, an effect reminiscent of an explosion of the irradiated material. The outer layer of the heat shield is blown off, possibly leaving insufficient ablative material to protect the weapon on re-entry. That, however, is not the full extent of the possible damage. Because the pulse is so short, a shock runs into the warhead. Behind the shockwave comes a tension wave sufficient to stress free surfaces beyond their mechanical strength. In the heat shield this can cause chips to flake off, or cause the inner layers to delaminate, further reducing its integrity.

The threat posed by X-rays depends upon the X-ray photon energy and hence in turn on the temperature of the defensive nuclear explosion. Unsurprisingly, the fear among the British weapons scientists of the mid-1960s would soon focus on the risk from so-called 'hot bombs'.[501]

X-rays were not, however, the only capability of the Galosh system to destroy incoming western ballistic nuclear weapons.[502] The neutrons from a Galosh detonation would arrive at the Polaris warhead shortly after the X-ray pulse, and they can cause fissions in the nuclear materials of the Polaris warhead. These fusions, although not likely to cause immediate destruction of the device, can produce significant heating of the fissile material – with the potential to cause unacceptable expansion, distortion or even melting of components whose precise, design-critical dimensions and configuration are therefore lost.[503]

This was the challenge that was becoming clear to the UK in the mid-to-late 1960s. As a consequence of the large number of weapons available to them, the Americans did not need to worry too much about the Galosh threat, but the British most definitely did. In addition to their overwhelming number of weapons, the Americans had a number of ways of protecting their warheads, using what they called 'socks'; they were able to put a disposable sock onto the outside of a re-entry vehicle to absorb the X-ray pulse. At re-entry into the atmosphere the sock could be explosively stripped off and then the warhead would run in towards its target with its heat shield undamaged.[504] This proposed system the Americans called 'Antelope'.

In May 1967 Defence Secretary Denis Healey recommended the Polaris-Antelope approach to Prime Minister Harold Wilson in place of the Poseidon missile alternative. He also recommended that the UK switch its Polaris missile purchase to the hardened A3T (Topsy) missile, as this benefit would be offered by the Americans at no cost, given that the US had ceased production of non-hardened A3 missiles. Despite the recommendation, no decision on Antelope had been made by December 1967; Healey therefore raised the matter again with Prime Minister Harold Wilson.[505] A six-month programme of work to assess vulnerabilities was initiated at Aldermaston, and the Polaris improvement studies were under way. The Cabinet had not been consulted, and perhaps as few as two Cabinet members (Healey and Wilson) knew about the decision at this stage. The V-Committee soon realised that they would need to do a lot better than the Antelope option, and the still vague ideas of what might indeed be needed started to be called 'Super Antelope'. It was the early thoughts around Super Antelope that would eventually become Chevaline. Despite the growth in the scale of the work, for both security and political reasons the 'non-project' remained firmly under wraps.

In the first weeks of 1968 the US Navy's Special Projects Office told the UK Polaris Executive that the US would not adopt Antelope or complete its development with US funds.[506] The US Navy recommended that the UK buy the newer and much more powerful Poseidon missile system. In June 1968 the US Navy further proposed a mini-Poseidon option, although this was later dropped.[507] Whatever the technical merits of the proposal, it would have been politically impossible for the inner core of the Labour government to hide such an advance in UK capability.

In September 1969 the US agreed to help the UK with its plans to harden the UK Polaris system, including moves to implement Antelope or Super Antelope. With such assistance available Aldermaston was able in January 1970 to write a report setting out the UK's strategic options. That report concluded that the benefits of Antelope were insufficient to solve the problems faced by the UK with its small number of Polaris missiles. Super Antelope appeared to have merit, but Poseidon looked better.[508] Once again the issues of Super Antelope were kept away from the full Cabinet. The report was considered at a meeting of Denis Healey, as defence secretary, Michael Stewart – the foreign secretary, Roy Jenkins –

by then chancellor of the exchequer – and Harold Wilson, the prime minister.[509] In agreeing to consider such sensitive nuclear matters in forums away from the full Cabinet, Wilson must have recalled the process led by Clement Attlee when he was Labour prime minister concerning the decision to develop Britain's atom bomb programme. In January 1947 Attlee had restricted that important decision to an inner group of the Cabinet. Wilson was merely following an established Labour government pattern when he chose to restrict the Polaris improvement decision to a core group. At the 1970 meeting no decisions were made; rather, decisions were deferred until after the election – an election won by the Conservative party under the leadership of Ted Heath.

The Royal Navy desperately wanted Poseidon and did not want Super Antelope. The Poseidon was a somewhat larger missile than Polaris, but it would fit the Polaris missile tubes on the submarines being built for the Royal Navy; the Polaris submarines had a liner in the missile tubes and if that were removed it would have been possible to fit the bigger Poseidon rocket into the same tube.[510] Importantly Poseidon had a bigger payload. The US planned to take advantage of this larger payload to deploy a Multiple Independent Re-Entry Vehicle (MIRV) system: several, perhaps as many as a dozen, separate small nuclear warheads could be deployed against different targets from one missile. The ability to MIRV the warheads on a ballistic missile greatly increased not only its destructive capability but also its ability to overcome advanced Soviet ABM defences, by separating the warheads so far out in space as to require 'one-on-one' defence, one ABM needing to be assigned to each incoming warhead.

Frank Panton has written that in August 1972 the US secretary of state Henry Kissinger during a visit to the UK offered the British a range of technologies suitable for Polaris improvement including Poseidon.[511] These options, however, were only for systems without MIRV capability. Subsequent analysis in Britain quickly revealed that de-MIRVing Poseidon would be a difficult task, and its cost would likely exceed that of continuing with a Super Antelope (Chevaline) approach. This concern with Poseidon turned out to be well placed, because US experience found the missile system to have numerous technical problems. In the event it was withdrawn from US service before the last of its predecessors, Polaris.

At the end of 1973 the Conservative government finally made the decision to push Super Antelope ahead to completion; but its decision was not implemented because the election intervened. In February 1974 Labour came back to power with a minority government. The electoral process was repeated in October 1974 yielding a workable, but very small, majority for Labour. It was in this context at the end of 1974 that the Labour government finally had to decide on Polaris improvement, and it decided to push ahead with the development and deployment of Super Antelope, which it decided would now be named Chevaline.

The reasons for Royal Navy's opposition to the development of Super Antelope were complex. The extra range and payload options offered by the Poseidon missile were clearly attractive. However, their concerns in the summer of 1974 over the safety issues associated with the proposed use of toxic liquid propellants in the modified 'front end' of the Polaris missile were very deep rooted.[512] The Royal Navy had developed an aversion to the chemical hydrazine. Simple hydrazine (without additional components) is a highly toxic and unstable material suitable for space applications when combined with an iridium catalyst.[513] The catalytic decomposition of the hydrazine into nitrogen and hydrogen releases large amounts of energy, causing the gases to be emitted as jets and the catalyst to reach very high temperatures. Chevaline required advanced fuels for propulsion and attitude control (itself a subject of much technical difficulty). Without speculating as to the fuels actually used, it is known that the choices worried those that would be close to them.

There was real concern in the Navy that Aldermaston, Farnborough and the Rocket Propulsion Establishment, Westcott, might not come up with the goods, risking the Royal Navy's status as the leading force in British defence. In fact, as we shall see, Chevaline was to be a success and the Navy status as the Senior Service (in every sense) was enhanced rather than undermined by its development.

The new Labour defence secretary, Roy Mason, took charge of the propellant safety issue and concluded that there were no significant concerns, but to assuage Navy fears he handed project management of Chevaline to the Navy.[514]

Frank Panton, the former deputy chief scientific adviser (nuclear) at the Ministry of Defence, has written of his recollections of a key visit with Roy Mason to the Royal Navy submarine facilities in Scotland to consider the Navy's concerns over hazardous propellants. Panton recalls:

> When we got back to Northolt after a very long day, Mr Mason offered me a lift back to London in his official car, and I accepted. As we sat in the back of the car with only his Private Secretary and his driver in the front, he asked me what I thought of the day. I said I thought that no-one we had spoken to, submariner or ordnance man, had shown any feelings that the presence of the liquid propellant would present unacceptable risks and on that showing the fears of Naval HQ seemed grossly exaggerated. Mr Mason then said, 'But they'll never have it you know'. 'Have what?' I asked. 'The Chevaline' he said, 'The Navy don't want it and you'll never force it on them'. Taking my courage and my career in both hands, I said, 'Yes, they don't want it and we scientists can't compel them to have it, but you can, Secretary of State. If you tell them they've got to do it, they will have to'. 'Why should I?' he asked.

> I cannot at this distance in time produce the exact wording of what I then said to convince him to order the Navy to go ahead fully with Chevaline, but the substance of my argument was as follows:

> 'It is clear that while, during the last five or so years, successive governments have tried, and failed, to make up their minds conclusively on which course to pursue to maintain the credibility of the UK nuclear deterrent, none of the three governments was prepared to consider a decision which meant not having a credible deterrent. That is presumably why, as all other options continued to be reviewed and re-reviewed

ad nauseam, the Chevaline option was kept in play by drip feeding. However, all improvement options other than Chevaline have now been discarded or are no longer available to us, and the choice is either to proceed full speed to completion with Chevaline, or do nothing. To do nothing, and simply keep the present unimproved Polaris system until it fell out of the water, would be taken as a signal by the US and the USSR that the UK was no longer a credible nuclear power, and was getting out of the nuclear deterrent business. Do you, S of S (Secretary of State for Defence), want to go down in history as the S of S who took the UK out of the nuclear deterrent business? If not, then you have no option but to instruct the navy to put its full weight behind the Chevaline programme.'

The very next day, Mr Mason ordered full speed ahead with Chevaline, and to make the order stick, he transferred the management of the project to the Navy.[515]

A VERY IMPRESSIVE PIECE OF KIT[516]

From 1965 until 1974 the UK had respected a self-imposed moratorium on nuclear testing following the successful development of the WE.177 warheads and the Polaris weapon. During that period Aldermaston went into research mode, including studies of the upcoming threats. It was during this period that the UK had very little to offer the United States under the 1958 Mutual Defence Agreement, and at that point the agreement almost died, as it relied on exchange to keep it going.

In 1974 the UK started testing again, and the intention was to develop a hardened warhead better able to cope with flash X-ray and neutron irradiation. The UK had to change its design very radically. The fission-based primary had to be smaller and narrower in order to pack around it the materials needed to protect it from incoming radiation. The heat shield had to be redesigned to cope with the X-ray problem. This work and its associated testing preoccupied Aldermaston in the years 1974–1976. The US assisted with this effort. For instance, the US granted the UK access to underground effects tests in Nevada; these required horizontal tunnels drilled into mountains with a smallish nuclear device at one end and an evacuated tube, mimicking the hard vacuum of space, running the length of the tunnel. Aldermaston scientists placed their samples and other bits and pieces at the other end of the evacuated tunnel to see how they would react in space to nuclear radiation.[517] This proved to be very helpful.

Leading defence civil servant Frank Panton has commented on the Polaris Improvement–Super Antelope–Chevaline work undertaken within defence science and engineering laboratories:

It was only due to the resourcefulness of *all* the Staff on Chevaline, and the risks we took in dealing with the contractors, that the government had a Chevaline Project to hand over to the Navy in 1975/76. Because of the secrecy, insufficient credit has been given to those who fought to keep Chevaline alive.' (Emphasis original.)[518]

In the end, the Chevaline warhead in its new RV was to become probably the hardest (i.e. most radiation-resistant) nuclear weapon that anybody had ever deployed.[519] However even that would not be good enough unless the UK was able to force the Soviets into a numbers game concerning a concept known as the 'exchange ratio'. The exchange ratio is the number of Galosh missiles it takes to intercept all the warheads on one Polaris missile. For the small British Polaris force the ratio was expressed as a number of Galosh missiles compared to one Polaris missile, and the challenge for the Chevaline project was to make that ratio as large as possible. Clearly if one Galosh could take out an entire missile payload, then the ratio would be 1:1. If the British had 16 missiles from a single submarine on patrol and the Soviets had 100 Galosh missiles (as the British feared they might) then with an exchange ratio of 1:1 the Soviets would have 84 defensive missiles left, after having intercepted the entire British strategic deterrent. A naïve calculation based on such numbers indicates that for British comfort the exchange ratio would need to be at least 7:1 – that is, the Soviets should be required to expend at least seven Galosh missiles in order to be sure of intercepting the threat from one Polaris missile.

But for Polaris A3T the ratio was the unacceptable figure of 1:1 – it was entirely possible that one Galosh missile could effectively intercept a Polaris A3T with all three of its warheads.

In order to achieve a high exchange ratio, the Polaris front end would need to be completely re-engineered. This would be Chevaline – Britain's nuclear weapons spacecraft.

The Chevaline front end consisted of a motoring penetration aid carrier, called a 'PAC'. The designers at Farnborough and Aldermaston removed the three warheads from the standard Polaris package and replaced them by a unique device – the Chevaline PAC. The testing of the PAC was to be a major undertaking and something, in the spirit of deterrence, that would need to be seen and understood by the Soviet Union. The testing programme necessitated the development of a rather special British rocket system known as 'Falstaff'. There are reports of more than 4000 Falstaff launches from Woomera, Australia, in the period 1969–1979.[520] Falstaff was key to the Chevaline programme, and it made use of the British Stonechat II solid-fuelled rocket design motor.[521] Solid rocket technology was well suited to large production runs and the very large numbers of launches that Chevaline development and testing would require.

Just as Galosh was designed to fight nuclear battles in space, so was the Chevaline weapon system designed to perform its most crucial tasks in space. Once the Chevaline-equipped Polaris missile left the upper atmosphere the PAC would separate from the missile and carefully orient itself. The task for the Chevaline spacecraft is to form in space a very long 'threat tube' where the entire tube can be expected to fall to a single target. The detailed composition of the Chevaline threat tube remains a sensitive matter, but it is known to have relied heavily on decoys. Jeremy Stocker has reported that the Chevaline decoys came in two types 'hard' and 'soft'.[522] The hard decoys were such that the X-rays from a Galosh detonation would not damage them.

The core capability of Chevaline was that it was able to fill a long threat tube with convincing radar echoes. Some of the echoes would be from the decoys and some from the hardened weapons themselves. Kate Pyne has suggested that the Aldermaston and Farnborough engineers were particularly clever in planning the nature of the threat and the use of decoys. She attributed the cleverness to an Aldermaston expert named Sid Barker, who served on the Polaris Re-Entry Systems Study Group.[523] Some of the key issues and concerns of the time were revealed by Richard Garwin and Hans Bethe in their March 1968 article published in *Scientific American*.[524]

If ever used, the Chevaline system would have deployed its penetration aid carrier in space. The PAC would motor in space for two to three minutes, releasing two real warheads at separate and essentially random points in its long threat tube.[525] Once its job was done the PAC would exit, leaving behind it the threat tube which when fully deployed could stretch between 100 and 200 miles.[526] The Chevaline PAC really was a spacecraft. The threat tube would be full of radar objects, and somewhere within it would be two real warheads. The Chevaline system had only two warheads per Polaris missile in place of the original three. This was because of the need to avoid any major increase in the weight of the missile front end. To have done otherwise would have reduced the range of the missile to unacceptable levels.

Kate Pyne has described the origins of this British idea when she reported:

> In early April 1968, AWRE [Aldermaston] staff paid a visit to the Polaris missile maker, Lockheed, to discuss ideas on Polaris improvement. ... One UK Polaris improvement scheme featured multiple ReBs [re-entry bodies] deployed from a maneuverable 'master dispenser system' or MDS. This had been 'designed' on the spot by the UK team, since Lockheed would only respond to specific proposals. The MDS would separate from the Polaris second stage, and accelerate along a prescribed path, dropping off ReBs as it went. A month later, Lockheed told the British that of the various options described by the UK team, only Antelope and the MDS were 'worthy of serious consideration'.[527]

The crews of the Moscow ABM system would have seen a very long threat tube coming at them, full of a large number of plausible objects. In principle there are two choices they might have made. The first option was termed 'shoot, look and shoot'. In this plan the Russians might have fired off one or two Galosh missiles and hope to 'blow away' all the decoys.[528] Then only the substantial re-entry vehicles would have shown themselves, and these could be have been hit with a second round. The problem that Chevaline could give to such a strategy was that its hard decoys would survive the first attack. Any Russian shoot, look and shoot plan would also have suffered a second problem. The first shot would have involved detonating many megatons of nuclear weapon in the exosphere, and that would disrupt the ionosphere such that the Russian target acquisition radars would not be able to see clearly.[529] The Moscow ABM personnel would then need to wait for the ionosphere to clear in order to look again in order to be able to target the missiles for the second shot. All this would take precious time, and by the time the ionosphere cleared it might be too late for a safe or effective second engagement given the very high yields involved.[530]

Aldermaston calculated that 'shoot-look-shoot'[531] simply would not work for the Russians, because of the different types of decoys available. The only other plan available to the Moscow ABM defenders would have been to seek to sterilise the whole threat tube. Because it is so long and full of credible objects, the Russians would need to expend significantly more than seven Galosh missiles to be sure of destroying both of the real hardened warheads hidden in the threat tube. This is how Chevaline achieved the necessary exchange ratio – and all of this was a unique British development, admittedly with some important assistance from the US under the 1958 Mutual Defence Agreement.[532] For example, the US, having given the Chevaline team early access to its nuclear effects testing facilities as mentioned above, subsequently assisted with achieving a UK warhead hard enough to work with Chevaline.[533]

We have repeatedly observed that the Cold War was a technological game of chess. The metaphor appears to be invoked in Garwin and Bethe's March 1968 *Scientific American* article.[534] For instance, they write: 'For purposes of discussion let us ask what responses a White side might make to various moves made by a Black side.' There then follows an extended discussion of hypothetical options and counter-options available to White and Black before concluding: 'it is considerably cheaper for White to provide more offensive capability than it is for Black to defend his people and industry against a concerted strike'.

Chevaline, like TSR2, was a truly remarkable British technological achievement. Chevaline restored the credibility of the UK deterrent, but it did so in complete invisibility. The Britain that mourned the loss of the TSR2 sadly knew almost nothing about the remarkable technical achievements of Chevaline.

The existence of Chevaline was first revealed by the British government in an announcement in Parliament by the defence secretary, Francis Pym, on 24 January 1980:

> The programme, which has the code-name Chevaline, is a very major and complex development of the missile front end, involving also changes to the fire control systems. The result will not be a MIRVed system, but it includes advanced penetration aids and the ability to manoeuvre the payload in space. The programme has been funded and managed entirely by the United Kingdom with the full co-operation of the United States Government, including the use of some of their facilities for trials and tests.[535]

It was remarkable that so little had been known publicly about the programme until then, although it has to be said that George Wigg had revealed a few ideas in his 1972 autobiography. He records:

> Ten years ago (1962) when the nation's money was being gambled on the Blue Streak project, the value of the Polaris missile-firing submarine was being called into question. Although it fired its sixteen missiles while under water the question arose: How long would it remain undetectable and invulnerable?

All this changed and, indeed, is still changing. The Polaris submarine, of which we have four armed with the A-3 (planned according to the Americans, to have a range of 2,500 nautical miles), is to remain equipped with a version of the A-3 specially designed to penetrate ballistic missile defences. In plain English, this implies that the Russians are almost certainly capable of destroying the original A-3 missile by the use of an anti-ballistic missile.[536]

Of course, even without the threat posed by the Galosh system, the end would come eventually for Polaris, Chevaline and all subsonic re-entry-based deterrents aiming to achieve the Moscow Criterion when, and if, the Soviet Union managed to develop a very fast short-range interceptor missile able to attack incoming ballistic missiles in the atmospheric re-entry stage. The fear was that the Soviet Union would acquire an equivalent of the US Sprint system, and hence the possible Soviet challenge was known as 'sprintski' in British defence circles. The successor to Chevaline was the Trident II D5 system, acquired for Britain during the Conservative governments of prime ministers Margaret Thatcher and John Major. Trident is designed to beat sprintski technology by the use of MIRVed re-entry vehicles. The Russians decided to develop a sprintski capacity in 1978, achieving the capability in the 1990s.[537] The UK acquired its first Trident submarine, HMS *Vanguard*, in 1994, and Polaris-Chevaline was withdrawn from service in 1996.

SERIOUS MONEY

In the context of the long technological race with the Soviet Union, one can appreciate the competing ideas in play during the weak government of Sir Alec Douglas-Home (October 1963–October 1964). TSR2 was evolving from a mere tactical weapons system into something with the potential to become a strategic nuclear weapons system. As such, it represented the only truly competitive way in which the Royal Air Force might preserve serious nuclear weapons capability with manned bombers after the retirement of the V-force, whose role was looking ever more difficult.

While if taken into service TSR2 would have been expensive, the Chevaline Polaris upgrade programme was also expensive. The Conservative defence secretary (1981–1983) in Margaret Thatcher's government was Sir John Nott, and he is reported to have said, when in office, that the cost of Chevaline had 'gone bananas'.[538] As R.L. Dommett points out, a key difficulty in assessing the costs of Chevaline relates to the very high rates of domestic UK inflation in the crucial R&D period when the work was led by Aldermaston and Farnborough.[539] General retail inflation exceeded 24 per cent in 1975, and in technical areas prices were rising at perhaps twice that rate. It is unsurprising therefore that the costs of Chevaline were higher than first predicted.

Many involved in the Chevaline programme were upset and angry about the 1982 findings of the Public Accounts Committee.[540] Frank Panton was assistant chief scientific adviser (nuclear) to the Ministry of Defence in 1969 to 1975, and in the period 1972–1975 he had responsibility for oversight of the Chevaline programme. He wrote to Sir Frank Cooper, permanent secretary of the MoD, in 1982 to comment on the recent PAC report:

> I cannot accept the criticism in the report, and I refute any imputation it may have for my own conduct and performance, and for those under me during those years. As a serving civil servant I am obviously, severely restricted in what I can do openly to defend myself, and I am taking the only course which seems open to me at the present time; to put my views on record to you.
>
> It was simply not possible before 1975 to manage the project in any concerted fashion. … It would obviously have been better to have set up a full-time integrated project management, vested with full technical managerial authority, but lack of decision by successive governments made that quite impossible to achieve. Nor in the drip feed, hand to mouth, three to six month instalment funding was it ever possible to introduce a Prime contractor into the management scheme. Management was made all the more difficult by the opposition of the Navy to the project. … When the project was confirmed in 1975 my hand-over report quite clearly shows non-nuclear parts of the project up to two years behind the nuclear.

The decisions surrounding the Polaris improvement studies and Chevaline were hugely difficult for Labour party politicians. The party, including the parliamentary party and much of the Cabinet, were firmly opposed to nuclear weapons, and took the view that the UK should unilaterally withdraw from the nuclear weapons club. Such a policy later appeared in the party 1983 election manifesto, acerbically dubbed by Gerald Kaufman as 'the longest suicide note in history'. For Labour politicians any decision to invest in, and to strengthen, the Polaris system would be an extremely difficult step. The MoD civil servants and the Aldermaston scientists were sometimes annoyed by these realities, and they were especially upset with the 1982 Public Accounts Committee report which, prepared by members of Parliament, failed to stress these aspects or to focus their investigations on their parliamentary colleagues. Sir Frank Cooper, in his 2 June 1982 reply to Frank Panton, said:

> I understand very well your concern over the terms of the report. … I hope you will agree that our evidence makes quite clear that it is wrong to doubt the dedication of those involved in the project in its early period or to decry their efforts. Indeed, far from the PAC's criticism being directed at the 'nuclear scientists', I am clear that, whether well founded or not, their criticism is directed at the MOD's management as a whole. What the PAC failed to do was to direct their criticism at the shilly-shallying of successive governments and my own belief is that they were determined to do so – this was apparent too in their criticism of officials (particularly me) in failing to disclose costs, which is a matter for ministers.[541]

The late Ken Johnston, a senior technical expert at the Atomic Weapons Establishment at Aldermaston in Berkshire, kindly shared his insights into the Chevaline programme during the research for this book. He allowed me to appreciate the scale of the invisible success of Chevaline that followed the highly visible cancellation of the TSR2. Johnston observed, regarding the value for money provided by Chevaline for the UK in the Cold War:

> Expenditure of £1Bn by the UK resulted in providing the capability to penetrate and defeat a vast defensive system which probably cost in the region of £50 Bn – an even better 'exchange ratio'! (The figure of £50 Bn was estimated by PGEF Jones at the time: I have no idea how he derived the figure, but the sheer scale of the Radars, missiles, and associated warheads, and battle management software made it entirely plausible.)'

The Moscow ABM was never intended to block a US attack; it could not conceivably have done that. It was more reasonably established to protect the Russian heartland from ballistic missile attack by France, the UK or even China. Perhaps the Russians believed that the United States was unlikely to allow a European nuclear conflict to tip from the tactical to the strategic, but they could not be so confident in connection with France and the UK, whose options in a major European war would present the British or French with limited flexibility and major strategic risks.

THE COLD WAR CHESS GAME

We have considered a Cold War story. The development and cancellation of the TSR2 and the successful development of Chevaline are not best understood as preparations for a war – they were the war itself. Technology moved so fast. Project initiation and project cancellation were a central part of the military tactics of the Cold War. Such decisions were the movement of pieces on a chess board. Cancelling one project allowed another to be viable: a technology-based Cold War gambit would open up another possibility through which the opponent's position might be challenged more effectively. One occasionally encounters bemusement as to why Cold War planners made weapon systems operational while it seems they were clearly ineffective or even dangerous to those that might be asked to use them. Garwin and Bethe offer some thoughts relevant to such considerations: 'An operational system is not threatened by a system that is still in development; the threat is not real until the new system is in fact deployed, shaken down and fully operative.'[542] They added later: 'One must distinguish clearly between the *possibility* of development and the development itself, and similarly between development and actual operation.' These observations naturally lead one to observe that the advice to be clear about realities rather than perceptions is a sign of the power of perceived realities. There is a strong incentive for a player in the Cold War chess game to signal capabilities early, and before they truly exist. It brings to mind an old aphorism about deterrence:

> In order to secure local governmental support for nuclear deterrence development there needs to be a 90% certainty that the weapons can be delivered successfully. However to deter the targeted adversary one need only achieve a 10% chance of success – such is the destructive potential of nuclear weapons.

Misperceptions and bluff were part of the Cold War chess game, but so is, of course, real technological innovation.

It seems clear that there were indeed compelling budgetary and technical reasons to cancel TSR2 in the spring of 1965. Perhaps when Denis Healey entered government in early 1964 he had already started to form the view that concerning the tasks for which the TSR2 had been designed the UK would need to keep an eye on European needs (which might be manageable with the Blackburn Buccaneer) and to keep a separate eye on East of Suez, where the F-111 would be helpful if they were to maintain defence commitments so far from home. Healey served Britain well when he retained the F-111 option at no cost to the taxpayer.[543] The alternative of continuing the TSR2 just in case would have been a very expensive and risky prospect indeed.

From the perspective of the mid-1960s two issues could be seen on the horizon: first, Britain was to receive a state-of-the-art submarine-launched nuclear deterrent, greatly reducing the need for advanced RAF nuclear strike capability and eliminating any RAF need to satisfy the Moscow Criterion; and second, Britain would need to withdraw from its extensive commitments East of Suez. As Guy Finch has observed, the British responsibilities East of Suez represented the theatres of possible conflict in which the TSR2 (or F-111) would have been hugely valuable.[544] Denis Healey devotes a chapter of his autobiography to the East of Suez decision, and he opens it with the words:

> When I took over the Defence Ministry in 1964 Britain had more troops East of Suez than in Germany … . All these bases were necessary because of our political commitments – our responsibility for defending our dependent territories or our treaty obligations to other sovereign states such as Kuwait or Malaysia or Australia. We could not give them up until our colonies had become independent or we had renegotiated our treaties with our allies.[545]

It seems probable that Denis Healey had held an ambition to reduce the East of Suez commitments from his earliest days in office, and perhaps even before. He was clearly aware of the scale of that military and diplomatic challenge, and he must have recognised the possibility that he might fail. In the event he successfully achieved the policy shift for British withdrawal from 1968 to 1969, and the F-111K option was never needed. As also mentioned in Chapter 8, Denis Healey denied early intentions for an East of Suez withdrawal. He records in his autobiography:

> On this first visit to Canberra [February 1966] I still believed it was right and possible for to stay East of Suez. I told the National Press Club, 'We intend to remain, and shall

remain, fully capable of carrying out all the commitments we have at the present time, including those in the Far East, the middle east and in Africa and other parts of the world. We do intend to remain in the military sense a world power.'[546]

Such words are, however, not entirely inconsistent with the notion that Healey already had the idea that Britain might be able to extricate itself from its East of Suez commitments. Healey looks back on the East of Suez decision, and notes:

> In Britain itself, the more common criticism nowadays is that we were too slow to recognise the facts, and should have announced our intention to withdraw immediately we took office in 1964. That would have been impossible. Our troops were fighting in both South Arabia and Borneo. Four independent Commonwealth countries were fighting with us during Confrontation. Even if we had intended to go, we could not have revealed our intention without the consent of our partners.[547]

Denis Healey was a shrewd tactician. He played the Cold War chess game well. In the spring of 1965 he leveraged the TSR2 investment into a remarkable no-cost option for the UK on a similar aircraft, the F-111. The UK could access that aircraft for the 1970s in the event that either it retained its commitments East of Suez or perhaps if there were to have been a serious problem with UK access to Polaris. As we have seen, there were already clues that there could be a serious problem with Polaris, but in the event those issues would eventually be resolved via the Chevaline upgrade. As we have seen, in the section 'Forced to Choose', the economic realities finally caught up with Denis Healey on 5 January 1968; his dilemma was the choice between his aircraft option or a highly capable independent British nuclear deterrent in the form of an upgraded Polaris system. The choice had to be made – and he made it. He chose Polaris and the journey to Chevaline. In a European or NATO context at least, the RAF would preserve some level of nuclear strike capability via the Buccaneer. Healey later made clear that the Buccaneer choice should have been made from the start.

In the mid-1960s, defence thinking was still extremely fragmented, with fierce rivalries between the Royal Air Force, the Royal Navy and the Army. For those involved in air force test work the bigger picture, visible to Healey in Whitehall, would not have been apparent. Hence Beamont was puzzled and bemused by the decisions he had observed. It is my intention, however, to reveal that even Roland Beamont's understanding of the issues surrounding his beloved TSR2 project was incomplete. Based on what he could see, he expressed strong opinions, in 1968 he wrote:

> At the time of the election of the 1964 Labour Government, and subsequently at the end of that year, at the reprieve in January 1965 and right up to the point of cancellation two months before the promised review date, it had been apparent to people closely concerned with the development of this aircraft that the programme was being endangered by lack of knowledge of the relevant facts at Government level,

or else by some motivation which took no account of the military and technological issues involved.

Perhaps these matters will never come clearly into the open, but it was a strange experience to visit the Ministry of Defence regularly between flights from January to April 1965, and to see in the offices of the Operational Requirements Branch men whom I had known and worked with over twenty-five years of service flying and test flying for the Service- people who I knew as personal friends- now talking riddles without frankness and clearly covering up for something which I could never really reach the bottom of.[548]

Healey was clearly struggling with a British military that was not yet joined up, despite key steps in 1964 which combined the Admiralty, the War Office and the Air Ministry into the Ministry of Defence.[549] The real achievement of truly joined-up defence planning would come much later with the abolition of separate Army, Air Force and Navy ministers in favour of the present position of armed forces minister.

Whatever the details of policy making, it is clear with hindsight that the United Kingdom in the 1970s had the resources to follow only one of two paths: TSR2/F-111 or Chevaline. The UK took the latter path, strengthened Polaris, and retained a strong nuclear deterrent against potential Soviet aggression. This was a powerful and important choice. In my opinion that importance far outweighs the real, and understandable, nostalgia one sees surrounding the history of the TSR2.

The decision in favour of Polaris-Chevaline also had consequences concerning the preservation and strengthening of British capabilities in military science and technology, but – unlike the very visible exploits of the supersonic test pilots – this would all be done in near total secrecy. If you mention Chevaline today, even those people familiar with the term struggle to associate an image with the phrase. It is a technology without iconography. Perhaps the best they can do is to imagine a Polaris A3 missile launching from a submarine. The TSR2 alternative, however, would have been so very different: TSR2 was visible, it was iconic and it was British. We may find ourselves imagining a path that was not followed, but in so doing it is important to reflect on the path that actually was followed.

Favouring the Royal Navy submarines over the Royal Air Force low-flying bombers may have been a shrewd move in defence policy terms, but as we shall see it had the potential to affect the very sense of national identity. While the UK did so much in secret (on Chevaline and other things), it created a society that thought it couldn't do difficult mechanical things any more, when the reality was far more nuanced and subtle. Over the last 50 years the UK has become simultaneously nostalgic and curious about the TSR2. A popular model manufacturer has released several versions of a TSR2 model aircraft over the years. In contrast very few people knew of the story of Chevaline, and even fewer had any sense of what it looked like. TSR2 was the thing that people remembered. British engineering excellence subverted by politics.

Early in this book we considered the relationship of Cold War aviation technology with popular culture and fine art. The TSR2 was clearly well known to aviation British enthusiasts and the popular press, but it never truly achieved the status of fine art object. The great rival to the TSR2, the General Dynamics F-111, arguably achieved that status, a status that comes from being presented in contemporary art galleries. Pop artist James Rosenquist chose the F-111 for a central role in his artistic opposition to the Vietnam War.

Rosenquist has described his giant four-part painting. His F-111 is 'flying through the flak of consumer society to question the collusion between the Vietnam death machine, consumerism, the media, and advertising'.[550] Back in the UK, shrouded by its cloak of secrecy, Chevaline would cleverly avoid all that.

CHAPTER ELEVEN – HISTORY REPEATS

The optimist proclaims that we live in the best of all possible worlds;
and the pessimist fears this is true.

James Branch Cabell

Why are stories from the 1960s relevant today? The stories of moves in the Cold War technological chess game have at least two contemporary resonances. The first is in the domain of industrial policy, as in recent years Britain has heard political rhetoric recommending a 'rebalancing of the economy'. The second area lies in strategic defence, as the UK moves to meet the challenge of 'Trident replacement'. The 2010–2015 coalition government postponed the Trident replacement decision, giving Britons an opportunity to ask: what is Trident for? What exactly is Trident? And … is there a better alternative? Various ideas were proposed, but the central notion of continuous at-sea deterrence delivered by submarine-launched ballistic missiles endured, and in the post-Brexit-referendum turmoil the new prime minister, Theresa May, moved quickly to win parliamentary approval for the new weapons system comprising, at its heart, four enormous new Dreadnought class submarines.

Despite the decision, the debate continues. Nuclear weapons are an important aspect of British national life. Something we do not generally see, but something we should never ignore. It a widely held view in UK defence circles that if the UK did not have the Bomb, we would surely not develop it now. The reality is that we do have the Bomb, and we have worked very hard over more than 60 years to ensure that we do, and that it presents the greatest retaliatory threat of which our small island might be capable.

For many people the question never gets beyond whether or not to have the Bomb. Arguably government has supported such absolutist consideration of the issues; too often the debate oscillates between such weapons being absolutely essential in the form recommended by government, or alternatively being absolutely immoral and to be completely renounced at the earliest possible opportunity. One can, however, consider a middle ground: a new more flexible nuclear deterrent, better suited to current strategic interests – and, importantly, suitable for gradual downscaling as a move towards disarmament. It is important to ask what the UK deterrent is, and why it exists.

By its very nature a nuclear weapons system is associated with high levels of secrecy. As a consequence, key decisions tend to be made by relatively small groups of similar people talking amongst themselves. The issues at stake, however, are profound and expensive. As such, they demand more open public debate.

My position as an academic without access to classified defence material allows me to comment relatively freely, but with the risk that my understanding of the issues is incomplete or even erroneous. To those that know the inner truths of these topics, and who might disagree with the ideas presented here, I simply ask that they put their ideas, in an appropriate form, into the public discourse so that the British people have a better chance of informed decision making.

ORIGINS

The origins of the issues underpinning today's Trident replacement process date back, as we have seen, to the mid-1960s. Then, the balance of Britain's nuclear defence effort was shifting away from the Royal Air Force and towards the Royal Navy. The mighty Avro Vulcan bombers, with their giant delta wings and their Blue Steel missiles made by the British Aircraft Corporation, had no future. The future of nuclear weaponry was to be hidden below the sea. The Resolution class submarines carrying Polaris missiles would be the true guarantors of British security in the late 20th century. Slowly our submarine-based nuclear missiles shifted from being a part of the deterrent to being the deterrent. Today the notion of the British nuclear deterrent has become synonymous with Trident, the successor to Polaris, and its very British upgrade, Chevaline.

I am not the first to argue that the British public deserves to understand better the issues inherent in the Trident replacement. Dr Lord (David) Owen, foreign secretary from 1977 to 1979, has made similar calls. He draws inspiration for his recommendations from his involvement in nuclear weapons policy at the time of the development of the Chevaline system and the choices concerning its successor. He advances his views forcefully and persuasively in his 2010 book *Nuclear Papers*,[551] and he has kindly provided the foreword to this book.

REPLACE TRIDENT WITH TRIDENT?

The current Trident force provides for Continuous At Sea Deterrence (CASD), using a fleet of four Vanguard class submarines each technically capable of carrying 16 Trident II D5 ballistic missiles, each with MIRV capability. The Non-Proliferation Treaty puts pressure on the UK to negotiate towards disarmament. Perhaps as a consequence of such considerations, and despite the great capability of the Trident system, the British Trident force was initially deployed with only around 48 warheads per submarine. Of the four submarines, at least one would always be at sea and ready. This was the same number of submarines, the same philosophy of readiness, and arguably the same level of deployed naval nuclear weaponry, as the Polaris system had had back in the 1970s. In the 2010 Strategic Defence and Security Review it was declared that the Trident figure would be reduced to 40 deployed warheads per submarine.

The Trident II D5 missile with its full US-developed MIRV capability has since 1994 represented a significant enhancement to UK offensive capability beyond the earlier UK-developed threat-tube approach of Chevaline. Each MIRV and its enclosed warhead is presumed to be capable of rapid lateral movements, avoiding short-range high-speed terminal defence missiles (see the discussion of Soviet 'sprintski' capacity in Chapter 10). One can probably assume that Trident D5 is able to evade the older threats posed by slow-moving nuclear-tipped interceptors of the Galosh type, and which had led to the development of Chevaline warhead delivery system. Chevaline had been arguably the most impressive British technology project of the late 20th century, while simultaneously perhaps the least known.

OTHER OPTIONS

In recent years UK commentators and experts have discussed various options by which the cost of Trident replacement might be reduced. One idea has been to drop entirely the notion of CASD, which, as mentioned earlier, currently requires that at all times a minimum of one of the four UK nuclear-powered ballistic missile submarines is on operational patrol. With echoes of a 1960s Labour government decision to reduce the Polaris force from five to four submarines, the Labour government of Gordon Brown in 2009 considered the possibility of reducing the Trident replacement fleet to just three vessels while maintaining CASD. However, in February 2011 coalition government defence secretary Liam Fox advised that in the opinion of his department four submarines would be required for assured CASD capability.

Nick Ritchie, lecturer in international security at the University of York, and Paul Ingram, executive director of the British–American Security Information Council, have commented on options for Trident replacement.[552] For instance, one proposal considered by Ritchie has been an 'Emergency Alert' posture without CASD; the plan would be to put a vessel to sea at short notice as a crisis developed.[553] While it seems probable that any attack that the British deterrent is capable of deterring might reasonably be expected to result from an escalation of tensions over several weeks, the act of putting a Trident-equipped submarine to sea could itself be escalatory in a crisis. It is noteworthy that in the Cuba crisis of 1962 the Royal Air Force strategic nuclear bombers were not dispersed from its home bases, as had been planned for the lead-up to a crisis. Presumably this was as a consequence of a concern regarding the signals that such an act would send at a moment of extreme tension.

The replacement, in essence, of Trident with Trident would, or will, necessarily involve the construction of a new fleet of submarines known in the jargon as Ship Submersible, Ballistic missile, Nuclear-powered vessels, or 'SSBNs'. The need for new SSBN submarines is driven by the limited hull life of today's Vanguard class SSBN vessels which carry the Trident missiles. On 18 July 2016 Parliament voted by a majority of 35 to renew the nuclear deterrent.

One issue at the heart of the Trident replacement decision related to the nuclear propulsion system to be used. These issues, previously discussed only among experts, have started to be published in the mainstream press. It has long been reported that the first British submarine propulsion reactor system was termed 'PWR1'. The acronym PWR corresponds to Pressurised Water Reactor, the world's most common type of nuclear power reactor and a technology originally developed in America for naval purposes. The UK PWR1 system was based heavily on US Westinghouse ideas and saw service with the Valiant, Resolution, Churchill, Swiftsure and Trafalgar class submarines. The current Trident SSBNs and the recently deployed Astute class hunter killer submarines both used variants of a second design known as PWR2. The PWR2 has proved to be somewhat controversial, having been assessed by the Ministry of Defence's senior nuclear safety regulator, Commodore Andrew McFarlane, as being wanting in safety terms; the concerns centring on a possible major loss of reactor coolant accident.[554] Such an accident scenario is perhaps not entirely dissimilar to the problems encountered at the Fukushima-Daiichi nuclear power plant following the north-east Japan earthquake and tsunami of 11 March 2011. However, given that the mechanical capabilities and the resilience to attack of Royal Navy submarines are rightly not public knowledge, the precise basis and the true importance of Commodore McFarlane's concerns are impossible for us to assess. That said, in April 2011 the tabloid press reported on a Ministry of Defence blunder which had briefly made classified PWR2 safety issues available for all to see: the newspapers reported that the PWR2 system could be vulnerable to the wilful acts of a lone sailor intent on causing harm. Previously such a scenario would have appeared somewhat hypothetical, but the murder that same month of one HMS *Astute* submariner by another put the risks of insider threats into stark focus.[555]

Initial government assessment had pointed to three possible reactor options for the Trident-replacement SSBNs. Noting the concerns with the PWR2 design, one option had been a slight modification of that system, as deployed in the Astute class hunter killer submarines. Another option was to enhance that design to create a variant, PWR2b, with significant benefits in platform safety and survivability. A third option was to build upon US experience, and develop a wholly new reactor to be known as PWR3. After much deliberation the MoD selected the PWR3 option for the new Dreadnought class boats – a major step indeed.[556]

In considering subsystem costs (such as the propulsion reactor) it is important to remember that the Trident nuclear weapons system is not just a fleet of four submarines. It is an entire military–industrial complex. It involves ports, dockyards, missiles, warheads, training establishments and much more. These capabilities have been built up over many decades in support of the SSBN force, and any move away from such a basis for the deterrent could itself be very disruptive and potentially expensive. Despite these realities, the issue of a cruise missile deterrent has repeatedly been suggested.

A CRUISE MISSILE DETERRENT?

The 21st-century version of a cruise missile-based deterrent might reasonably be expected to contain certain elements. The idea was considered during the 2010–2015 coalition government. One suggestion was that such missiles might be launched from vessels very similar to the Astute class hunter killers. The costs of extending the current production run of seven Astute class vessels might have, at least initially, been less than that associated with building a small fleet of new next-generation Dreadnought SSBNs. If the UK were to deploy variants of Astute in a strategic and potentially offensive nuclear role, then various new factors would come into play. First the patrol areas of the new offensive vessels would be different from those of the current Astute class hunter killers, and this might motivate some design differences. One could expect that there might be a greater need to be able to break through Arctic ice than is the case for the hunter killer force. The offensive variant would presumably also face greater pressure for silent running and extended slow-running.

It is important to note that in some ways a modified strategic-offensive Astute might in some ways be a simpler vessel than today's version. For instance, it seems unlikely that the offensive version of Astute would ever need to deploy special forces, and hence there would be no need for the hunter killer Astute's 'dry deck shelter' capability.[557]

When thinking of cruise-missile-launched nuclear weapons, modification of Astute's capabilities is not the only possibility. Now that the decision to build four new Dreadnought SSBNs has been made, it would be conceivable that these could be set up so as to launch cruise missiles vertically rather than rely on ballistic systems similar to that of the Trident D5. The scenarios in which such a choice might make sense are, however, rather hard to anticipate.

RETURN TO THE ROYAL AIR FORCE?

Beyond the enhancement of Astute submarines, in order to maximise force flexibility it might be beneficial to return part of the nuclear deterrent to the Royal Air Force, from whom such responsibilities were removed in 1998. One possibility would be to develop a nuclear-tipped version of the small Storm Shadow cruise missile used so effectively by RAF aircraft in the 2011 Libya crisis. Consideration of a nuclear version of Storm Shadow would take defence thinking back more than 20 years to the earliest days of that programme.

The operational version of the Eurofighter Typhoon is a single-seat aircraft. If such an aircraft from the RAF were to be permitted to carry nuclear weapons it would be a rare example of UK operational nuclear weapons deployed on a single-seat aircraft, although other NATO air forces have done so. Previous UK single-crew nuclear weapons experience is limited to the Jaguar fighter-bomber and the small Wasp helicopter, which needed to go down to one crew member to take the weight of the WE.177 weapon. Procedurally, for these aircraft 'take-off 'equated to 'launch' in nuclear weapons policy. That is not the same with other aircraft, where one crew member readies (arms) the weapon in the air while the other retains fire control. In principle, single-crew operation brings with it greater risks, requiring special management.

Generally, the larger the number of platforms with nuclear weapons the greater the risk of an accident, or the occurrence of other problems. Despite well-developed systems and procedures, problems do still occur. On 30 August 2007 a US B52 bomber carrying six nuclear-tipped cruise missiles flew across the United States from Minot Air Force Base in North Dakota to Barksdale Air Force Base in Louisiana. The aircraft had not been authorised to carry nuclear weapons. This incident represented one of the most significant breaches of nuclear military discipline in western military experience.

Importantly, developing a nuclear-tipped version of Storm Shadow for Eurofighter Typhoon and for the Royal Navy Tomahawk cruise missiles would presumably bring with it the need for the UK to develop a new nuclear warhead – not a small task.

Britain first considered issues of submarine-based nuclear deterrence in the 1960s, and then again in the late 1970s. Now we are considering the issues for a third time, but in a very different geopolitical and social context.

THE DUFF–MASON REPORT

The option of moving the UK nuclear deterrent to cruise missiles is known to have received consideration as far back as the late 1970s as part of the British government process which led it to seek Trident as a replacement for Polaris-Chevaline. At the heart of the process was a report in 1978 by Sir Anthony Duff and Professor Ronald Mason, now known as the Duff–Mason Report. In 2006 Part I of the report was located in the UK National Archives, from where it was briefly publicly available before being hastily removed. It was later returned to public viewing in a heavily redacted form. In 2009 more papers were released, again in redacted form.

Lord Owen has been a prominent voice calling on the UK government to release more of the 1978 Duff–Mason Report. The report considered UK nuclear deterrent options going forward into the 1980s. One option considered was the construction of dedicated cruise missile carrying submarines. Owen writes that at the time the cruise missile option was considered to be much less effective than the Trident alternative, and no cheaper. Owen adds, however, that the cruise missile option never had any serious adherents in the late 1970s. More recently, in the years of policy development for the successor to the original UK Trident system, and what is now known as the Dreadnought programme, Lord Owen reprised the idea of a submarine-launched cruise missile alternative to a ballistic-missile-based deterrent.[558]

MOSCOW CRITERION REDUX

During the Cold War the dominant and most difficult goal of British nuclear strategic forces had been the ability credibly to threaten Moscow and its hinterland so as to render key places within the zone unusable for a minimum of several months: the Moscow Criterion. It is important because arguably for decades the region around Moscow was, and perhaps is, the most heavily defended place on the planet. For Britain in the second half of the Cold War, it would have been the hardest target to hit by far. The UK wanted, and perhaps still wants, to *be able to* hit it and destroy it.

Looking back, the Moscow Criterion emerged in the years after the Cuban Missile Crisis. It was a product of the Cold War that ended in 1991. The Chevaline system was developed at great cost and in total secrecy to preserve (or perhaps restore) the Moscow Criterion after Polaris had lost, or was about to lose, the capability to deliver that level of threat. Following Chevaline, the Trident system further preserved these British capabilities. One might assume that this remains a goal for an upgraded replacement of Trident with the new Dreadnought class submarines.

It seems probable that a British system relying on nuclear-tipped cruise missiles launched from either hunter killer submarines and/or aircraft would not with certainty preserve Moscow Criterion capability. Such a clear reduction in capability might, however, bring with it several benefits.

John Ainslee of the Campaign for Nuclear Disarmament, has pointed out that the Duff–Mason report considered three groups of options. The first was essentially the Moscow Criterion; option two involved lesser damage to Moscow and to one other Soviet city. Importantly two forms of a third option were presented in the report, which, using the terminology of the day, might be summarised respectively as 'attacks on ten cities' and '30 bangs in 30 places'. It is the attacks on ten cities sub-option which would appear to be achievable via a cruise missile-based capability. Importantly the Duff–Mason report concluded: 'Option 1 would provide greater certainty of deterrence; but we believe that any one of them would be adequate.' Despite option 3 being adequate as a deterrent, option 1 would appear to have been selected, leading to Trident and presumably preserving the Moscow Criterion in British policy, perhaps even up to the present. If option 3 might reasonably have formed the basis of a deterrent for the 1980s, then it seems reasonable to infer that it might still represent a sufficient deterrent today. That said, of course, one might forcefully argue that the British nuclear deterrent is not simply intended to deter the Russian Federation but rather any power that might threaten the existence of the United Kingdom. However, the risk that an emergent nuclear power might attain the missile defence capabilities of the former Soviet Union, and hence be a harder target than Moscow, also appears to feel somewhat unlikely. As regards the Moscow Criterion, Ken Johnston remarked:

> All the UK ever wanted to do was to be able to threaten unacceptable damage. We couldn't deploy a force that would destroy the Soviet Union, but as an independent

deterrent the Duff Mason criterion, … was basically that you had to hold a proportion of the things that the Soviets held dear at threat, and that threat had to be credible. And all that Chevaline did was it made it very credible until such time as we got Trident.

MOVING TO A WORLD WITHOUT NUCLEAR WEAPONS

In the United States four prominent statesmen known affectionately as the four horsemen (of the apocalypse) – George Schultz, William Perry, Henry Kissinger and Sam Nunn – have argued repeatedly that the nuclear defence doctrine of Mutually Assured Destruction no longer effectively militates against the threat of the use of a nuclear weapon, and that there is therefore a pressing need to move towards a world free of nuclear weapons.[559] A similar cautionary call was made by prominent British statesmen Douglas Hurd, Malcolm Rifkind, George Robertson and David Owen in a 30 June 2008 letter to *The Times* newspaper.

If the UK were to replace its nuclear weapons system with a more flexible, and perhaps somewhat less threatening, system, then perhaps this might reasonably be presented as an act of disarmament. It could also perhaps form a key part of a journey towards a world without nuclear weapons. Even if the system was incapable of achieving the Moscow Criterion, there is reason to believe that it would be capable of deterring the Russian Federation even in those unlikely scenarios where NATO support could not be relied upon. It also seems probable that any such new British system would be acceptable to NATO as part of Britain's contribution to the alliance. Lastly, if the intention were to move to a cruise-missile-based deterrent, then it might be possible to spread the UK nuclear weapons across a larger number of delivery systems than is envisioned for the four proposed Dreadnought class SSBNs. Notwithstanding the long range of Trident ballistic missiles, arguably Britain could even perhaps achieve a more global reach for its nuclear forces via a more dispersed approach. For many decades the UK has relied on an independent deterrent based on a single launch point. British strategic interests are increasingly global, and the issues surrounding Brexit put further pressure behind such ideas. In such future scenarios there could even be benefit in reversing the retrenchment of British capability associated with the 1967 decision to withdraw from all bases East of Suez except Hong Kong. That said one needs to be cautious in confronting any Brexit-era thoughts along the lines of resurrecting the notion of a Fourth British Empire (see Chapter 4). That idea was rightly rejected in the 1950s, and there are so many reasons that Britain's economic and security future cannot be tied to the notion of 'southern dominions'.

The official estimates of success probabilities associated with the Moscow Criterion rightly remain a sensitive matter, but it was not the British sense of success that mattered most; it was the Russian assessment of such things. We noted earlier that if a nuclear weapons system was going to frighten the potential enemy then it need only have a 10 per cent chance of working, but in order for that same weapons system to give comfort to the country paying for its development, then it needed to have a 90 per cent chance of working.

The equivalent thinking in today's world is perhaps difficult to assess, but as regards nuclear weapons it is probably still the case that perceptions can be at least as important as reality. Such considerations matter when asking, for instance, whether a cruise missile nuclear deterrent would be of sufficient capability to be frightening to a potential enemy.

In positing the possibility of a cruise missile-based deterrent it is important to recognise the controversy surrounding the prospect of hypersonic glide vehicles and hypersonic cruise missiles. The Rand Corporation in the United States has been warning of the dangers inherent if weapons systems with speeds above 5,000 kilometres per hour were to enter service.[560] The Rand researchers caution that the very high speeds of hypersonic technology could dangerously compress the timescales available for decision making, and lead the potential enemies to put their retaliatory capabilities on a hair trigger. The report further comments on the capabilities of many countries and observes that such technologies do not appear to be a priority for the UK Ministry of Defence. They report also reminds its readers, however, that the UK is home to a relevant cadre of expertise in respect of the dual use world of hypersonic technology, in the form of the company Reaction Engines, based at the Culham Science Centre in Oxfordshire, a place associated with the site of a major UK national laboratory famous for its researches into civil energy generation from nuclear fusion energy.

As things stand the UK is not moving towards a hypersonic cruise missile-based deterrent. Rather, the Dreadnought ambitions are for the CASD ballistic-missile technology described earlier. One problem, however, associated with CASD in a world seeking to eliminate nuclear weapons is the consequence that each UK Trident replacement SSBN would in some senses be strangely under-armed. Each of today's Trident submarines is capable of carrying approximately 160 independent re-entrant warheads, but as mentioned earlier only one quarter of this capability is deployed by the UK. No public transport company in Britain would buy new buses with the proviso that only a quarter of the possible seats would be ever fitted; someone, somewhere, would surely suggest the use of minibuses instead. One might also imagine buying a larger number of these smaller buses permitting service on a wider range of routes. I suggest a similar reassessment is now needed for UK nuclear weapons and the deterrent. Perhaps such thoughts are already shaping design choices for the Dreadnought-Trident replacement system.

WHERE ARE WE NOW?

Despite the end of the Cold War, strategic nuclear deterrence continues to be a chess game. The movement of pieces in the game is not a metaphor for actions that would be taken during a hot conflict; they are moves in the here and now. They are real actions. We live in a world where all sincerely hope none of these weapon systems will ever be used; as such, the actions are of development, deployment and with obsolescence, decommissioning. The greatest chess gambits relate to the preservation of options and the ability to make bold future moves.

A LITTLE-DISCUSSED IDEA

Looking across the various options for the future of the UK deterrent, none of them is overwhelmingly compelling. Arguably the Dreadnought class Trident replacement option is the least bad idea, whereas the torpedo tube-launched cruise missile option from a modified Astute vessel brings with it more problems than it solves. Any return of the deterrent to the RAF brings back memories of the V-force and Blue Streak, and appears to be so anachronistic as to be verging on risible. With that said, one must always be open to the possibility of radically different future scenarios and technological innovation. In such a space of ideas lies the possibility of 'transparency of the oceans'. As things stand, the laws of physics would appear to ensure that SSBNs can indeed hide in deep blue ocean water, but if for some reason there were to be a breakthrough rendering the oceans transparent, then the whole logical basis of the SSBN-based deterrent would be undermined. Some commentators have suggested that unmanned submersible vehicles, essentially maritime drones, might be part of such future risks. Indeed in 2015 an anti-submarine exercise entitled Operation Mongoose deployed NATO naval drones in the hunt for submarines for the first time.[561]

In considering the chosen Dreadnought approach, I fear that it could be incompatible with a later phased journey to a zero-nuclear-weapon Britain. As conventionally conceived, the British SSBN is already arguably at the lower limit of credible deterrence, and any reduction from current capability could render the whole Dreadnought approach worthless.

I suggest, however, that it might be possible to conceive of the new Dreadnought SSBNs in a new and more flexible way, akin in some ways to the US Ohio class vessels, sometimes known as 'SSGNs' – with the 'G' standing for 'guided'. A UK SSGN would have the same hull and propulsion system as that conceived for a conventional 'replace Trident with Trident' SSBN approach, but it might be designed with future flexibility in mind. For instance, if defence policy sought to reduce the extent, or capability, of UK nuclear forces, then some missile tubes might be reconfigured to permit the vertical launch of cruise missiles, whether nuclear or eventually conventional. Furthermore, from the outset the vessel might be designed such that while it might start life running slowly in blue water, hiding from all those seeking to find it, it might in later decades emerge from hiding to find a use in more littoral battle spaces, or even in diverse non-offensive future roles for which a large self-supporting Royal Navy vessel with global capabilities might be very valuable. It could be that decisions made in the current decade could preserve better some important potential future options. When thinking of future options, one can imagine a future flexible SSGN configuration for the new Dreadnought programme being converted relatively easily to play a role in prompt global strike. This would allow for a highly accurate, long-range and destructive retaliatory capability using conventional capabilities and without any recourse to nuclear weapons.

As concerns the use of an SSGN vessel as a major multi-purpose naval platform, from an early-21st-century perspective it might appear inconceivable to risk a multi-billion-pound SSBN in hostile coastal waters or to expose it deliberately to attack from hostile great powers, but at this stage we simply do not know what lies ahead. I merely suggest that the UK should position itself as a Non-Proliferation Treaty weapons state clearly capable, if circumstances should later permit, of moving credibly and carefully towards complete nuclear disarmament in a phased and secure way without rendering multi-billion pound investments immediately worthless.

While on a first impression the Dreadnought decision represents more of the same, the way ahead is likely to represent a repositioning of the United Kingdom's strategic defence bringing in the possibility of new purposes and capabilities. Such aspects are perhaps so sensitive that it will be decades before they can be understood and appreciated by the public. In the face of an uncertain future there could be benefit in designing for flexibility from the start.[562] In this way we might hope for a more flexible capability, better suited to meeting the widest range of future threats and challenges and, in addition, having the possibility of developing a deterrent better positioned for later progressive steps towards full nuclear disarmament. Such a more flexible and disaggregated deterrent might even mitigate the need to make difficult 'replacement' decisions every 25 years.

In considering the nuclear deterrent, we must prepare for unknown scenarios of the middle of the 21st century. Such thinking motivates my interest in system flexibility, and arguably the need to finally move away from an anachronistic Moscow Criterion-based mindset, if it still holds sway.

As Niels Bohr famously reminded us, '*Prediction is very difficult, especially about the future.*'

I note that flexibility might in the future require the design of a new nuclear weapon, and this is no trivial matter, especially in a world without nuclear weapons testing – but I venture it would not be as difficult as previous challenges presented by government to AWE Aldermaston. There is perhaps a certain irony in my recommendation that the UK should better position itself for phased nuclear disarmament while simultaneously remembering the need to be able to design and build a new nuclear weapon.

CHAPTER TWELVE – SELF-AWARENESS

George Kerevan, MP, asked the new Prime Minister: 'Can we cut to the chase? Is she personally prepared to authorise a nuclear strike that could kill a hundred thousand innocent men, women and children?'

Prime Minister Theresa May replied: 'Yes.'

House of Commons, 19 July 2016

Today in the early 21st century the challenges of industrial development parallel those of the mid-1960s, but the broader contexts are very different. One key difference has been the end of the Cold War. If someone from 1960 were to be transported to the present they would find our current defence and security challenges completely unfamiliar. They might have expected a world dominated by an adversarial conflict between two similarly matched great power blocks, differing in their secular visions for economic prosperity and social justice. But in contrast, our current multi-polar challenges are characterised by asymmetry, ambiguity and religious factors which would appear deeply disconcerting, perhaps even unbelievable, to a a time traveller from that era.

To a time traveller from the mid-19th century, however, our recent situation would appear to be a continuation of familiar battles, with small groups of beleaguered British infantry fighting off fanatical tribesmen in Afghanistan, fears of anti-western religious conflict in Sudan, and failing states in the horn of Africa. Such military challenges of the 21st century can read more like something from a Flashman novel by George MacDonald Fraser than Ian Fleming's *Thunderball*. In addition our time traveller would be familiar with the notion of multiple empires in collision. The clear rise of China and India, and the rather more uncertain emergence of Brazil, pose challenges to established dominance. Russia sees this evolving world and appears to like what it sees as it seeks to re-establish its own position after the perceived humiliations endured at the end of the Cold War. In some ways the modern world feels a bit like the year 1900, but this time with nuclear weapons (and indeed a very large number of nuclear weapons).

Away from the concerns of international relations and defence, lie the industrial policy questions we face in the early decades of the 21st century. Competitiveness and worries about jobs and growth in times of lingering austerity appear to mirror those of the early 1960s, but it is clear that the dominant challenges facing the world are different now. For example, worsening climate change is a major driver of future global risk and uncertainty, and the defence technology sector has arguably many capabilities which could usefully be reoriented to address such threats.

At the time of writing Britain feels particularly unsure about the future. The Brexit process is under way, but not complete. Perhaps Brexit will herald a complete re-alignment of British interests or perhaps very little will change. Interestingly the prospect of change has within it both hopes and fears. It seems that the UK could be part-way through a process as important as that described in this book – the retreat from Empire in the 1950s and 1960s. It is hard to know what the future will hold, but it now seems clear that the end of the Cold War was not 'the end of history', to use Francis Fukuyama's memorable phrase.[563]

In this book we have considered the history of nuclear weapons in a relatively small country with modest means and in turbulent times. It is hoped that by reflecting on stories from the past one can gain a better appreciation of the inter-relationship between the philosophy of nuclear deterrence and the practical realities facing policymakers. In Britain there is much debate about 'the deterrent', but there can be a somewhat unhelpful ambiguity to the debate: are we talking about the decision to have a deterrent, or are we talking about the choice of one particular deterrent? Both can be difficult questions. The answers to them can be altered as a consequence of externally changing circumstances. That reality can be as much part of our future as it has been part of our past.

The history of the TSR2 aircraft reminds us of the past role of nuclear weapons as a tactical capability. Today it seems unimaginable that the UK would seek to use its nuclear weapons in such a manner. However, in the rapidly evolving world of the 21st century it is far from unimaginable that emerging powers might see a battlefield role for their weapons. Indeed, their weapons might have as much to do with war fighting as they do with deterrence. Does not the Iraq experience after 2003 reveal the reluctance of the west to engage in true nation-building in large, complex and war-ravaged countries? If a country did break the nuclear taboo and use a nuclear weapon, what would the long-term impact really be?

In Britain the 1960s and 1970s are widely remembered as years of national decline and eroding competitiveness, especially in manufacturing. For defence technology enthusiasts the very public, and highly politicised, abandonment of the TSR2 project in 1965 is still a source of great regret. This book seeks to challenge such assessments by exploring the deeper logic behind the decisions and also revealing that the UK continued to develop amazing defence technologies, albeit in complete secrecy. It wasn't that our ambition and greatness were lost – it was that the technologies were removed from public view.

Back in the 1960s there was a widespread sense that the future quite simply had to be supersonic. That assessment was clearly flawed, but I fear that we in Britain are now suffering from a lack of technological ambition born out of a misunderstanding of national decline. Just as we need heroes we need grand challenges, and it is not inappropriate for the government to help the country in defining and achieving grand ambitions – because without a doubt we face grand challenges in environmental security and economic prosperity similar in importance to those of the Cold War. We should not forget that the Cold War was a conflict fought and won through science and engineering; and science and engineering can help us tackle big challenges once again.

REFERENCES

1 Royal Navy, http://www.royalnavy.mod.uk/the-equipment/submarines/future-submarines/successor-class accessed 12 March 2017.

2 Barack Obama, *Remarks by President Barack Obama in Prague As Delivered*. Available at: https://www. whitehouse.gov/the-press-office/remarks-president-barack-obama-prague-delivered accessed 4 August 2015.

3 Mary Elise Sarotte, 'A Broken Promise? What the West really told Moscow about NATO expansion', *Foreign Affairs*, September/October 2014, available at: https://www.foreignaffairs.com/articles/russia-fsu/2014-08-11/broken-promise accessed 6 August 2015.

4 Uwe Klußmann, Matthias Schepp and Klaus Wiegrefe, 'NATO's Eastward Expansion: Did the West Break Its Promise to Moscow'? *Der Spiegel*, 26 November 2009, available at: http://www.spiegel.de/international/world/nato-s-eastward-expansion-did-the-west-break-its-promise-to-moscow-a-663315.html accessed 6 August 2015.

5 Steven Pifer, 'Did NATO Promise Not to Enlarge? Gorbachev Says "No" ', *Up-Front*, Brookings Institution, 6 November 2014, available at: http://www.brookings.edu/blogs/up-front/posts/2014/11/06-nato-no-promise-enlarge-gorbachev-pifer accessed 06 August 2015.

6 The autumn of 1983 saw a dangerous rise in fear of NATO attack in parts of the Soviet government. The Iran–Iraq war was generating much tension in the Persian Gulf; the seemingly hawkish Reagan administration was pushing for new nuclear missiles in western Europe; there was the shooting down of a Korean airliner over Russia; there was the highly realistic 1983 NATO Able Archer command post exercise; and there was a dangerous Soviet early warning error indicating incoming US intercontinental ballistic missiles, luckily quickly interpreted by operators as a false alarm. It was a tense time.

7 There is some debate as to whether the designation 2 in TSR2 referred to its planned capability to fly at Mach 2 at altitude or rather that it is an acknowledgement that it followed the Canberra as a tactical strike and reconnaissance aircraft, i.e. that in some sense the Canberra was TSR1.

8 Dominic Sandbrook, *White Heat: A history of Britain in the swinging sixties*, Little, Brown, London, 2006, pp.52–53.

9 A leading advocate of High Value Manufacturing has been Sir John Rose, former chief executive of Rolls-Royce. See for instance his lecture of 10 November 2009 to the Royal Society of Arts, London http://www.thersa.org/events/audio-and-past-events/2009/creating-a-high-value-economy accessed May 2010.

10 Charlemagne column, 'Perfidious Albion Again', *The Economist*, 20 May 2010, available online at: http://www.economist.com/node/16163218 accessed 24 June 2010.

11 Gordon Bowker, *Inside George Orwell: A biography*, Palgrave Macmillan, London, 2003.

12 BBC news report on 'Keep Calm and Carry On' (a 1939 British wartime motivational poster), http://news.bbc.co.uk/1/hi/magazine/7869458.stm accessed 19 June 2010.

13 J.G. Ballard, *Miracles of Life,* Harper Perennial, London, 2008, p.123.

14 Francis Spufford, *Backroom Boys: The secret return of the British boffin*, Faber & Faber, London, 2003.

15 J.G. Ballard, op. cit. p.124.

16 Nigel Calder, New Scientist, 24 November 1966.

17 J.G. Ballard op. cit. p.187.

18 Richard Hamilton and Reyner Banham, exhibition catalogue, 'Man, Machine and Motion', Durham University at Newcastle upon Tyne, 1955.

19 Richard Hamilton interview with the author, November 2009.

20 Richard Hamilton interview with the author, November 2009.

21 For a fuller description of these issues, see for instance Corelli Barnett, *The Audit of War*, op. cit.

22 *Eagle*, 'Prisoners of Space', artwork by Desmond Walduck, Vol. 5 No. 34, 1954, p.2.

23 Dominic Sandbrook, *White Heat: A history of Britain in the Swinging Sixties*, op. cit. p.197.

24 Stanley Cohen, *Folk Devils and Moral Panics,* Third Edition, Routledge, Abingdon, Oxon. UK, 2002.

25 Don Hughes, *Friday on my Mind,* Armadillo, 2010.

26 T. Rawlings, *Mod: A very British phenomenon,* Overlook-Omnibus, 2001.

27 Don Hughes, op. cit., p.267.

28 Roland Beamont, *My Part of the Sky,* Patrick Stephens Ltd, Northamptonshire, England, 1989, p.86.

29 James Stuart, London Evening Standard, 21 June 1944, *Big percentage of Fly Bombs Killed,* reproduced in *My Part of the Sky,* ibid.

30 Roland Beamont, *Testing Years,* Ian Allan Ltd, London, 1980.

31 Roland Beamont, *My Part of the Sky*, op. cit. pp.61–62.

32 Roland Beamont, *My Part of the Sky*, op. cit. p.102.

33 Roland Beamont, *My Part of the Sky*, op. cit. pp.139–140.

34 Roland Beamont, *My Part of the Sky*, op. cit. p.46.

35 Richard Pike, *Beaufighter Ace,* Pen and Sword Aviation, Barnsley, UK, 2004.

36 Sir Douglas Lowe, interview with the author 10 May 2011.

37 Sir Douglas Lowe, memoirs, Chapter 13, *Commissioned and Life at Newmarket 1 Feb 1943–30 June 1943,* unpublished. As provided to the author by Sir Douglas Lowe 2011.

38 Sir Douglas Lowe, memoirs, Chapter 14, *Bombing Operations 1942–1943*, unpublished. As provided to the author by Sir Douglas Lowe 2011.

39 Sir Douglas Lowe, ibid.

40 The *Miles Magazine*, 17 August 1943, as reproduced in Sir Douglas Lowe, ibid.

41 Sir Douglas Lowe, ibid.

42 Denis Healey, *The Time of My Life,* Penguin Books, London, 1990, Chapter 3.

43 Kevin Dell, interview 15 January 2010.

44 As quoted in BBC news website: http://news.bbc.co.uk/2/hi/uk_news/1779996.stm 28 January 2002, accessed July 2011.

45 BBC News, *On This Day 3 February 1960,* http://news.bbc.co.uk/onthisday/hi/dates/stories/february/3/newsid_2714000/2714525.stm accessed 28 September 2012.

46 SEATO was formally dissolved in 1977.

47 Wayne M. Reynolds, 'Whatever Happened to the Fourth British Empire? The Cold War, empire defence and the USA, 1943–1957', chapter of *Cold War Britain, 1945–1964: New perspectives*, ed. M.F. Hopkins, M.D. Kandiah and G. Staerck, Palgrave Macmillan, New York, 2003.

48 Wayne M. Reynolds, °ibid. p.129.

49 Wayne M. Reynolds, '°ibid. p.136.

50 Wayne M. Reynolds, ''ibid. p.139.

51 Guy Finch, *Replacing the V-Bombers,* PhD thesis, Department of International Politics, University of Wales Aberystwyth, 2001, Chapter 5.

52 British Pathe Newsreel, available at: http://www.britishpathe.com/record.php?id=30908 accessed August 2009.

53 George Edwards had to struggle to get the Vickers Valiant approved for production as it did not match the requirements of specification B.35/46. He argued successfully that the Vickers aircraft had fewer risks and would be quicker into service than its Avro and Handley Page rivals. A new cut-down specification, B.9/48, was issued to allow Vickers to proceed: Reference: http://www.thunder-and-lightnings.co.uk/valiant/history.php accessed August 2009.

54 *Flight* magazine letters, 6 August 1988, Vol. 134, No. 4125, p.43 http://www.flightglobal.com/pdfarchive/view/1988/1988%20-%202065.html accessed August 2009.

55 W.T. Gunston, 'Spadeadam: space springboard or white elephant?', *Flight* magazine, 16 September 1960, http://www.flightglobal.com/pdfarchive/view/1960/1960%20-%201991.html accessed August 2009.

56 Roland Beamont, *My Part of the Sky,* op. cit. pp.181–182.

57 Roy Dommett, 'The Blue Streak Weapon', *Prospero: The journal of British rocketry and nuclear history.* Oral History Project, Issue 2, Spring 2005, pp.1–33.

58 C.N. Hill, *A Vertical Empire,* Imperial College Press, London, 2001, Chapter 5.

59 C.N. Hill, ibid.

60 C.N. Hill ibid., Chapter 4.

61 Space UK website (HTP page) http://www.spaceuk.org/htp/htp.htm accessed 27 September 2012.

62 Discussion at British Rocketry Oral History Project, Nuclear History Conference, Charterhouse School, 2010.

63 As quoted in: Peter Hennessy, *Having it so Good,* Allen Lane-Penguin, London, UK, p.407.

64 As quoted in: Peter Hennessy, ibid., p.442.

65 Peter Hennessy, ibid, p.451.

66 Peter Hennessy, ibid, p.452.

67 Thunder and Lightnings website: http://www.thunder-and-lightnings.co.uk/valiant/history.php accessed August 2009.

68 Colin Hughes, *Blue Danube: An inside story of Britain's first atomic bomb,* unpublished memoir.

69 RFE Audience Analysis Section, *The Hungarian Listeners of Western Broadcasts,* Munich, October 1957, available from: 1956 Digital Archive, Hoover Institution, www.osaarchivum.org accessed 28 September 2012.

70 Sir Douglas Lowe, *Memoirs,* Chapter 38, 'The British Aircraft Industry Post War Politics and OR 339 1945–1956', unpublished, as supplied to the author 2 May 2011.

71 Sir Douglas Lowe, ibid.

72 Sir Douglas Lowe, ibid.

73 Sir Douglas Lowe, ibid.

74 Sir Douglas Lowe, ibid.

75 Sir Douglas Lowe, interview with the author 10 May 2011.

76 HM Government, *Defence: Outline of future policy* (The Sandys White Paper), Cmnd 124, HMSO, April 1957.

77 Richard Moore, *Nuclear Illusion, Nuclear Reality,* Palgrave Macmillan, Basingstoke, Hampshire, UK, 2010, p.11.

78 Richard Moore, ibid. p.13 (with embedded quotation from *Central Organisation for Defence,* Cmnd 476, via Michael Howard's *The Central Organisation of Defence,* RUSI, London, 1970, p.8).

79 Derek Wood, *Project Cancelled,* Jane's Publishing Company Ltd, London, 1986, p.140.

80 Robert Gardner, *From Bouncing Bombs to Concorde: The authorised biography of aviation pioneer Sir George Edwards OM,* Sutton Publishing 2006, p.9.

81 Robert Gardner, ibid., pp.147–148.

82 Derek Wood, *Project Cancelled,* Jane's Publishing Company Ltd, London, 1986,p.141.

83 Robert Gardner, *From Bouncing Bombs to Concorde* op. cit., p.149.

84 Robert Gardner, ibid., p.150.

85 Robert Gardner, ibid, p.151.

86 Robert Gardner ibid., p.152.

87 Roland Beamont, *Phoenix into Ashes,* William Kimber and Co. Ltd, London 1968, p.101.

88 The Beamont Files, http://www.airsceneuk.org.uk/oldstuff/2005/bee/bee.htm, accessed 17 November 2009.

89 Roland Beamont *Phoenix into Ashes,* op. cit. p.102.

90 Roland Beamont, *Phoenix into Ashes*, op. cit. p.131.

91 Air Commodore (ret'd) Neil Taylor interview with the author, 9 November 2010.

92 Neil Taylor, ibid.

93 Neil Taylor, ibid.

94 Paul Dickson, *Sputnik the Shock of the Century,* Walker Publishing USA, 2001, p.133.

95 Paul Dickson, ibid., p.139.

96 Paul Dickson, ibid., p.129.

97 Nevil Shute, *On the Beach,* House of Stratus, Thirsk, Yorkshire, 2000.

98 Nevil Shute, ibid., p.36.

99 W.H. Kyle, 'Why the RAF Needs these Aircraft', *RAF Flying Review*, July 1958, pp.13–15.

100 W.H. Kyle, ibid.

101 William Green, 'Supersonic Scrapheap!', *RAF Flying Review*, Vol. XVII, No. 1, September 1961, pp.23–26 & 49.

102 UK–US Mutual Defense Agreement 1958, main public text available at: http://www.fco.gov.uk/resources/en/pdf/pdf7/fco_pdf_usmilitarydefenceagmt537, accessed 9 November 2010.

103 An official history of Aldermaston's plutonium programme was published in 2000 and is available from the UK National Archives at: http://webarchive.nationalarchives.gov.uk/+/http://www.mod.uk/publications/nuclear_weapons/aldermaston.htm accessed 9 November 2010.

104 Absolute Astronomy: http://www.absoluteastronomy.com/topics/1958_US-UK_Mutual_Defence_Agreement accessed 17 November 2009.

105 Bob Fairclough, 'TSR2: Triumph and Tragedy', *Air International*, Vol. 72, No. 4, pp.32–39, April 2007.

106 Commons Hansard, Vol. 580, Col. 1295, 23 Jan 1958, and as quoted in Richard Moore, *Nuclear Illusion, Nuclear Reality,* Palgrave Macmillan, Basingstoke, Hampshire, UK, 2010, pp.10–11.

107 Damien Burke, *TSR2: Britain's lost bomber,* The Crowood Press, Marlborough, 2010, p.68.

108 Robert Gardner, *From Bouncing Bombs to Concorde: The authorised biography of aviation pioneer Sir George Edwards OM,* Sutton Publishing, 2006, p.145.

109 Ian Speller, 'Inter-service rivalry: British defence policy, 1956–1968', RUSI Analysis, 19 August 2010, available at: http://www.rusi.org/analysis/commentary/ref:C4C6D2A628B79D/#.UOAH3Gcn2M4 , accessed 30 December 2012.

110 Interestingly, the 21st-century Queen Elizabeth class carriers will be larger still, but they are not without controversy.

111 Eric J. Grove, *Vanguard to Trident: British naval policy since World War II,* The Bodley Head, London, 1987, pp.274–279.

112 Keith Hayward, Government and British Civil Aerospace, Manchester University Press, Manchester, 1983, and Keith Hayward, The British Aircraft Industry, Manchester University Press, Manchester, 1989.

113 *Report of the Committee of Inquiry into the Aircraft Industry*, Chairman Lord Plowden 1964–1965, December 1965, Cmnd 2853, HMSO.

114 Nevil Shute, *No Highway,* New Windmill Edition (abridged with glossary), Heinemann, London, 1962, p.52.

115 Draft Defence White Paper 1959, Cabinet Paper C (59) 12, 30 January 1959, National Archives.

116 This item is discussed by Jeff Daniels, Fly Past magazine, issue May/June 1981.

117 Bob Fairclough, 'TSR2: 'Triumph and Tragedy', *Air International*, Vol 72, No. 4, pp.32–39, April 2007.

118 Fairclough, ibid.

119 Robert Gardner, *From Bouncing Bombs to Concorde: The authorised biography of aviation pioneer Sir George Edwards OM,* Sutton Publishing, 2006.

120 1 knot is equivalent to 1.85 km/hour.

121 Brian Mann, IET Lecture, *TSR2: Too ahead of its time,* Cranfield, Bedfordshire, 30 September 2009.

122 Brian Mann, ibid.

123 Robert Jackson, *High Cold War,* Patrick Stephens Limited (Haynes Publishing), Yeovil Somerset, 1998, pp.128–129.

124 AFC Hunter (ed.), *TSR2 With Hindsight,* Royal Air Force Historical Society, 1998, p.176.

125 John Forbat, *TSR2: Precision attack to Tornado,* Tempus Publishing Ltd, Stroud, Gloucestershire, 2006.

126 John Forbat, ibid., Chapter 3.

127 John Forbat, ibid., Chapter 4.

128 John Forbat, ibid., Chapter 4.

129 Illustrated well in a fine cutaway diagram by Mike Badrocke, *Air International*, Vol. 72, No 4, April 2007, pp.34–35.

130 John Forbat, ibid. Chapter 12.

131 *TSR2: The untold story*, Classic British Jets DVD, DD Home Entertainment 2005.

132 Jeff Daniels, op. cit.

133 I am most grateful to Hironori Matsunaga, Nicholas Oliver and Matthias Holweg for assistance with this section. All responsibility lies with the author.

134 Günter Endres, *British Aircraft Manufacturers since 1908*, Ian Allan Publishing, Shepperton, England, 1995.

135 Corelli Barnett, *The Audit of War*, Pan Macmillan, London, 1996, p.145.

136 Corelli Barnett, ibid., p.154.

137 Corelli Barnett, ibid., p.147.

138 Peter Lewis, *The British Bomber since 1914*, Putnam, London, 1980, pp.348–349, and Corelli Barnett, ibid., p.147.

139 Corelli Barnett, *The Audit of War*, Pan Macmillan, London, 1996, p.148.

140 George L. Bernstein, *The Myth of Decline: The rise of Britain since 1945*, Random House Pimlico, London, 2004.

141 Bernstein ibid., citing Crafts and Woodward, *The British Economy since 1945*, p.12.

142 Charles Gardner, *British Aircraft Corporation*, Batsford, 1981.

143 Charles Gardner, ibid., p.25.

144 *TSR2: The untold story*, Classic British Jets DVD, DD Home Entertainment 2005.

145 *TSR2: The untold story*, ibid.

146 *TSR2: The untold story*, ibid.

147 Keith Hayward, *The British Aircraft Industry*, Manchester University Press, Manchester, 1989, p.51.

148 *TSR2: The untold story*, op. cit.

149 *TSR2: The untold story*, op. cit.

150 George L. Bernstein, *The Myth of Decline – The Rise of Britain Since 1945*, Pimlico-Random House, London, 2004, p.149.

151 BBC, On This Day website: http://news.bbc.co.uk/onthisday/hi/dates/stories/june/5/newsid_2660000/2660375.stm , accessed 13 March 2013.

152 George Wigg, *George Wigg by Lord Wigg*, Michael Joseph, London 1972, p.17.

153 George Wigg, ibid., chapters 1–3.

154 Christopher Andrew, *The Defence of the Realm: The authorized history of MI5*, Allen Lane, London, 2009.

155 George Wigg, op. cit., p.218.

156 George Wigg, op. cit., p.263.

157 George Wigg, op. cit., p.264.

158 George Wigg, op. cit., p.273.

159 Christine Keeler with Douglas Thompson, *Secrets and Lies*, John Blake Publishing 2002, p.107.

160 Christopher Andrew, op. cit.

161 George Wigg, op. cit., p.273.

162 Christopher Andrew, op. cit., p.499.

163 Christine Keeler with Douglas Thompson, op. cit., p.126.

164 Douglas Thompson, *Stephen Ward, Scapegoat: They All Loved Him …* John Blake Publishing, 16 Dec 2013, Chapter 2.

165 http://www.dailymail.co.uk/news/article-2323094/Stephen-Ward-Hidden-50-years-Secret-Profumo-scandal-portraits-humble-clerk-defied-order-dispose-revealed-time.html, accessed 18 January 2018.

166 http://www.telegraph.co.uk/news/2017/11/28/mi5-files-reveal-mysterious-case-john-profumo-glamorous-nazi/, accessed 18 January 2018.

167 Keith Hayward, *The British Aircraft Industry*, Manchester University Press, Manchester, 1989, p.84.

168 Sir Frederick Page, 'A Project Overview', in *TSR2 With Hindsight*, Royal Air Force Historical Society, A.F.C. Hunter (ed.), 1998, p.75.

169 Stephen Hastings, *The Murder of the TSR-2*, MacDonald, London, 1966, p.188.

170 Derek Wood, *Project Cancelled*, revised edition, Jane's Publishing Company Ltd, London, 1986, p.155.

171 Roland Beamont, *Phoenix into Ashes*, William Kimber and Co. Ltd, London, 1968, p.136.

172 Roland Beamont, ibid., p.137.

173 Robert Gardner, *From Bouncing Bombs to Concorde: The authorised biography of aviation pioneer Sir George Edwards OM*, Sutton Publishing, 2006, p.153.

174 Robert Gardner, ibid., p.155.

175 Interview by Nikolai Kulin, *Trud*, October 1996, as reported by Sergei Khrushchev and William C. Wohlforth, *Nikita Khrushchev and the Creation of a Superpower*, Pennsylvania State University Press, 2001, p.379.

176 Stephen I. Schwartz, Letter to *Time* magazine, 22 December 1997 (available at: http://205.188.238.181/time/magazine/article/0,9171,987578-3,00.html accessed December 2009.

177 Как сбили Пауэрса, Russian website: http://www.webslivki.com/u11.html accessed December 2009.

178 Stepan Anastasovich Mikoyan, *Memoirs of Military Test-Flying and Life with the Kremlin's Elite,* Airlife Publishing Ltd, Shrewsbury, England, 1999, p.261.

179 Sergei Khrushchev and William C. Wohlforth, *Nikita Khrushchev and the Creation of a Superpower,* Pennsylvania State University Press, 2001, pp.365–379.

180 S.R. Twigge, *The Early Development of Guided Weapons in the United Kingdom, 1940–1960,* Harwood Academic, 1993, p.193.

181 S.R. Twigge, ibid.

182 C.N. Hill, *A Vertical Empire,* Imperial College Press, London, 2001, p.115.

183 Frank Barnett Jones, *Phoenix or Folly,* p.158.

184 Denis Healey, *The Time of My Life,* Penguin Books, London, 1990, p.260.

185 C.N. Hill, op. cit., Chapter 10.

186 Although it is interesting to note that the British later launched a very large number of solid-fuelled 'Falstaff' rockets from Woomera, South Australia, in support of the Chevaline programme - see Chapter 10.

187 C.N. Hill, op. cit., p.81.

188 Richard Moore, *Nuclear Illusion, Nuclear Reality,* Palgrave Macmillan, Basingstoke, UK, 2010, p.116.

189 Richard Moore, ibid., p.117.

190 Richard Moore, ibid.

191 Harold Macmillan, text of 'Winds of Change' speech to South African Parliament, 3 February 1960, available at: About.com African History: http://africanhistory.about.com/od/eraindependence/p/wind_of_change2.htm accessed 5 November 2012.

192 Chris Gibson and Tony Buttler, *British Secret Projects Hypersonics, Ramjets and Missiles,* Midland Publishing, Hinckley, England, 2007, p.116.

193 Discussion at British Rocketry Oral History Project, Nuclear History Conference, Charterhouse School, 2010.

194 Robert S. Norris and Hans M. Kristensen, 'The Cuban Missile Crisis: A nuclear order of battle, October and November 1962', *Bulletin of the Atomic Scientists* 68 (6), 2012, pp.85–91.

195 Robert S. Norris and Hans M. Kristensen, Bulletin of the Atomic Scientists, 2012, op. cit.

196 It is sometimes argued that the autumn 1983 Able Archer NATO command post exercise prompted a particularly dangerous situation in which parts of the Soviet government believed that a NATO nuclear first strike was imminent, and they acted by escalating Soviet defence capabilities. The level of the actual danger is, however, somewhat contested. A recent overview of the issues has been presented by Gordon Barrass, 'Able Archer 83: What were the Soviets thinking?' *Survival: Global Politics and Strategy*, December 2016-January 2017, pp.7–30. See reference 6.

197 John Boyes, *Project Emily, Thor IRBM and the RAF,* The History Press, Stroud, Gloucestershire, 2008.

198 John Boyes ibid. p.48 quoting TNA, DEFE 13/594.f.E33.

199 'Engineering Britain's Superweapons (V-Bombers)', Channel 4, UK, first shown 22 July 2009.

200 John Boyes, op. cit., Chapter 7.

201 John Boyes, op. cit.

202 Jim Wilson, *Launch Pad UK: Britain and the Cuban Missile Crisis,* Pen and Sword Aviation, Barnsley UK, 2008, p.5.

203 Jim Wilson, *Launch Pad UK,* ibid., p.165.

204 Cabinet Papers relating to Defence White Paper 1962, C. (62) 23 9 February 1962, UK National Archives.

205 BBC News, *Cold war bomb warmed by chickens,* BBC News website 1 April 2004, reporting on comments originally made to *The Times* amidst heavy and authoritative denials that it all represented an April Fool.

206 Richard Moore, *Nuclear Illusion and Nuclear Reality,* Palgrave Macmillan, London, 2010, p.100.

207 Conclusions of a Meeting of the Cabinet held at Admiralty House SW1 on Friday 3 August 1962 at 11a.m., Cabinet Papers CC. (62), 53rd Conclusions, National Archives.

208 Conclusions of a Meeting of the Cabinet, ibid.

209 Ian Q.R. Thomas, *The Promise of Alliance: NATO and the political imagination,* Rowman and Littlefield, Lanham, Maryland, USA, 1997, p.72.

210 Conclusions of a Meeting of the Cabinet, op. cit.

211 Derek Wood, *Project Cancelled*, Jane's Publishing Company Ltd, London, 1986, p.151.

212 Neil Taylor (RAF air commodore ret'd), private communication August 2009.

213 Malcolm Davis entries in *Weapons of Mass Destruction: An encyclopedia of worldwide policy, technology and history, Vol. 2*, eds Eric A. Croddy and James J. Wirtz, ABC-CLIO Santa Barbara, CA, USA, 2005.

214 Guy Finch, *Replacing the V-Bombers*, PhD thesis, Department of International Politics, University of Wales Aberystwyth, 2001, section 2.8.1.

215 David Edgerton, *Warfare State: Britain, 1920–1970*, Cambridge University Press, 2006, p.43.

216 Corelli Barnett, *The Audit of War*, Pan Books (Macmillan), London, 1986, p.146.

217 David Edgerton, op. cit., p.102.

218 Sir Douglas Lowe, interview with the author, 10 May 2011.

219 Sir Douglas Lowe, ibid. NB: the First Viscount Trenchard (Hugh Trenchard) was the first chief of the air staff and a key figure in the formation of the Royal Air Force in 1918.

220 Conclusions of a Meeting of the Cabinet, op. cit.

221 Conclusions of a Meeting of the Cabinet, held at Admiralty House SW1 on Thursday, 3 January 1963, at 5pm. Cabinet Papers C.C. (63) 2nd Conclusions, National Archives.

222 Cabinet Meeting 3 January 1963. ibid.

223 George Edwards, *Under The Radar Screen*, Battle of Britain Souvenir Book 1963, Thomson Printers Ltd, London, pp.12–13.

224 Bill Gunston 'TSR.2: What went wrong?' *Aeroplane* Monthly, September 1973, pp.216–220.

225 Philip Ziegler, *Mountbatten: The official biography*, Book Club Associates, London, 1985, under agreement from William Collins Sons and Co. Ltd.

226 *TSR2: The untold story*, Classic British Jets DVD, DD Home Entertainment, 2005.

227 Richard Moore, private communication, 2016. The Australians were keen to acquire the F-111C variant.

228 *TSR2: The untold story*, op. cit.

229 Derek Wood, *Project Cancelled*, Jane's Publishing Company Ltd, London, 1986, p.158, citing the *Sunday Times*, London, 10 November 1963.

230 Robert Gardner, *From Bouncing Bombs to Concorde: The authorised biography of aviation pioneer Sir George Edwards OM*, Sutton Publishing 2006, p.167.

231 Richard Moore, 'A Proliferation of Royal Air Forces', *The Nonproliferation Review*, Vol. 21, No. 2, 2014, pp.167–187.

232 With thanks to Richard Moore for sharing research materials on such matters.

233 Derek Wood, 'op. cit., p.160.

234 Message from Harold Macmillan to Robert Menzies, 4 October 1963. Source: National Archives of Australia online material: http://www.naa.gov.au, tag: F-111 Aircraft, accessed 26 March 2010.

235 Message from Robert Menzies to UK deputy PM R.A. Butler, 14 October 1963, source: ibid.

236 Denis Healey, *The Time of My Life*, Penguin Books, London, 1990, p.226.

237 Vietnam Veterans of Australia, Vietnam: Australia's longest war: A calendar of military and political events, http://www.vvaa.org.au/calendar.htm , accessed 31 December 2012.

238 Message from Mr Athol Townley to PM Robert Menzies, 22 October 1963, source National Archives of Australia op. cit.

239 *Daily Telegraph*, London, 13 November 1963.

240 Letter from E.J. Bunting to Sir Allen Brown, 22 November 1963, information kindly supplied to the author by Richard Moore, July 2012.

241 Message from Sir Robert Menzies to Sir Alex Douglas-Home, 24 October 1963, source National Archives of Australia, op. cit.

242 Robert Gardner, *From Bouncing Bombs to Concorde: The authorised biography of aviation pioneer Sir George Edwards OM*, Sutton Publishing 2006, p.164.

243 Robert Gardner, ibid., p.165.

244 Atomic Weapons Establishment website: http://web.archive.org/web/20070607120057/www.awe.co.uk/main_site/about_awe/history/timeline/1961b/index.html accessed August 2009.

245 Eric J. Grove, *Vanguard to Trident: British naval policy since World War II,* The Bodley Head, London, 1987, p.222.

246 Eric J. Grove, *Vanguard to Trident,* ibid. p.223.

247 Carolynn Langley, *Roll of Honour,* http://www.roll-of-honour.com/Dorset/PortlandHMSSidon.html , accessed 19 October 2018.

248 Conclusions of a Meeting of the Cabinet held at 10 Downing Street, SW1, on Tuesday, 18 February 1964 at 10.30 a.m., Cabinet papers C.M. (64) 12th Conclusions, National Archives.

249 Daniel Tatarsky (ed.), *The Eagle Annual of the Cutaways,* Colin Frewin and Associates Ltd/Orion Books London, 2008, Colin Frewin, Preface, p.4.

250 Daniel Tatarsky (ed.), ibid., Jonathan Glancey, Introduction, p.7.

251 Tatarsky (ed.), *The Eagle Annual of the Cutaways,* ibid.

252 *The Times,* 'Survey of British Aviation 1964', London, 7 September 1964.

253 Society of British Aerospace Companies.

254 Society of British Aerospace Companies Ltd, *Farnborough '64 Official Publication,* London 1964, Design and production by Scott-Turner and Associates Ltd, London, p.30.

255 Rotax alternator advertisement, March 1965. Source: Damien Burke, *TSR2: Britain's lost bomber,* ibid. p.184, citing Brooklands Museum.

256 Bill Gunston, '*Beyond the Frontiers, BAC TSR.2',* in *Wings of Fame* Vol. 4, Aerospace Publishing Limited, London, 1996, pp.122–137.

257 Richard Moore, private communication, 2016.

258 Labour Party Manifesto 1964, Section C, available at: http://www.labour-party.org.uk/manifestos/1964/1964-labour-manifesto.shtml , accessed 6 January 2013.

259 Stephen Hastings, The Murder of TSR-2, Macdonald & Co. London, 1966, p.18.

260 Stephen Hastings, *The Drums of Memory,* Leo Cooper (Pen and Sword Books), Barnsley, Yorkshire, 1994, pp.148–149.

261 Timothy Green, 'Little Harold' Knocks at No. 10', *Life* magazine, Vol. 54, No 15, April 12, 1963, p.37.

262 Roland Beamont, *Phoenix into Ashes,* William Kimber and Co. Ltd, London 1968, pp.95–96.

263 Roland Beamont, *Testing TSR-2, Aeroplane Monthly,* Vol. 10, No. 4, Issue, 108, April 1982, pp.184–189.

264 V-stop is the decision point on take-off at which, should one engine fail, pilot can elect to abandon or continue (this note is original to the *Aeroplane Monthly* article).

265 Roland Beamont, 'Testing TSR-2', *Aeroplane Monthly,* Vol. 10, No. 4, Issue, 108, April 1982, pp.184–189.

266 Roland Beamont speaking in *TSR2: The untold story,* ibid.

267 Robert Gardner, *From Bouncing Bombs to Concorde: The authorised biography of aviation pioneer Sir George Edwards OM,* Sutton Publishing 2006, p.172.

268 Robert Gardner, ibid. p.157.

269 Roland Beamont, *Phoenix into Ashes,* William Kimber and Co. Ltd, London 1968, pp.139–141.

270 In *Flying to the Limit,* Patrick Stephens Ltd, 1996, Roland Beamont refers to a total of three engine explosions, p.134.

271 Roland Beamont, op. cit., p.142.

272 Roland Beamont, op. cit., p.144.

273 Roland Beamont, op. cit., p.145.

274 Roland Beamont, op. cit., p.145.

275 Roland Beamont, *Testing Years,* Ian Allen Ltd, Shepperton, Surrey, 1980, pp.143–145, also Roland Beamont, 'Testing TSR-2', *Aeroplane Monthly,* April 1982, pp.184–188.

276 Roland Beamont, *Phoenix into Ashes,* op. cit., p.150.

277 *TSR2: The untold story,* Classic British Jets DVD, DD Home Entertainment 2005.

278 'TSR-2: The most important weapon in Britain's armoury', *Air Pictorial,* Vol. 26 No. 11, November 1964, pp.347–348.

279 'TSR-2: The most important weapon in Britain's armoury', ibid.

280 Roland Beamont, *Phoenix Into Ashes,* William Kimber and Co. Ltd, London, 1968, p.151.

281 Roland Beamont, 'Testing TSR-2', *Aeroplane Monthly,* April 1982, pp.184–188.

282 Roland Beamont, *Phoenix into Ashes,* William Kimber and Co. Ltd, London, 1968, p.143.

283 Robert Gardner, *From Bouncing Bombs to Concorde: The authorised biography of aviation pioneer Sir George Edwards OM*, Sutton Publishing, 2006, p.171.

284 Stephen Hastings, *The Murder of the TSR-2*, MacDonald, London, 1966, p.78 and Derek Wood, *Project Cancelled*, Jane's Publishing Company Ltd, London, 1986, p.161.

285 Peter Wright with Paul Greengrass, *Spycatcher*, Dell Publishing, New York, USA, 1988, p.347.

286 George Wigg, op. cit., p.202.

287 Wigg, ibid., p.321.

288 Denis Healey, *The Time of My Life*, Penguin Books, London, 1990, pp.302–303.

289 Healey, ibid., p.303.

290 Richard Worcester, *Roots of British Air Policy*, Hodder and Stoughton, 1966, p.47.

291 Richard Worcester, ibid. p.156.

292 Richard Worcester, ibid. p.157.

293 Derek Wood, *Project Cancelled*, Jane's Publishing Company Ltd, London, 1986, Chapter 12.

294 Richard Worcester op. cit.. p.163.

295 C.G. Milner, letter to *Flight International*, 8 April 1965, p.535.

296 Robert Gardner, *From Bouncing Bombs to Concorde: the authorised biography of aviation pioneer Sir George Edwards OM*, Sutton Publishing, 2006, p.176.

297 Roland Beamont, *Flying to the Limit*, Patrick Stephens Ltd, Yeovil, Somerset, 1996, p.136.

298 Jeff Daniels, *Fly Past* magazine, issue May/June 1981.

299 Jeff Daniels, ibid.

300 Jeff Daniels, ibid.

301 Roland Beamont, *Phoenix into Ashes*, William Kimber and Co. Ltd, London 1968, p.102.

302 Roland Beamont, ibid., p.156.

303 *Air Pictorial* Editorial, February 1965, pp.35, 36.

304 Peter Lewis, *The British Bombers since 1914*, Putnam, London, 3rd edn, 1980, pp.373–374.

305 Peter Lewis, ibid., p.375.

306 Thunder and Lightnings website: http://www.thunder-and-lightnings.co.uk/valiant/history.php accessed August 2009.

307 Cabinet Paper C. (65) 19, National Archives 1965.

308 Derek Wood, *Project Cancelled*, Jane's Publishing Company Ltd, London, 1986, frontispiece.

309 Conclusions of a Meeting of the Cabinet held at 10 Downing Street SW.1. on Monday 1 February 1965, at 11 a.m. Cabinet papers CC. (65) 6th Conclusions, National Archives ,1965.

310 Precursor to the extremely successful Harrier Jump Jet.

311 Robert Gardner, *From Bouncing Bombs to Concord:– the authorised biography of aviation pioneer Sir George Edwards OM*, Sutton Publishing 2006, p.175.

312 Robert Gardner, ibid., p.176.

313 Quotes from Conclusions of a Meeting of the Cabinet held at 10 Downing Street SW1 on Thursday 1 April 1965, at 10 a.m. Cabinet papers CC. (65) 20th Conclusions, National Archives.

314 Conclusions of a Meeting of the Cabinet held at 10 Downing Street S.W.1. on Thursday 1 April 1965, at 10 p.m. Cabinet Papers CC (65) 21st Conclusions, National Archives.

315 Cabinet Papers C(65) 58, 1 April 1965, National Archives.

316 'TSR.2: It has got to be stopped', *Flight International*, 15 April 1965, pp.550–551, article quotes MoD statement at length.

317 Evan Davies, *Made in Britain*, Little, Brown, and Hachette, London, 2011.

318 Cabinet Papers C.(65) op. cit.

319 Jeff Daniels (with contributions from Roland Beamont), 'TSR2: The martyrdom of a superjet', *Fly Past*, Key Publishing Ltd, May/June 1981, pp.4–10.

320 Matthew Jones, *The Official History of the UK Strategic Nuclear Deterrent – Vol. 2 The Labour Government and the Polaris Programme, 1964–1970*, Routledge 2017, Kindle edition p.239 of 560, location 6672.

321 Derek Wood, *Project Cancelled*, Jane's Publishing Company Ltd, London, 1986, p.158.

322 *The Times*, Weather Forecast, 6 April 1965, p.13.

323 Kevin Dell, interview with the author, 15 January 2010.

324 Based on the first flight of XR219, 24 September 1964, ref: Roland Beamont *Testing Years,* Experimental Flight Report pp.143–145.

325 Source Frank Barnett-Jones *TSR2: Phoenix or Folly?* pp.152–154, Steve Broadbent *TSR2 Memories Project* http://www.stevebroadbent.net/540a.pdf and Thunder and Lightnings website: http://www.thunder-and-lightnings.co.uk/tsr2/survivor.php?id=1 .

326 Former Boscombe Down ground crew – private communication.

327 Jeff Daniels (with contributions from Roland Beamont), *Fly Past,* Key Publishing Ltd, May/June 1981, pp.4–10.

328 Jeff Daniels, ibid.

329 6 April 1965, Budget Hansard Report available at: http://hansard.millbanksystems.com/commons/1965/apr/06/budget-statement .

330 The distinction between BBC1 and BBC2 was at that stage very new. BBC2 launched broadcasting from London on 20 April 1964 amidst power cuts, chaos and distraction. Much insight can be gained from this 1989 parody by Rowan Atkinson: http://www.youtube.com/user/rosiethedog#play/uploads/3/ABsA8GJTSjo accessed 5 April 2019.

331 *TSR2: The untold story,* Classic British Jets DVD, DD Home Entertainment 2005.

332 Kevin Dell, interview 15 January 2010.

333 Frank Barnett-Jones, *Tarnish 6: The biography of test pilot Jimmy Dell,* Old Forge Press, King's Lynn, UK, 2008, p.138.

334 Hansard Budget Report 6 April 1965 (xi) Tobacco and Alcoholic Drink, http://hansard.millbanksystems.com/commons/1965/apr/06/xi-tobacco-and-alcoholic-drink .

335 Roland Beamont, *Phoenix into Ashes,* William Kimber and Co. Ltd, London, 1968.

336 Frank Barnett-Jones, 'op. cit., 2008, p.37.

337 Frank Barnett-Jones, op. cit., pp.226–227.

338 Kevin Dell, interview, op. cit.

339 Frank Barnett-Jones, 'op. cit., p.37.

340 Roland Beamont, op. cit., p.118.

341 Roland Beamont, *Testing Years,* Ian Allan Ltd, Shepperton, 1980, p.146.

342 Kenneth Owen, Parliament Column, *Flight International,* 15 April 1965.

343 Conclusions of a Meeting of the Cabinet held at 10 Downing Street SW1 on Thursday 8 April 1965, at 10a.m. Cabinet papers CC. (65) 24th Conclusions, National Archives.

344 *TSR2: The untold story,* Classic British Jets DVD, DD Home Entertainment 2005.

345 eBay item # 130383698185.

346 Robert Gardner, *From Bouncing Bombs to Concorde: The authorised biography of aviation pioneer Sir George Edwards OM,* Sutton Publishing 2006, p.179.

347 Antony Jay and Jonathan Lynn, *The Yes Minister Miscellany,* Biteback Publishing, London, 2009, p.81.

348 Special Executive for Counter-intelligence, Terrorism, Revenge, and Extortion (SPECTRE).

349 Derek Wood, *Project Cancelled,* Jane's Publishing Company Ltd, London, 1986, pp.161–162.

350 *Flight International,* 15 April 1965, editorial, editor-in-chief: Maurice A. Smith, DFC.

351 Roland Beamont, *Phoenix into Ashes,* William Kimber and Co. Ltd, London 1968.

352 Roland Beamont, op. cit., p.126.

353 David Hoffman, 'press' column, *Flight International,* 22 April 1965, p.626.

354 'TSR2: It has got to be stopped', quoting MoD statement 6 April 1965, *Flight International,* 15 April 1965, p.550.

355 'The Questions Begin', *Flight International,* ''15 April 1965, p.551.

356 'General Dynamics F-111', *Air Pictorial,* January 1966, pp.4–7.

357 Thunder and Lightnings website: http://www.thunder-and-lightnings.co.uk/phantom/history.php accessed 8 February 2013.

358 *Air Pictorial,* January 1966, ibid.

359 Pete Arnold Defence Research Establishment Shoeburyness, speaking in *TSR2: The untold story* DVD, DD Home Entertainment 2005.

360 Frank Barnett-Jones, *Phoenix or Folly* p. 228.

361 Cabinet Papers C(66) 35, 11 February 1966, National Archives.

362 'TSR2: "It Has Got to be Stopped" ', op. cit., p.550.

363 Denis Healey letter to the author 7 August 2009.

364 Denis Healey letter to the author 5 December 2009. The word 'created' is hard to read and has been inferred.

365 Denis Healey, *The Time of My Life*, Penguin Books, London, 1990, p.274.

366 'TSR.2 The Case for Cancellation: Mr Healey's Policy Statement', *Flight International*, 22 April 1965, pp.624–625.

367 'The Questions Begin', *Flight International*, 15 April 1965, p.551.

368 'TSR.2 The Case for Cancellation – Mr Healey's Policy Statement' op. cit.

369 Cabinet Papers C(66) 35, 11 February 1966, National Archives.

370 Denis Healey, *The Time of My Life*, Penguin Books, London, 1990, p.301.

371 Denis Healey, ibid., p.279.

372 Denis Healey, ibid, p.292.

373 Denis Healey, ibid., p.300.

374 Denis Healey, ibid., p.274.

375 Guy Finch, PhD thesis, *Replacing the V-Bombers*, University of Wales at Aberystwyth, December 2001.

376 'World Air News', *Air Pictorial*, November 1968, pp.404–406.

377 Norman J. Vig, *Science and Technology in British Politics*, Pergamon, Oxford 1968.

378 Norman J. Vig, ibid. p.38.

379 Norman j. Vig, ibid. p.42.

380 Norman J. Vig, ibid. p.82.

381 Norman J. Vig, ibid. p.82.

382 As quoted by Norman J. Vig, ibid. p.89.

383 Graham Spinardi, 'Civil Spinoff from the Defence Research Establishments', in *Cold War Hot Science,* ed. Robert Bud and Philip Gummet, Science Museum, London, 1999.

384 Norman J. Vig, *Science and Technology in British Politics*, Pergamon, Oxford 1968, p.146.

385 Norman J. Vig, ibid. p.150.

386 Norman J. Vig, ibid. p.151 referring to Plowden Report, op. cit.

387 National Archives: http://www.legislation.gov.uk/ukpga/1966/32/enacted accessed July 2011.

388 Bill Gunston, 'TSR.2: What went wrong?' *Aeroplane Monthly*, September 1973, pp.216–220.

389 Bob Fairclough, 'TSR: Triumph and Tragedy', *Air International*, April 2007, pp.32–39.

390 C.G. Milner, Letter to Flight International, 8 April 1965, p.535.

391 Roland Beamont, *Flying to the Limit*, Patrick Stephens Ltd, Yeovil, Somerset, 1996, p.178.

392 Roland Beamont, ibid., p.173.

393 BBC News website http://news.bbc.co.uk/1/hi/uk/71226.stm accessed 28 July 2009.

394 Robert Gardner, *From Bouncing Bombs to Concorde: The authorised biography of aviation pioneer Sir George Edwards OM*, Sutton Publishing 2006, p.180.

395 Stephen Hastings, *The Murder of TSR-2*, Macdonald & Co. London, 1966.

396 *TSR2: The untold story*, Classic British Jets DVD, DD Home Entertainment 2005.

397 *TSR2: The untold story*, ibid.

398 *TSR2: The untold story*, ibid.

399 *TSR2: The untold story*, ibid.

400 Eric Brown and Dennis Bancroft, *Miles M.52: Gateway to supersonic flight*, Spellmount (The History Press), Stroud, Gloucestershire, 2012, p.117 and 211.

401 Eric Brown and Dennis Bancroft, ibid., Chapter 12.

402 Eric Brown (with Dennis Bancroft), ibid., p.99.

403 Eric Brown (with Dennis Bancroft), ibid., p.107.

404 Eric Brown, postscript in Eric Brown (with Dennis Bancroft), ibid., 2012.

405 Eric Brown (with Dennis Bancroft), ibid, p.212.

406 *TSR2: The untold story*, Classic British Jets DVD, DD Home Entertainment 2005.

407 Geoffrey Goodman, 'Obituary: Aubrey Jones', *The Guardian*, 12 April 2003 (available at: http://www.guardian.co.uk/news/2003/apr/12/guardianobituaries.obituaries accessed December 2009.

408 Bill Gunston, 'TSR.2: What Went Wrong? *Aeroplane Monthly*, September 1973, pp.216–220.

409 Richard Moore, 'Replacing Red Beard: Early Development History of WE.177', presentation to UK Space Conference, British Rocketry Oral History Project (BROHP), Charterhouse School, May 2009.

410 Richard Moore, ibid.

411 Richard Moore, ibid.

412 Andrew Brookes writes in *RAF Canberra Units of the Cold War*, Osprey, 2014, on p.65: that Mike Knight was given command of No. 32 squadron in 1961, and Knight observed: 'Our CENTO nuclear role involved last-minute loading and target study. We had targets in the Southern USSR which we regarded as "one-way tickets".'

413 Philip Goodall, *My Target was Leningrad: V-Force: Preserving our democracy*, Fonthill Media, 2015.

414 Richard Moore, BROHP, Charterhouse, 2009, ibid.

415 Paul Lucas, *TSR2: Lost tomorrows of an eagle*, SAM Publications, Bedford, UK, 2009, p.23.

416 Paul Lucas, ibid, p.23.

417 Chris Gibson and Tony Buttler, *British Secret Projects Hypersonics, Ramjets and Missiles*, Midland Publishing, Hinckley, England, 2007, p.110.

418 Chris Gibson and Tony Buttler, *British Secret Projects: Hypersonics, ramjets and missiles*, Midland Publishing, Hinckley, England, 2007, p.116.

419 Chris Gibson and Tony Buttler, ibid., pp.94–95.

420 Derek Wood, *Project Cancelled*, Jane's Publishing Company Ltd, London, 1986, p.155.

421 John Simpson, private communication, April 2010.

422 Richard Moore, BROHP, Charterhouse 2009, op. cit.

423 Richard Moore, BROHP, Charterhouse, 2009, ibid.

424 Derek Wood, *Project Cancelled*, Jane's Publishing Company Ltd, London, 1986, p.155.

425 Chris Gibson and Tony Buttler, op. cit., pp.116–117.

426 From 1945 to 1971 the major western economies operated according to an agreement negotiated at Bretton Woods, New Hampshire, USA, in the summer of 1944. The arrangements sought to maintain stable currency exchange rates between the major economies; the system effectively pegged the exchange rates between member currencies and the US dollar. For the British government planning major defence projects, it meant that dollar spending was always hard to justify to colleagues responsible for maintaining Bretton Woods compliance.

427 Chris Gibson and Tony Buttler, op. cit., p.117 and MBDA website: http://www.mbda-systems.com/mbda/site/ref/scripts/siteFO_contenu.php?lang=EN&noeu_id=120&page_id=115 accessed 22 April 2010.

428 A cruise missile flies through the atmosphere under computer control, benefiting from advanced map-based guidance. The weapon typically flies close to the ground, relying on aerodynamic lift, in an attempt to get below enemy radar. The attributes are in contrast to the very high-speed and high-altitude trajectories of ballistic rockets.

429 Chris Gibson and Tony Buttler, op. cit., p.116.

430 *Flight International*, Thursday 10 December 1964, Vol. 86, No. 2909, p.985.

431 Tony Buttler, *British Secret Projects: Jet bombers since 1949*, Ian Allen Publishing Limited, Hinckley, England, 2003, p.116.

432 Bill Gunston, 'Beyond the Frontiers, BAC TSR.2', in *Wings of Fame* Vol. 4, Aerospace Publishing Limited, London, 1996, pp.122–137.

433 'TSR-2, The Most Important Weapon in Britain's Armoury', *Air Pictorial*, November 1964, pp.347–348.

434 Charles G. Keil, 'Scrap TSR-2 and Concord at Britain's Peril!', *Air Pictorial*, January 1965, p.7. (note the lack of an 'e' at the end of the name 'Concorde'. This is because the precise name of the aircraft had not been agreed between the UK and France. 'Concord' is an English word, whereas 'Concorde' is not. On this point the French, as we now know, were to prevail.

435 B47 Strato-jet, GlobalSecurity.net, http://www.globalsecurity.org/wmd/systems/b-47.htm , accessed 2 December 2010.

436 Richard Moore, 'The Real Meaning of the Words: A pedantic glossary of British nuclear weapons', *Prospero*, No. 1, Spring 2004, pp.71–90, British Rocketry and Oral History Programme.

437 Richard Moore, *Prospero*, ibid.

438 Richard Moore, *Prospero*, ibid. (and private communication 2016).

439 John Baylis, 'The Development of Britain's Thermonuclear Capability 1954–61: Myth or reality?', *Contemporary British History*, 8: 1, 1, 1994, pp.59–174.

440 Richard Moore, *Prospero* 2004, op. cit.

441 US–UK Mutual Defence Agreement (without secret amending annexes) available at: http://www.basicint.org/nuclear/1958MDA.htm , accessed December 2009.

442 Kenneth Hubbard and Michael Simmons, *Operation Grapple – Testing Britain's First H-Bomb,* Guild Publishing, London, 1985.

443 Lorna Arnold with Katherine Pyne, *Britain and the H-Bomb,* Palgrave Macmillan, 2001.

444 Lorna Arnold with Katherine Pyne, ibid.

445 Ken Johnston, private communications 2009–2010.

446 Ken Johnston, ibid.

447 Ken Johnston, ibid.

448 Richard Moore, BROHP, Charterhouse, 2009,op. cit.

449 Paul Lucas, *TSR2: Lost tomorrows of an eagle,* SAM Publications, Bedford, UK, 2009, p.64.

450 Paul Lucas, ibid.

451 Having judged the American design (Mark 58 Mod 1) to be insufficiently safe, the UK decided to base its Polaris primary on a design developed for the WE.177B high yield RAF laydown bomb. See: Matthew Jones, *The Official History of the UK Strategic Nuclear Deterrent: Vol. 1: From the V-Bomber era to the arrival of Polaris*, Cambridge University Library EDeposit version, Routledge, 2017, pp.631/740.

452 Ken Johnston, op. cit.

453 Arguably there are parallels to the stress problems affecting the RAF Valiants (see Chapter 6, and later the RAF Vulcans after they were also forced into low-level operations following the Gary Powers incident).

454 J.J. Kohout, 'A Post B-1 Look at the Manned Strategic Bomber', *Air University Review*, July–August 1979 Available at: http://www.airpower.maxwell.af.mil/airchronicles/aureview/1979/jul-aug/kohout.htm accessed 3 December 2010.

455 J.J. Kohout, ibid.

456 Derek Wood, *Project Cancelled,* Jane's Publishing Company Ltd, London, 1986, p.163.

457 Literally 'anti-aircraft defence of the homeland', though it may be translated as the Soviet Union's Radiotechnical Troops for Air Defence.

458 Boeing company history, http://www.boeing.com/defense-space/ic/awacs/e3svcww/history.html, accessed 2 December 2010.

459 Bill Gunston, 'TSR.2: What went wrong?' *Aeroplane Monthly*, op. cit.

460 Peter Jones, 'Chevaline Technical Programme 1966–1976', *Prospero,* No. 2, Spring 2005, pp.179–191, British Rocketry and Oral History Programme.

461 Ken Johnston, private communication 2010. Note: the radiation flux would be an unattenuated mix of thermal X-rays, gamma rays and neutrons.

462 Denis Healey, 'The Need for an Option on the F-111A', paper presented to the evening meeting of the Cabinet on 1 April 1965 *Cabinet Papers* CC. (65) 21st Conclusions, National Archives.

463 'Not the Same Beast!', *Air Pictorial*, February 1965, p.40.

464 BBC, On This Day website: http://news.bbc.co.uk/onthisday/hi/dates/stories/december/21/newsid_3815000/3815251.stm, accessed 17 March 2013.

465 Denis Healey, *The Time of My Life,* Penguin Books, London, 1990, p.273.

466 Denis Healey, ibid., p.274.

467 Denis Healey, ibid., p.274.

468 Atomic Weapons Establishment website http://web.archive.org/web/20070607112707/www.awe.co.uk/main_site/about_awe/history/timeline/1973/index.html accessed August 2009.

469 Matthew Jones, *The Official History of the UK Strategic Nuclear Deterrent: Vol. 1: From the V-Bomber era to the arrival of Polaris 1945–1964*, Routledge, 2017, Chapter 12: 'The Origins of a Polaris Improvement Programme, HR 169 and the Emergence of the Moscow ABM System'; Cambridge University Library EDeposit version, p.617/740.

470 Matthew Jones, ibid., p.639/740 ff.

471 Matthew Jones, *The Official History of the UK Strategic Nuclear Deterrent: Vol. 2: The Labour Government*

and the Polaris Programme, 1964–1970, Routledge, 2017, Kindle edition, pp.151 and 156 of 560, locations 4425 and 4533.

472 Matthew Jones reports that the V-Committee was established in November 1965. See: Matthew Jones, ibid., Kindle edition p.175/560 and p.333/560.

473 Peter Jones, 'Chevaline Technical Programme 1966–1976', Prospero, No. 2, Spring 2005 pp.179–191, British Rocketry and Oral History Programme.

474 Ken Johnston, private communications 2009–2010.

475 Ken Johnston, ibid.

476 Matthew Jones, Vol. 2, op. cit., quoting Sunday Telegraph 22 January 1967, Kindle edition p.158 of 560, location 4603.

477 Matthew Jones, ibid., quoting Daily Telegraph 19 May 1967, Kindle edition p.241 of 560, location 6729.

478 Ken Johnston, op. cit.

479 Frank Panton, 'The Unveiling of Chevaline', Prospero, No. 1, Spring 2004, pp.91–108, British Rocketry and Oral History Programme.

480 Matthew Jones, Vol. 2, op. cit.

481 Labour Party Manifestos Archive http://www.labour-party.org.uk/manifestos/1964/1964-labour-manifesto.shtml accessed January 2010.

482 Labour Party Manifestos Archive, op. cit.

483 Frank Panton, 'Polaris Improvements and the Chevaline System 1967–1976', Prospero, No. 1, Spring 2004, pp.109–128, British Rocketry and Oral History Programme.

484 Frank Panton, ibid.

485 See for example the 'trigger arguments' advanced by Henry Kissinger, in: Matthew Jones, The Official History of the UK Strategic Nuclear Deterrent – Vol. 2 The Labour Government and the Polaris Programme, 1964–1970, Routledge, 2017, Kindle edition, p.439 of 560, location 11938.

486 In December 1964 Solly Zuckerman used a memorable turn of phrase: 'No enemy would ever know if a submarine missile that was fired had a Union Jack painted on it, or the Stars and Stripes' – See: Matthew Jones, ibid., Kindle edition p.199 of 560, location 5654.

487 Matthew Jones, ibid., p.336 of 560, location 9195.

488 Matthew Jones, ibid., p.311 of 560, location 8586.

489 Peter Jones, 'Chevaline Technical Programme 1966–1976', Prospero, No. 2, Spring 2005 pp.179–191, British Rocketry and Oral History Programme.

490 Peter Jones, Prospero, 2005, ibid.

491 Peter Jones, Prospero, 2005, ibid.

492 Matthew Jones, Vol 2, op. cit., Kindle edition, p.363/560, location 9919.

493 Matthew Jones, ibid., Chapter 10: 'The Press Gang at work and the birth of Super Antelope, January–June 1968'.

494 Ken Johnston, private communications 2009–2010.

495 Frank Panton, 'The Unveiling of Chevaline', op. cit.

496 R.L. Dommett, 'Engineering the Chevaline Delivery System', Prospero, No. 5, Spring 2008, pp.99–121.

497 Dr Strangelove, Columbia Pictures, January 1964, screenplay by Stanley Kubrick, Terry Southern and Peter George, based on the book Red Alert by Peter George, a continuity transcript, available at: https://www3.nd.edu/~dlindley/handouts/Dr%20strangelove%20script.doc accessed 05 April 2019.

498 Hans A. Bethe and Richard L. Garwin, 'Anti-Ballistic Missile Systems', Scientific American, March 1968, Vol. 218, No. 3, pp.21–31.

499 Garwin and Bethe, ibid.

500 Garwin and Bethe ibid. See also: Matthew Jones, Vol 2, op. cit., Kindle edition p.210 of 560, location 5997.

501 Matthew Jones, ibid., Kindle edition p.115 of 560, location 3460.

502 Garwin and Bethe, op. cit.

503 Garwin and Bethe, op. cit.

504 Ken Johnston, private communications 2009–2010.

505 Frank Panton, 'The Unveiling of Chevaline', op. cit.

506 Frank Panton, 'The Unveiling of Chevaline', op. cit., p.112.

507 Frank Panton, 'The Unveiling of Chevaline', op. cit., p.112.

508 Frank Panton, 'The Unveiling of Chevaline', op. cit., pp.112–113.

509 Frank Panton, 'Polaris Improvements and the Chevaline System 1967–1976', *Prospero*, No. 1, Spring 2004, pp.109–128, British Rocketry and Oral History Programme p.119.

510 Ken Johnston, private communications 2009–2010.

511 Frank Panton 'The Unveiling of Chevaline', op. cit., p.115.

512 Ken Johnston, op. cit.

513 For a good overview of 1960s rocket fuels see: John D. Clark, *Ignition! An informal history of liquid rocket propellants,* Rutgers University Press, New Brunswick, New Jersey, USA, 1972, available at: https://archive.org/details/ignition_201612 accessed 26 March 2017.

514 Frank Panton 'The Unveiling of Chevaline', op. cit. p.118.

515 Frank Panton, 'Polaris Improvements and the Chevaline System 1967–1976', op. cit., pp.122–123.

516 See Peter Jones, 'Chevaline Technical Programme 1966–1976', *Prospero,* op. cit, 2005, for source of the phrase 'a very impressive piece of kit'.

517 Ken Johnston, private communications 2009–2010.

518 Frank Panton, 'Polaris Improvements and the Chevaline System 1967–1976', *Prospero,* op. cit., p.125.

519 Ken Johnston, op. cit.

520 Sanjida O'Connell and Patrick Barkham, 'Australia used for secret tests of UK ballistic missile', *The Guardian,* 1 April 2002, available at: https://www.theguardian.com/uk/2002/apr/01/physicalsciences.australia accessed 19 October 2018.

521 Jean-Jacques Serra, *Falstaff Vehicles,* available at: http://fuseurop.univ-perp.fr/falsta_e.htm accessed 19 October 2018.

522 Jeremy Stocker, Britain and Ballistic Missile Defence 1942–2002, Routledge, 2004.

523 Kate Pyne, 'More complex than expected: The Atomic Weapons Research Establishment's contribution to the Chevaline payload', *History of the UK Strategic Deterrent: The Chevaline programme*, Proceedings of the RAeS Conference, 28 October 2004.

524 Hans A. Bethe and Richard L. Garwin, 'Anti-Ballistic Missile Systems', *Scientific American*, March 1968, Vol. 218, No. 3, pp.21–31.

525 Matthew Jones, *The Official History of the UK Strategic Nuclear Deterrent: Vol. 2: The Labour Government and the Polaris Programme, 1964–1970*, Routledge, 2017, Kindle edition p.378/560.

526 Matthew Jones, ibid. p.371/560, location 10118.

527 Kate Pyne, op. cit.

528 Ken Johnston, private communications, January 2010.

529 Matthew Jones reports that the UK analysts never trusted such blackout effects to the point that they should be relied upon. See: Matthew Jones, *Vol 2*, op. cit., pp.379/560, 522/560.

530 Ken Johnston, op. cit.

531 Hans A. Bethe and Richard L. Garwin, op. cit.

532 Ken Johnston, op. cit.

533 Ken Johnston, op. cit.

534 Richard L. Garwin and Hans A. Bethe, op. cit.

535 Hansard, Nuclear Weapons, HC Deb, 24 January 1980, Vol. 977 cc672–784.

536 George Wigg, *George Wigg by Lord Wigg*, Michael Joseph, London, 1972, p.211.

537 Peter Jones, 'Chevaline Technical Programme 1966–1976', op. cit.

538 Frank Panton 2004 *The Unveiling of Chevaline* op. cit.

539 R.L. Dommett, 'Engineering the Chevaline Delivery System', *Prospero*, No. 5, Spring 2008, pp.99–121.

540 Public Accounts Committee, House of Commons, Ninth Report, *Improvements to the Polaris Missile System*, HC269, session 1981–1982.

541 Frank Panton 'The Unveiling of Chevaline', op. cit, p.105.

542 Richard L. Garwin and Hans A. Bethe, op. cit..

543 Healey had negotiated a no-cost option for the UK, but in fact the UK would end up paying out for F-111, as aircraft were later requested only to be cancelled incurring a cancellation fee. With thanks to Richard

Moore – private communication 2016.

544 Guy Finch, Presentation on TSR2 at British Rocketry Oral History Project/UK Space Conference, Charterhouse School, March 2010.

545 Denis Healey, *Time of My Life,* op. cit. pp.278–279.

546 Denis Healey, op. cit. p.292.

547 Denis Healey, op. cit. p.300.

548 Roland Beamont, *Phoenix into Ashes,* William Kimber and Co. Ltd, London, 1968, p.161.

549 Ministry of Defence, History of the Ministry of Defence online, available at: http://www.mod.uk/DefenceInternet/AboutDefence/History/HistoryOfTheMOD/ accessed December 2009.

550 Museum of Modern Art, New York, NY, USA, website: https://www.moma.org/calendar/exhibitions/1233?locale=en accessed 19 March 2017.

551 David Owen, *Nuclear Papers,* Liverpool University Press, Liverpool, 2009.

552 Nick Ritchie and Paul Ingram, 'A Progressive Nuclear Weapons Policy: Rethinking Continuous-at-Sea Deterrence', *RUSI Journal,* Vol. 155, No. 2, May 2010.

553 Nick Ritchie, *Stepping Down the Nuclear Ladder: Options for Trident on a path to zero,* Bradford Disarmament Research Centre, Department of Peace Studies: University of Bradford, May 2009. http://www.york.ac.uk/media/politics/documents/research/Trident_Options.pdf, accessed 17 March 2013.

554 Rob Edwards, 'Flaws in Nuclear Submarine Reactors could be Fatal, Secret Report Warns', *The Guardian,* 10 March 2011, http://www.guardian.co.uk/world/2011/mar/10/royal-navy-nuclear-submarine-reactor-flaws accessed 17 March 2013.

555 Chris Greenwood and Ian Drury, 'Video games-obsessed submariner killed officer after threatening to go on 'Grand Theft Auto-style' shooting spree', *Daily Mail,* 20 September 2011, http://www.dailymail.co.uk/news/article-2039125/Sailor-Ryan-Samuel-Donovan-murdered-officer-nuclear-submarine-HMS-Astute.html accessed 17 March 2013.

556 Ministry of Defence, UK, *The United Kingdom's Future Nuclear Deterrent: The submarine:* Initial Gate Parliamentary Report, May 2011, https://www.gov.uk/government/uploads/system/uploads/attachment_data/file/27399/submarine_initial_gate.pdf accessed 17 March 2013.

557 Joseph Dempsey, HMS Astute – a special deployment? International Institute for Strategic Studies website, https://www.iiss.org/en/militarybalanceblog/blogsections/2014-3bea/april-7347/hms-astute-153f accessed 1 December 2015.

558 Richard Norton-Taylor, 'Trident Replacement Plan No Longer Credible, says Former Foreign Secretary', *The Guardian,* 25 October 2009, available at: https://www.theguardian.com/uk/2009/oct/25/trident-defence-policy-david-owen accessed 19 October 2018.

559 See the work of the Nuclear Security Project: http://www.nuclearsecurityproject.org/ accessed 17 March 2013.

560 Richard H. Speier, George Nacouzi, Carrie Lee, Richard M. Moore, *Hypersonic Missile Nonproliferation: Hindering the spread of a new class of weapons,* Rand Corporation, Santa Monica, CA, 2017. https://www.rand.org/pubs/research_reports/RR2137.html accessed 18 October 2018.

561 Jonathan Beale, BBC News website, 14 May 2015, available at: http://www.bbc.com/news/uk-32715299, accessed 3 February 2018.

562 For further insight into the role of flexibility and options in engineering systems see: R. de Neufville and S. Scholtes, *Flexibility in Engineering Design,* MIT Press, 2011.

563 Francis Fukuyama's 1989 essay 'The End of History' is often misunderstood, but nevertheless the post-Cold War context that prompted so much interest in his ideas is not so far from the realities that we see emerging in the world. Arguably Fukuyama's essay is more important as a historical document in itself rather than as a comment on human history.

INDEX